WHERE HAVE YOU GONE . . .

Ernie Banks: He went from a major league power hitter with 512 career homers to a major league power broker in one of Chicago's big-time banks.

Warren Spahn: He left baseball the 5th winningest pitcher in history to build his own bullpen on his 3000 acre Oklahoma cattle ranch.

Mickey Lolich: After years of whipping batters at the plate with 2832 lifetime strikeouts, he now whips batter into donuts in his Michigan bakery.

Orlando Cepeda: Sixteen years a slugging superstar, then 10 months in jail for smuggling dope, he now runs a baseball clinic for kids.

You'll be happy, you'll be sad,
you'll be surprised . . . and you'll never again
have to ask the question . . .

WHERE HAVE YOU GONE,
VINCE DIMAGGIO?

BASEBALL IS A FUNNY GAME by Joe Garagiola
FERNANDO! by Mike Littwin
GIFFORD ON COURAGE by Frank Gifford
INNER GAME OF TENNIS by Timothy Gallwey
INNER SKIING by Timothy Gallwey and Bob Kriegel
NEW CROSS-COUNTRY SKI BOOK
    by John Caldwell
RULES OF THE GAME by the Diagram Group
THE UMPIRE STRIKES BACK by Ron Luciano and
    David Fisher

WHERE HAVE YOU GONE, VINCE DIMAGGIO?

by Edward Kiersh

Photographs by Harvey Wang

BANTAM BOOKS
TORONTO · NEW YORK · LONDON · SYDNEY

WHERE HAVE YOU GONE, VINCE DIMAGGIO?
A Bantam Book / May 1983

"Before" photos:
Curt Flood by Mul Emmons—copyright © 1960
George Altman by Russ Reed—copyright © 1970
Mudcat Grant by Bob Schranck—copyright © 1959
Willie McCovey by Ron Mrowiec—copyright © 1969
Karl Spooner by Barney Stein—copyright © 1954
Dusty Rhodes and Willie Mays by Bill Greene—copyright © 1954
Blanchard and Marris by Bill Greene—copyright © 1954
Elroy Face by Kilingensmith—copyright © 1960
All other "before" photos are from The Sporting News.
"After" photos by Harvey Wang copyright © 1982.

Title inspired by the song, "Mrs. Robinson," copyright © 1968 by
Paul Simon.
"Astros Players" song on pages 47 and 49, copyright © 1970, 1981
by Jim Bouton from the book Ball Four Plus Ball Five. Reprinted
with permission of Stein and Day Publishers.

Book designed by Renée Gelman.

ISBN 0-553-23131-6

Published simultaneously in the United States and Canada

Bantam Books are published by Bantam Books, Inc. Its trademark,
consisting of the words "Bantam Books" and the portrayal of a
rooster is Registered in U.S. Patent and Trademark office and in
other countries. Marca Registrada. Bantam Books, Inc., 666 Fifth
Avenue, New York, New York 10103.

Since many of the men in this book filled his life with excitement, I would like to dedicate this book to my father, Irving Kiersh. I would also like to acknowledge the loving support of my mother, Gloria Hecht; the assistance of my editor Peter Guzzardi, and initial help from *Inside Sports* editor Jay Lovinger.

CONTENTS

FOREWORD
by Phil Rizzuto

Holy Huckleberries!

Time sure passes. It seems like only yesterday that I was playing alongside the guys in this book, yet here they are, making doughnuts, working on a tugboat, and doing all sorts of crazy things. Cy Young Award-winner Dean Chance is on the carnival circuit, and Bobby Shantz is making ice cream cones—amazing! I can't believe it.

For years, just like a lot of fans, I've been wondering about my old friends. What had happened to them? What were they up to, how was life treating them? I never thought I'd see most of them again. But this book, it's like a great detective story, it has solved the mystery: "What happens to yesterday's heroes?"

Geez! I'm really glad to see that lots of the guys are doing so well. I know Yankees were special, and that the uniform was the closest thing to heaven, but imagine, Bronx Bomber Gene Woodling has found oil in his backyard, while Hector Lopez still has the kids cheering. And while I remember Vic Power's bat flashing, Dick Allen's long home runs, or Jim Bunning's fastball, they're scoring even bigger victories today—helping kids in Puerto Rico, getting ready for the Kentucky Derby, or suiting up for the White House. As my old sidekick Mel Allen would say, "How 'bout that?"

Anyone who ever twirled a ball or had a favorite team will also be thrilled to read these success stories. I certainly was. And surprised, as well. Back in the 1940s and '50s, none of us ever thought of the future, or what we'd do after baseball. We were living in a dream world, a place where we were rubbing elbows with immortals like DiMaggio, Williams, and Feller, so why bother thinking about tomorrow? We already had it made.

That's why the business world—or the "reality" the players in this book talk about—was always so far off. And such a difficult adjustment. No one was ever prepared.

I was one of the lucky ones. I stepped out of my Yankee pinstripes and moved right into the broadcasting booth. I never had to worry about mortgage payments, starting up a business, or crashing into a new pin-striped league, that attache-case world where you have to speak the King's English, and not my Brooklynese. Can you picture me in some fancy bank like Ernie Banks, or conducting business negotiations in China like Walt Dropo? Thank God the Yankees have been so good to me.

I'm the exception, though. Most guys have to really struggle for years—and that's why this book is so exciting, it's fun to read about guys finally making it off the field. I never thought a lot of them would, the odds were so stacked against them. Without any business training or help, they've shown themselves to be winners, they've survived. They've entered a totally new ballpark, and are doing a lot more than scratching out a few hits. George Altman, Jay Hook, Willie McCovey, Mel Stottlemeyer, they're all prospering and enjoying life. And don't forget, none of these guys made $800,000 a year, fell into a business, or had the benefit of Madison Avenue lawyers or agents. They all made it on their own.

It doesn't matter that not everyone's a millionaire, or as happy as when they were playing. You have to miss the game. But that's why I liked this book so much. It's not a fairy tale. Ballplayers are real people, they go through ups and downs and have emotions just like the average fan. As this book shows, when it comes time to hang up those spikes, players start out on a new adventure, and all of them must have lots of courage.

And for pointing that out, "Where Have You Gone, Vince DiMaggio?" deserves a loud Holy Cow!

INTRODUCTION

Our dreams, strivings, and day-to-day routines are filled with their heroics. What American boy can forget Willie Mays' dramatic catch in the 1954 World Series; antics of a Doug Rader; the Monster, Dick Radatz, coming in from the Boston bullpen; or the constant controversy swirling around baseball's bad boy, Dick Allen? Even today, most of us remember Curt Flood's courageous stand against the reserve clause, Vic Power's flamboyant grabs at first base, or Willie McCovey's career home run totals.

How could we forget? These men were special. They were our heroes. Long before the megabucks era of free agency arrived—when players' loyalty to a club vanished, we showed our own allegiance by going to bed with our transistors glued to our ears, hoping to hear one last crack of the bat, or tucked our gloves under a pillow, as if this would affect the next morning's box scores.

Then we got older. The summer game lost some of its interest—our heroes retired, a group of *nouveaux* millionaires replaced them, baseball expansion watered down the game, and, most importantly of all, we got down to the business of our own lives. We went on to school, marriages, and careers. Fantasies of the baseball diamond were now inappropriate—hitting a home run suddenly meant a new BMW, a fat raise, or a killing on the stock market.

But part of our childhood will never die. We are who we rooted for. Names like Daddy Wags, the Moose, Stonehands, the Red Rooster, Thunder, and Dr. Strangeglove will always conjure up their own special magic. Mention Vinegar Bend Mizell. Boog Powell, King Karl Spooner, or Harmon "Killer" Killebrew to any fan, and immediately the pinball machine in his mind starts to flash, the wires trip a kaleidoscope of memories—we're adolescents again.

If only we could go back in time. Or, failing that, at least catch a glimpse of our favorite players today—to see what has happened to the men who shaped our lives. How have the years treated them? Are they happy? What struggles have they gone through? When the crowds stopped cheering, how did they adjust to a simpler, more mundane life?

As a baseball addict—or someone who used to rub Yankee Stadium gravel into my Roger Maris glove for a better pocket—I felt a real need to answer these questions. My entire boyhood had been wrapped up in these men, yet it seemed as if they had all vanished. Where were they, what were they doing? I had a feeling that they had become heroes again, on a different type of ballfield—it's not easy starting over at age thirty-five or so, after being forced to leave a game you love so dearly, and becoming a rookie in some strange, new business. While researching a magazine article for *Inside Sports* in 1981, I met men who had thrilled crowds of 50,000 or more who were now playing out a more private drama—that of providing for families, overcoming personal problems like failed businesses or alcoholism, and in essence leaving the make-believe world of sports for the realities of workaday living.

To capture more fully this true slice of Americana— like its used cars, America also abandons its heroes—I set out on a trip across the United States, along with photographer Harvey Wang. I knew the Mantles and Aarons got their share of speaking engagements or

Burma Shave commercials, so I only wanted to track down those guys who weren't in the headlines every day. (This took some doing, since a lot of players just seemed to disappear, and it often meant a lot of door-to-door bell-ringing.) Of course, the players I sought all had recognizable names; I didn't want to interview men who only had a cup of coffee in the major leagues. But what does a Mantle or Mays have in common with the average working man? I hoped to explore a different league, those men who were no longer in the public eye, but loomed large in my own memory.

Consequently, this book helped me see the soul of America. Traveling from New York to California, through several Midwestern states, Texas, the South, Florida, and Puerto Rico (much of it in a beat-up Toyota), I saw more than Bobby Shantz's Dairy Freeze, Bernie Carbo's hairdressing salon, or Mickey Lolich's doughnut bakery. I met John Q. Baseball Fan—the gasoline attendants, restaurant owners, grocery store clerks, and other shopkeepers who turn to the baseball standings every morning, before they summon up enough courage to read the front page headlines.

And in the process of meeting these average citizens, along with reliving the glories of my former heroes—or suffering with them when they described their hurts or struggles over the years—I discovered a very basic truth. One that will always be emotionally moving.

I realized that the relationship between fan and player has an extra, normally hidden dimension. We certainly are tied to our heroes; we're thrilled to hear about their exploits, and their best moments will always fire our imaginations. But this relationship also has another side—ex-major leaguers are not only linked to fans, *now they are us*.

Because they have moved off the playing field, to pass through life the way we do, they've had to surrender all the pampering and special treatment of their youth, and have finally been exposed to the rigors of normal, everyday life. No longer stars in a special constellation, they don't buy a new car every year, stay in glamorous hotels, or think their future is a limitless rainbow. Instead, they're struggling, or fighting to evolve productive lives for themselves. We're engaged in the same pursuit, so following their progress is more than exciting reading. It's a mirror of ourselves.

ERNIE BANKS
Today a Wooden Indian, Tomorrow a Bank President

"Hurry, get E.B. on the phone. I need him to back me up with five million dollars. The Arabs need that to cover the exploratory research; that gas line from Riyadh to the Yemen border can't miss. We just need that money up front."

Sensing the urgency of the situation, the speculator's secretary dials the First African Bank and waits to be connected with the president. The moment his familiar voice comes on the line, she announces who's calling and switches him to her boss.

"Good afternoon, sir, this is Wayne Morgan at Oil Tech Consultants. I hope I'm not disturbing you, but I'd like your help on a deal with the Saudis. I know First African is very active in the Mideast, and that you have close relations with a few of the princes, especially Sheik Yamani, their OPEC minister. A $5-million line of credit from you could cement the deal. Whatever terms you want, that's okay, Mr. Banks, I just want you in on this."

Sounds too far-fetched? Though only a fantasy, it's still very plausible. Just as he entered the Hall of Fame with 512 homers, two home run titles, two RBI crowns, and two MVP awards, Ernie Banks is opening the doors of another exclusive club, the banking

A fan waves his scorecard to Ernie Banks after the Hall of Famer's 2,500th hit (9/23/69).

establishment. One year away from obtaining a finance degree from Northwestern University, the slugging shortstop-turned-first baseman wants to "uplift people, to get away from entertainment, and do something for the working man." Not content with being "a cigar-store wooden Indian," Banks is handling public relations for a local Chicago bank, and has already formed ties with the city's most influential power brokers. He's inspired by the challenge of becoming more than a jock, but, more importantly, says, "The downtrodden need access, they have to influence the decision-makers. Through banking, or meeting their money needs, I can and will get them this clout. Money is power."

Don't take Ernie Banks lightly. No matter what his goal is. Power has always been his specialty. Dubbed Mr. Chicago by the Wrigley Field faithful, he didn't get this nickname for his sweet smiles, saucy wit, or warm-hearted handshakes. Number 44 clobbered that ball. Never playing a day in the minor leagues, he went straight from the old Negro League to the Cubs (1953), and clubbed nineteen homers in his first full season. Over the next seventeen years, he had twenty or more homers thirteen times, so it's understandable why Chicago's bleacher bums called him Triple G—going, going, gone.

Fans needed this excitment. They had to take their minds off the Cubs. Always finishing at the bottom of the pack, Wrigley's chewing gum boys were much like Doublemint or Beechnut—they'd start off with a rush, then go totally flat. The worst example of this choking was in 1969. Already planning to print World Series tickets, the Cubs took a large first-place lead into September, then took a dive into Lake Michigan. Perhaps Chicago fans were used to the disappointment. But the team's collapse was especially bitter for Banks. He always dreamed of playing for a pennant winner, and had strained his thirty-eight-year-old body all that year. Yet, despite his twenty-three homers, and 106 RBIs in 155 games, the Cubs faltered, again. The "You Gotta Believe" Mets overtook them, and Banks was never more than a World Series spectator.

He deserved better. The game's premier first baseman for many years, Banks was not just a home run hitter. Possessing very strong wrists, he became synonymous with the line drive, or the timely base hit (129 RBIs in 1958, 142 in '59, 117 in '60). For a slugger, his strike-outs were relatively low (eighty-seven, seventy-two, sixty-nine in those same years); and from 1955 to 1962 he batted .292. And while the national exposure of a World Series eluded him, Banks did get a chance to shine in All-Star Games (thirteen of them, to be exact). Unlike Aaron, Mantle, or Berra, Banks was one big star who delivered in those games, hitting a crisp .303.

Even at the end of his career, Banks was special. Once those remarkable wrists started to fail him, he didn't try to hang on indefinitely for that proverbial "one more good year." He sensed it was time to quit. "I didn't want to go out the back door like most washed-up players," notes Banks, sitting in one of his bank's boardrooms. "I wanted to go out with my head up. When a pitcher got me out, I always thought, 'How did he do that to me? I gotta get that one back the next time up.' Well, that feeling was more than intensity. It was pride, a caring about yourself. Well, I don't like to talk about baseball, it's the '80s now, not the '50s. But the game's like the business world, actions speak louder than words. You had to get back at that pitcher, and when you couldn't it was time to go on."

Banks first tried coaching, but that didn't work out too well. A victim of the old baseball axiom, "the dug-out isn't big enough for two personalities," he had numerous run-ins with fiery Cub manager Leo Du-rocher. When the Lip lost his job (1972), Banks's life on the baselines became somewhat more tolerable. He still wasn't happy, however. It was one thing to be a name, a Cub fixture, and another to be "really productive, or to feel valuable."

Afraid of losing Banks, or his publicity value, the Cubs made him a roving instructor for their minor

Bank on it, Mr. Chicago is still a big deal.

league organization. He did this for a few years, then moved on to the Cubs' executive office, as a director of marketing. Essentially a ticket salesman, Banks was again a prisoner of name. At charity events or business conferences, a Mr. Chicago could sell companies half a grandstand, a few season tickets, or at least pitch an Elks or Rotary Club ballpark picnic.

Reduced to "a smiling face with a sweet voice," Banks felt cut off from major administrative decisions. And was left with a gnawing sense of insecurity. Or the feeling that he was a prisoner of his own name. Now he was suddenly deaf to any crowd's cheering—and frightened. It seemed as if the world viewed him as only an image, without any substance, or worth.

As Banks poignantly puts it, "There were times, especially in restaurants, when everyone wanted autographs, that I felt I had to leave, run away from everything, and be a fugitive from myself. I felt trapped. No one looked at me at a human being. There was no reality, just image, image, image. I couldn't get on with my life; I had to be this famous ballplayer, or what people wanted me to be. I couldn't be my own man."

Asserting himself or attaining some measure of freedom was not too easy. Banks was defined by the Cubs. With the team for twenty-five years, he had paid a heavy price for their pampering and financial support. Conditioned to be an organization man, he could only think in terms of the Cubs this, the Cubs that. Never able to put Ernie first, then the team, Banks eventually became alarmed by this dependency, quit the team, and went into psychotherapy.

He now says, "I had to see a psychologist. I didn't know how to deal with my environment, the real world. She helped me adjust, to get the right perspective on things. It's fabulous being a baseball star. But too many people direct your life. You're always doing what you're told. This hurts you. Functioning later on is so difficult. That's why I got tired of people recognizing my face, my voice, my walk. It's incredible. I just wanted to be alone so I could find some answers. Only recently have I regained some control of myself."

Banks can be more optimistic now. After a few years of emotional unrest and self-evaluation, he's pulled off the big switch. The conservative banking establishment doesn't expect a ballplayer, let alone a black grocer's son, to make it in their circle. Banking is a good-old-boys' club: white, rich, by invitation only. But Banks has worked hard for admission. Just as skeptics were silenced in 1962 by his smooth shift from short to first, Banks has "learned the language, the tempo, the right questions to ask," and is moving gracefully in this new, high-stakes world.

Looking like a Wall Street financier, in a stylishly cut pin-striped suit, he sits in a big leather chair, his hands tightly clasped, and says, "It's going to be a while before I get to play for this team. Blacks aren't exactly in the mainstream of banking. I'm getting there, though. I've turned things around since I got here (with the bank since 1979). You have to develop credibility, and I've done that by going to school, by getting a degree. It's hard to show the world that a ballplayer can be something else; we're put into these little slots. But all of us have some ideals, goals, needs, desires, just like the guy on the street. People see Liz Taylor as a beautiful actress. They don't understand she can also get fat or sick. Well, I want to be seen as something else, too, a thinking, highly competent banker. I want to see those reports, to get involved with people.

"Being a pathfinder, that's what I want. Right now I'm using this experience to get there. I'm focusing on new goals. I want to help people. Not just here, but around the world. That's my whole thrust. The baseball provided a little entertainment; now, through my own bank, I really want to do something for people. In my bank, people would get money based on sweat equity, not collateral. I'm especially interested in new business development, rising nations, the Third World. That's the big picture. Tapping an oil well in Nigeria or developing farms in Saudi Arabia, that's what I want to do.

"Sure, it's a few years off. Dreams don't become reality that easy. But the establishment, the top of the economic club, that's where I want to be. I don't want to be a pea brain. I remember kids asking me, 'Why do you want to be a banker? You're a big star.' I'd say 'Where is he?' The real bottom line of life is 'what have you done lately?' That's the only thing baseball and the business world accepts."

Banks now shuffles around in his seat. He looks concerned. Perhaps remembering that his father lost the grocery store and had to become a porter for a hotel, Banks tempers his optimism and seems more pensive. Staring intently ahead and speaking more softly, he continues, "Well, if I don't make it in banking, I always wanted to be a cab driver. They really get to know a city, its best restaurants, its clubs, the soul of a place.

"I don't know; I think I have what it takes to be a banker. Who knows how life works? As a ballplayer I was into numbers, I did graphology, and the numerology of pro players when I was a minor league scout. I knew who would have problems with drugs, who was nervous. I kept a dossier on everyone, but I never thought I'd be working with other charts. The million-dollar kind.

"Baseball is really the past now. I want it to go away, I want to forget the Cubs. Those years require a lot of questions, and I'm not into talking about that. I'll only say that I've met a lot of people through baseball, lawyers, judges, government people, all types from the Fortune 500. That's rewarding. Especially when I see plaques on the wall from Harvard, Yale, and there it is, an autographed Ernie Banks ball on the desk. Then, I say to myself, 'Yeah, Ernie, you're really special, one day you're going to have that bank.'"

WALT DROPO
As American as Apple Pie

The Dropo family circus, traditionally known in other quarters as the evening meal, usually begins with:

"Zurka, Zurka, where are the plates? Hurry, we need plates for the blini. Come on, Zurka, hurry. And don't forget my photos from China."

"Walter, don't you know where your own plates are?" screams Zurka Dropo, adding to the bedlam in her brother's wharfside Boston apartment. "You told me to find that hat you got in Manchuria. I'm doing that first. And I have to get ice for the wine."

"Come on Zurka, it's time to eat. Ice for the wine? You don't need ice, forget it. You have to taste this *mou t'ai*. This Chinese *mou t'ai* is great."

"Tell these guys about the pigeon-brain soup you were always having. I can't find the photos. You should know where they are. Mom, Mom, get off the couch. Help with the plates. Walt, the chicken's burning. The oven, Walt, the chicken. Hurry."

Enjoying the chaos that's rapidly resembling a Marx Brothers movie, Moose's plump, 84-year-old mother Maria mutters a few Serbo-Croatian words to herself, goes to the oven, and then takes a hefty gulp of slivovitz (a form of schnapps). "I heard you before. Walter, you're crazy. I wasn't born in Dubrovnik. That's where your father comes from. I was born in Mostar. That's

Walt "The Moose" Dropo was so awesome, a Yugoslavian tailor had to specially fit his uniform.

close to where the archduke was assassinated. You forgot? What's wrong, you going nuts?"

With everyone's sanity now in doubt, Dropo just keeps on talking. And not about baseball. Picturing himself more as a Marco Polo rather than as an Incredible Hulk, the six-foot, five-inch 235-pounder must be pressed to discuss his playing career. The American League's Rookie of the Year in 1950, he's admittedly "disappointed about not living up to expectations." So instead of focusing on baseball achievements, like his twenty-nine homers for the Red Sox and Tigers in 1952, or a still-standing record of twelve straight hits, he finds it easier to talk about his adventures in another world.

"China, that's the place to be. What a country, the people treat me like a giant. They love all the Dropos there. Nixon made my brother a millionaire. He opened the corridor up so people could trade there, and my brother has really taken advantage of that. We import fireworks, $5 million a year's worth, plus all kinds of other items, like porcelain vases, ashtrays, jewelry, and some clothes. I have to make a few trips a year there, and I love it. It's a whole new ballgame for me there. We own China. Bob Hope hit a golf ball over the Great Wall, but I'm the only player ever to hit a baseball over that thing. I do it every time I go. I'll drink to that. Bottoms up, *Kampei, kampei.*

"Hey Zurka, get some more *mou t'ai.* We need more *mou t'ai.*"

Now the diplomat and world trader who finesses complicated financial transactions, Moose has come a long way from belting either home runs (thirty-four in 1950), RBIs (144 that year), or Enos Slaughter (in a memorable 1954 Comiskey Park brawl). Today his world is one of Oriental furniture, a bottle of the best Russian vodka or *mou t'ai,* a bachelor's paradise on the thirty-first floor of one of Boston's most prestigious buildings, and a warm-hearted, belly-laughing approach to life that makes him say, "my baseball mementos, all that stuff isn't worth a s____."

Too busy running an insurance business and helping

two brothers with such all-American items as "flying cuckoos" and "jumping jacks," Dropo can't live in the past like most ex-ballplayers. Only after a few belts of schnapps will he grudgingly say, "I broke in with a bang, only to tail off to where I should have been, very average. Truthfully, I never thought I was going to be a Ted Williams. I only dreamed of having better-than-average stats." (.270 career batting average, with 152 HRs).

But give him three to four hours, and he becomes Chairman Walt of Chinese Tourism, promoting delights that are even better than the dumplings or sweet and sour pork.

"The Chinese are cultured people, they're class. They don't have violence there the way we do. If you forget your wallet somewhere, it'll either be there when you come back or someone will try to find you. It's a beautiful country. There's loyalty over there, too. I used to think baseball encouraged loyalty, but that's a thing of the past. Loyalty is dying all over America. But in China you give a handshake, and you have a handshake. You don't need lawyers. Life there isn't surviving. It's really being alive.

"The Chinese don't have baseball; they have ballet instead. That's fine with me. I haven't completely forgotten baseball, but it's a different life for me now. What do I care what Steinbrenner does, or what Winfield gets? I'm happy without the game. I'm not searching or groping for anything. When I was playing ball, in my wildest dreams I didn't think I'd become an international businessman."

Visions of future deals suddenly vanish, however, when Zurka deposits a tray of Yugoslav delicacies on the table. Confronted with mounds of spinach pies, cheese-filled appetizers called *kolach*, lamb chops, and four bottles of wine, Dropo forgets the millions he wants to make (his current yearly income is about $200,000) and shows that his own loyalty is not to be questioned. Like any other growing Yugoslav boy, he eats with a gusto that would've made Tito proud.

*A self-styled Marco Polo, Dropo
traded six packs of bubble gum for that
Chinese hat. He's now negotiating
for the Great Wall.*

Ignoring his mother's joking ("Walter was born big; when he was five years old I was buying him men's clothes"), Dropo more seriously adds, "I eat, I drink, what else is there? I can only wear one suit a day, so what else do I need? Our family's from royalty, and it's in our blood to eat.

"That's why, if I left this country, I'd only go back to Yugoslavia. I have no real roots in China. The Chinese are the cleanest people in the world. And I also love Hong Kong. You should see the women there. You go nuts in nightclubs. But except for America, I could only be happy in Dubrovnik. The Adriatic coast, it's God's country."

Then raising a glass, for what seems like the thousandth toast, Dropo prompts a chorus of oohs and ahs from his relatives, by loudly proclaiming, "Fireworks, it's an American way of life. They were at America's birth, and they show a pride in this country. Most of all, they make people happy, just like a game-winning home run."

RON BRYANT
Booze, Blackjack, Busted Dreams

What might have been, if . . . ?

That question has haunted Ron Bryant for years. Once a potential superstar with the San Francisco Giants, he lost his playing career in too many bottles of Jack Daniels—and nearly lost his life. He's now fighting his alcoholism, but the road back hasn't been easy. It winds through years of wine and roses, a blood-curdling swimming-pool accident, and a nightmare bordering on Skid Row.

The stockily built left-hander, nicknamed the Golden Bear by his Giant teammates, had great stuff, much like a Marichal or a Seaver. Before descending into hell, he was the 25-year-old boy wonder of the National League, compiling a 24-and-12 record, with a 3.54 ERA in 1973 (in 1972 he was 14-7, with a 2.90 ERA). That was good enough to place him third in Cy Young Award voting that year, just behind Tom Terrific and Mike Marshall. But even while greatness seemed within his grasp, there was always a devil lurking nearby. Bryant simply drank too much. A few beers or Scotches were never enough. To cope with the demands of success and lingering feelings of intellectual insecurity, he usually had to get blind drunk.

That led to disaster in 1974. As was his custom after a game, Bryant went on a drinking binge with a group of

Nowadays, aces are coming up for Ron Bryant.

reporters, joining them on a five-hour bus ride to Palm Springs during the exhibition season. Upon arriving at the hotel, admittedly "snookered out of my mind," he put on a swimsuit and splashed around the pool atop another player's back. The fun didn't last long. When the horseplay got rougher, Bryant crashed into the edge of the pool, sustaining a wound which required seventy-three stitches in his left side and nearly had him bleeding to death. Bryant did pitch again, three months later. But as his statistics show (3-15 that season, with a 5.60 ERA, and 0-1 in 1975, with a 16.00 ERA), he was never the same. Nerves in his shoulder had also been injured in the mishap, and by 1975, Bryant was washed up.

He then drifted around California for four years, from one odd job to another, from assorted gin mills to flea-bitten flophouses. Often contemplating suicide, he wound up crashing on friends' floors, working menial construction or supermarket jobs, and in the process splitting up with his wife and two daughters. He was then "desperate for any shred of hope, for just something to make life worth living." He finally wound up in Lake Tahoe, late in 1979, where he became involved with Alcoholics Anonymous. Eventually "sober for the first time in twenty or so years," he also got lucky, landing a job with Harrah's casino, as a poker and blackjack dealer.

Getting permission from a pit boss to leave his table, he stands away from a crowd of gamblers and admits, "Bumming around was the only thing I could do. I had to forget; I could only think of how close I got to really being a superstar. What a down it was to think of what I had lost. And for what? When I realized that I didn't have enough velocity on my fastball to break a pane of glass, that my baseball dream was over, I just scrounged up money for more drinking. Nothing mattered. I didn't care if I was a bum. I only thought booze. Eventually I had to ask myself, 'What's Ron Bryant going to do now? Was it worth it to keep on living?'

"Dealing cards has been a real life-saver. I don't want to do it the rest of my life; I've registered in school, and maybe I can get a job where I can teach baseball, with a minor league team or college. I hope they can see that I'm not a bum any more, that I've given up the booze. Well, if not, the casino is still exciting. You walk out there on the floor, it's crowded, lots of noise, the lights are flashing, and it seems like a ballpark. When people are winning, and there are thousands of dollars on the table, it's just like the ninth inning for me. I try to put on a mean face, get tough, and try to change the odds somehow. It's like pitching, it's do or die.

"I get baseball flashbacks all the time. How could I forget that super season? It was the only thing I had for so many years. I was drunk, lying in streets, but I still had that season. I can remember every pitch I threw that year, and what happened where. Not pitching anymore, that's still tormenting. I guess I'll always be frustrated. The game has such an impact on everyone.

"But baseball also has its down side. It gives you an opportunity to drink. Players have so much idle time on their hands, plus they're so wired from a game, they have to get snookered. I could never have only a few. I had to be carried out. Same thing with drugs; I did amphetamines. For most of my life I felt I needed something extra, a boost. I've always felt educationally inferior, or only capable of putting on a jockstrap. It's only recently that I've seen people being honest with one another, dealing with the truth. Reality is usually missing from baseball.

"At least now, though, I know I'm going to make it. I feel so much stronger. I'm not afraid of talking, or confronting most problems. There are still some things to clear up. My ex-wife and I have problems, and I'm not ready yet to face my kids. But I do like myself now."

Then smiling for the first time, Bryant adds, "and liking yourself is better than a twenty-game season."

MOE DRABOWSKY
Laughing Gas

What dresses up like a gorilla, throws cherry bombs at Indians, mounts sneak attacks from the bullpen, and wants to be known as the original Polish joke?

A Moe Drabowsky.

While most ballplayers get to the Hall of Fame because of their statistics or accomplishments, this self-described nut will get there by sneaking through a turn-stile, masquerading as one of the inductees, or popping out of a ballot box. If none of these maneuvers work, watch out, the Polish-born right-hander will undoubt-edly try some other kind of lunacy. With him, anything is possible. He never was much on the mound, as shown by his 88-105 record, with a career ERA of 3.71 for 7 clubs in seventeen years. But when it came to pranks, no one was wilder. Or more crazy.

Here are only a few of the reasons why Mo had a reputation for escaping from a madhouse.

1) During the 1969 World Series between the Mets and Orioles, Drabowsky wasn't content to sit on the sidelines. Feeling that "things had to be livened up," he hired a skywriter to send messages to his beloved ex-Baltimore teammates. Then, to psych them up even more, Drabo, as his closest friends called him, had a six-foot boa constrictor delivered to the clubhouse. Unfor-tunately for the Orioles, this wasn't much of a good-

A Moe-in-the-box!

luck charm. Or as Mo now says, "Gee, I didn't want it to work out that way, even though they had traded me away. They never won a game after getting my gift. I guess you could say they were 'snake bitten.'"

2) Mo would routinely dress up as a gorilla while sitting out in the bullpen and start throwing rocks, dirt balls, or splinters at opposing pitchers. He now gleefully remembers these impromptu battles, calling them "sneak attacks at 0400 hours. They were better than Pearl Harbor and the fighting at Iwo Jima."

3) A student of Che Guevara's guerrilla warfare tactics, Drabowsky manipulated the opposition one night by impersonating Kansas City manager Al Dark in a phone call to the KC bullpen. Athletics' pitcher Jim Nash had been pitching a two-hit shutout. But once he saw relief pitchers warming up, all hell broke loose. Nash flung his glove on the ground, walked around disgustedly, and, as Drabo recalls, "It didn't matter that Dark corrected the situation. Nash's concentration was lost, we went on to score a lot of runs, and I think my stats should include one more win."

4) Confusion in the hallways. That's the game Mo played in a San Diego hotel, during a 1971 Shriners' convention. The fun began when he erased all the numbers on temporary door tags, and renumbered dozens of hotel rooms. When the Shriners returned to their rooms, an evening of merriment became a night of pandemonium. Even now, after all the intervening years, the Joker remembers it as "the most berserk thing I've ever seen."

5) Before most of their 1971 home games, the Atlanta Braves had "Chief Nokahoma" do a war dance outside a teepee in left field. And Mo just couldn't resist staging his own version of the Little Big Horn. Ingeniously linking slow-burning cigarettes to cherry bombs, he deposited a dozen of these cannons next to the teepee, and "waited for the Chief to surrender." A huge explosion did occur, but after the cloud of smoke drifted away, and there still was no trace of the Indian, Mo only

thought, "By gosh, he's up there, he's with his ancestors in the Great Hunting Ground."

Habitually driven to scare the daylights out of people ("I can't help it if I'm sick"), Drabowsky couldn't really concentrate on pitching. In seventeen years, he barely eked out six winning seasons, and a 4.0 ERA was customarily combined with ten to fifteen losses. His greatest moment came in the 1966 World Series, as an Oriole, when he struck out eleven Dodgers in six and two-thirds innings, after coming in to relieve Dave McNally (those eleven Ks are still a record for a relief pitcher in a World Series game).

Earlier that same year, he had gone 6-0, with a 2.81 ERA, and had struck out ninety-eight batters in ninety-six innings of pitching. But Mo now says "All this went to my head. I thought I could get away with any pitch I wanted." And so the next four years were like his first ten seasons in the big leagues—terrible. He was so bad most of the time—5-10 in 1959, 3-7 in 1962, 7-13 in 1963, 5-13 in 1964—his greatest prank was "my staying around as long as I did."

When Drabo wasn't getting shelled or scaring teammates with snakes, electric shock devices, or exploding cigars, he spent most of his time computing "productivity factors." This equation was supposed to determine a relief pitcher's actual worth to a ballclub, by measuring effectiveness in terms of walks, base hits, and outs gained at specific points of a game. Most of the computations were done out in the bullpen, where this self-dubbed "Einstein of pitching" would draw up complicated charts or write long treatises on pitchers' monetary value. Drabo presented management with these tabulations to strengthen his case for salary increases. But execs in Kansas City, St. Louis, Cincinnati, Milwaukee, etc. were hardly impressed. They were more concerned with other numbers, like Drabowsky's completing only thirty-three games out of 154 starts, or his tendency to give up hits (1441 hits in 1640 innings), and invariably sent him packing.

Mo finally got tired of changing addresses in 1972,

and decided to "quiet down, to be more normal" with a Chicago paper company. While this job lasted nine years, he went straight for about two days. The blond, blue-eyed Danny Kaye lookalike admits, "I guess being a clown is in my genes. I couldn't fit into the business world like most people. I had to have a stage. I enjoy people, I like to make them laugh. All this made me a good salesman, but things were a little quiet for me. I couldn't be myself. Plus, paper products weren't the wave of the future."

After briefly considering a Hollywood acting tryout, as (you guessed it) a Danny Kaye impersonator, Drabo found his future, by becoming a sales representative for Gandalf Technology (in 1981). At this communications equipment company, which specializes in fiber optics and other high-speed data-transmission products, he's had to learn a whole new vocabulary of "nanoseconds," "pacs" (or private automatic computer exchanges), "contention problems," and "data accessing." But even though Drabo is now seriously studying engineering textbooks, he still sneaks up on his boss, crawls under a desk, and gives him a hotfoot.

"Hey, this is a new career, electronic-oriented equipment is the 1980s and '90s. But I'm always going to joke around with people, no matter what business I'm in. This stuff might be technical, but we have a good time here. It's loose. Everyone knows that this company is moving, that computer cable is being laid everywhere. Gandalf might be going out on a limb to hire me. I only have a sales orientation, without any technical background. I'm learning, though. And this place is G-R-O-W-T-H.

"Even in baseball I was a student, a true problem solver. I had to put my brain to work all the time, to figure out ways to trick people, or launch missions into the enemy's camp. Baseball really improved my mind. I had to be quick, alert at all times, ingenious. Not even Commissioner Kuhn could outsmart me. I ran a trail of lighter fluid all the way to his foot, lit that beauty, and he must've jumped four or six feet. Yowww! What a scream he gave out. He never figured out who did it. I guess I'm a frustrated soldier. I would have loved being in combat.

"Baseball was the next best thing. I could defeat the enemy with a good pitch, and also play my war games. The bad thing about the game today is that the players aren't doing it for fun. There aren't the characters, the hotfoots, or the wild hotel parties, because everyone is becoming a businessman. They all carry attache cases. In my day only Frank Robinson on the Orioles carried one. I fixed that. I put this rubber snake in it, and when he opened it up on a plane, the snake jumped into (Luis) Aparicio's lap. Both of those guys were petrified. What a sight! Wow!"

Recalling this incident gets him so excited, Mo impersonates that same jumping snake. He hops onto a chair and leapfrogs into a carton. Crouching inside the box, he remains silent for several minutes. Then, satisfied that everyone fears a surprise attack, he slowly lifts his head, and laughs devilishly, "That's Drabo, the king of the unexpected. I was a mediocre ballplayer, sure. But you know how I survived in a young man's game? I was an unknown quantity. I could strike out eleven guys in a World Series game, and I could give up three homers in one inning. Everyone had to watch out for a beautiful pitch on the inside corner, or a wild one at their ear. I did it all. Don't forget, Drabowsky was the second Polack to appear in a World Series. The first one carried a rake."

WARREN SPAHN
At War with General Patton

Down on the ranch, the Invincible One is having problems. His prized bull, Charley, won't eat.

"Hey Charley, what the hell's the matter? This is your favorite feed," demands Warren Spahn, outside the bullpen, on his 2800-acre ranch in Oklahoma. "Look at your buddies, they're all eating. What's with you today? Eat."

Pushing a bucket of feed towards Charley's mouth, Spahn shows why he was one of the greatest pitchers of all time. He would never quit. Compelled to be the best, even if that meant physical pain or exhaustion, Spahnie tapped incredible reserves of stamina to be a twenty-game winner at age forty-two. That same determination also made him the fifth winningest hurler in baseball history (363 victories and 245 losses, for a .597 percentage), and a Hall of Famer who can easily intimidate a Hereford bull.

"Don't be raunchy with me, just start chewing. I have to go take care of some fence mending, and I don't have the time for you to be fooling around. I'm going to leave this bucket here. This is it. There's no spinach today. And don't start with the noises."

Charley is Spahn's gentlest bull, so the tough talk soon pays off. Besides taking a few exploratory nibbles, the 800-pound Hereford gives off a short, seemingly

Jimmy Durante may have been funnier, but Warren Spahn made the Hall of Fame.

contrite roar. This makes Spahn laugh. He pats the bull on the head, then rushes off to his pickup truck—to take care of chores that he's neglected for forty-some-odd years. Concerned with baseball for all that time as either a player, coach, or manager, he's only recently become a full-time rancher, committed "to living like a normal human being."

"When my wife died a few years ago I knew I would have to make some basic decisions about my life, about where I was going," says the sixty-two-year-old Spahn, staring straight ahead at his cattle pastures. "I knew I was okay financially, I even lease some of this (land) to natural gas developers. I just had to decide where I'd live. I almost became a recluse at the time. But then I got a job as a minor league instructor with the Angels, and after the traveling became much too much I figured it was time to really take care of this place. All those suitcases and planes are behind me now. It's like a divorce, being away from baseball, but I want to be a big success here."

He undoubtedly will be. Spahn has not just been a baseball hero. Or a name constantly repeated in record books. The hawk-nosed left-hander was cited for bravery in World War II. During a battle at the Rhine River, he also suffered shrapnel wounds in a German bombardment, and was later awarded a Purple Heart.

Sent to Europe in 1943, Spahn had been drafted into the Army from the minor leagues after Casey Stengel dropped him from the Boston Braves. The Old Professor would later say, "Releasing him was the biggest mistake of my life." But in the meantime, Spahn's debut was hardly auspicious. National League batters pelted him for twenty-five hits in only fifteen innings of pitching, and, even more importantly, he had broken one of the cardinal rules of baseball. When Stengel called for a knock-down pitch, Spahn had refused.

"Casey wanted me to go after Pee Wee (Reese), but I just couldn't," recalls Spahn, who would later have another run-in with Stengel after the Braves sold him to the Mets in 1965. "I threw in front of Reese, behind him, only I didn't get one under his chin. Casey was furious. He came out to the mound and cursed me out. He was right. I guess I wasn't ready for the big leagues."

Even though that eventually meant three years of military service, Spahn goes on to say, "Going from the minors to the army did me a lot of good. I was just a green-eyed kid in Boston. The Army makes you grow up, fast. It's the discipline. That had to help me in baseball. I found out that you didn't get pneumonia if you were lying in a trench or on the ice. I fought the fatigue barrier, and developed stamina. In other words, I learned that I could do what I made up my mind to do. When you're at maximum effort, which a war demands, you're not cognizant of anything else around you, and that's the same in baseball. You just go out and do it."

National League batters weren't ready for the return of baseball's General Patton. Spahn wiped them out the same way the Allies cut through Germany. Though only 8-5 during his first year back (1946 with the Braves), he soon combined a scroogie with his already-proven fast-ball, and became a one-man blitzkrieg.

Especially devastating in 1947, Spahn whipped off a 21-10 mark, leading the league in both ERA (2.33) and innings pitched (289.2). From then on, there wasn't a more consistent performer in baseball. A twenty-game winner for the next twelve out of sixteen seasons, he also led the league in complete games nine times, and recorded 2,583 lifetime strikeouts (tenth on the all-time list). And while his 14-19 season in 1952 or 17-14 mark in 1955 prompted retirement talk, Spahn always fought back to beat out younger players for a starting slot, or to "silence those who constantly wanted to write my obituary."

Particularly disturbed by managers who treated him as though he was "in the grave already," Spahn defended his interests in a variety of ways. He either pitched no-hitters (two after reaching age thirty-nine), or got into angry shouting matches with managers like Charley Dressen or Birdie Tebbetts. This outspoken behavior infuriated club owners (Spahn didn't reach the coveted $100,000 salary mark until the late 1950s)—and baseball people say it barred him from managing. But Spahn continued to air his feelings, especially when managers wanted to assign him to the bullpen for short relief stints or mop-up duty.

"If you don't take pride in yourself, or speak up for what you can do, you're conceding defeat, you're a loser," says Spahn, jumping out of his flatbed truck to toss some hay into a pasture (he owns 250 head of cattle). "I spoke what I thought, I didn't go for snow jobs. In my advanced years managers wanted to give me five days rest. But I felt, if I was going to be effective, I had to pitch every four. I finally convinced them of that, but everyone was always writing me off, or looking to retire me. I'm proud of the way I battled them."

One of Spahn's notorious altercations was with Braves manager Bobby Bragan. In preparation for the team's move to Atlanta, the Milwaukee boss had traded away Lew Burdette, Spahn's long-time roommate, and was also hoping to waive Eddie Mathews. Spahn criticized both of these moves, and the two men nearly came to blows when Bragan "was going to punish me by shipping me off to the bullpen." Emotions ran so high in 1964, Spahn told general manager Bob McHale that he couldn't pitch for the Braves anymore, and was soon traded to the Mets—after twenty years in a Braves uniform.

Sparks flew again in New York. Stengel also wanted to use him as a reliever, or spot starter, and this led to several quarrels. Spahn was only 4-12 by the All-Star Game break, so management had little patience for his complaints. In a straight cash deal, they sent him to San Francisco. A few months later, after going 7-16 for the year (1965), Spahn retired from major league baseball.

But not from active competition. Uncomfortable at home, feeling like "a cow in a strange pasture," he didn't know what to do with himself. There were always fences to mend, or cattle auctions to attend, but this "wasn't the same as a one-one ballgame going into the ninth." So when the Mexico City Tigers offered him a coaching position (1966) he grabbed it.

The Tigers also asked him to pitch one day, and this immediately started rumors about a comeback. Though only a publicity stunt to help increase attendance, sports writers played up the game as "a second coming . . . another Satchel Paige" (the fifty-year-old-plus Negro League star). In fact, comeback stories appeared in newspapers throughout the late 1960s (for wherever Spahn coached or managed, he'd pitch one game). And as a result, Spahn now feels, "I could've made it into the Hall of Fame in 1970 during my first year of eligibility. I guess people thought I was really serious about returning, so my induction was delayed (to 1973)."

To get away from the hullabaloo, Spahn became a pitching instructor in Japan, for the Hiroshima Toyo Carp. He worked there from 1973 to 1978, and was about to give up baseball when his wife suddenly died. That unnerved him. And wrecked all of his plans. Now the prospect of staying in his sixteen-room house, alone, became impossible. Fortunately, the Califormia Angels came to his rescue. They made him a minor league pitching coach, a position Spahn enjoyed for two years, until "it was time for me to settle down. I had been away from home for so long, I had to get my bags unpacked and take better care of Charley."

After settling a deal for some barbed wire fencing, Spahn continues, "I feel great these days. I'm doing everything myself, the housekeeping, the ranch chores, everything. There are lonely spots, being away from the game. But you get adjusted. I'm not frothing at the bit to get to a baseball stadium, like I used to. I sort of think there's a new world to see, a world I think I can fit into.

"Anything is possible. I've always felt capable of doing what I set out to do. And, thanks to baseball, I certainly have a lot to do. My Herefords have to be fed at eight AM, there's management of the soil to think of, and you got to know where the money's going. It's almost like baseball, being a rancher. It's constant strategy, you have to know what your strengths and weaknesses are. And while I'm not staying ahead of batters any more, you still have to know what your ranch hands are doing, or else you really strike out."

Spahn then laughs and brings the truck to a stop. Pointing to a few jeeps and men on the horizon he says, "I gave a lot to baseball, all I had, and baseball was good to me. It was great. Those men over there, they're paying me a pretty price to lease my land; they're looking for natural gas. Everyone around here is making loads of money. And baseball got me all of this.

"Yeah, I'm disappointed that I didn't get 400 wins. I really wanted that. But it's okay, look at the company I'm in. Cy Young, (Walter) Johnson, (Christy) Mathewson, and (Grover) Alexander (the only four pitchers with more lifetime victories). Not too bad, eh?

"And you know what? I did it all my own way. Maybe I could've become a manager if I had kissed ass. But who wants that? Not me. I wanted to be my own person, to speak out for what I believed. Anyway, that's the past. All in all, I'm really grateful to baseball. Look at what it did for me.

"Everyone in the United States knows my name."

Leon Wagner teams up with sluggers Joe Louis and Archie Moore in this 1962 photograph.

LEON WAGNER

Brooks Brothers, Pacino, or the Hall of Fame?

Back in the '60s, it was the hottest, mind-blowingest, zaniest rage, "Get Your Rags at Daddy Wags."

No lie, Jack, the Soul Man was on fire. They came from everywhere to look at Leon's threads, to touch the silks, to ooh and ah. Kings, princes, dudes of every description, shuffled to his tune. Daddy Wags was their hero, their one and only. He was the brother who did it all—a flashy clothing store that was the black man's Brooks Brothers; million-dollar deals, Hollywood parties—you name it, the man was T-E-R-R-O-R. Especially in left field. When Leon was here, opposing pitchers cowed in fear.

Yes, Lethal Leon did hammer that ball. As a California Angel from 1961 to 1965, and then as a Cleveland Indian, Wagner's home run stats read twenty-eight, thirty-seven, twenty-six, thirty-one, twenty-eight (his entire career spanned 1958-69). He was also a member of the ninety-plus RBI club three times, and while 121 strikeouts in 1964 don't fit his image of being the game's most notorious hitter, other deeds add up to a special Big W folklore. He was one of the first men to jazz up outfielding with eyes-closed, one-handed grabs. The self-crowned carnival king of the Angels, he flexed the straw that stirred pranksters like Bo Belinsky, Ken Hunt, and Ryne Duren into madness. And, last but not least, long before Ali or Reggie, Leon's message echoed across the land: "I'm a superstar, I deserve my own candy bar."

Little has changed since those halcyon days. Leon is still Daddy Wags. Whether it's his slick-talking, Madison Avenue, pinstripe approach to selling Oldsmobiles in San Francisco, or his late-night, high-fiving, silky-jiving on the disco floor, Cheeks Wagner still dances to different kind of music. One song especially swells his head. On any given occasion he can be heard shouting, "That's it, clap your hands, stomp your feet. Come on brother, listen to the beat. Daddy Wags knew how to play that game. He should be in the Hall of Fame."

Sitting bare-chested in his San Francisco condo, Leon only starts to talk after examining his muscles in a mirror. Pleased that "I'm in better shape than ever," he then exclaims, "I was a raw hitter, a gladiator who had to face 50,000 booing fans and still perform under pressure. That took guts, the strength to deal with the unknown. You never knew if you'd have to go up on the wall the first play of the game, or if you were going to get your brains scrambled by a beanball. But I played on the same terms with the best of them. Aaron, Mays, McCovey, Clemente. I hit the ball with arch, just like Ted Williams.

"Not only was I a gladiator, but I also had the heart of a lion. I had to; I was always bouncing back from humiliations and frustrations. That was the only way I could be a hero the next day. Dogs would bite you, and old ladies cursed you out. So I had to be a super human being, a perfect human specimen. Just think about it, I was platooned for years. I had to be great to hit 211 homers in twelve years. Think about that.

"But I'm glad I got out of the game when I did (in 1969 at age thirty-five). Few guys come out on their own. I didn't want to take any crap from reporters about why I was still hanging on. It wasn't worth it to me to be shown up by youngsters. Look, guys like Monbouquette, Ford, Pierce, they never saw a dude like me. Yastrzemski will never be the hitter I am. He's a

A quiet moment of reflection for Daddy Wags.

singles hitter. I didn't hit singles up the middle. I hit towering homers. Yet he's going to the Hall of Fame. I'm better, the real people around the country know that.

"Most black athletes really have to push for everything they get. Especially when it comes time to hang 'em up. But I guess I was lucky. I was looking for a job when I left baseball that would give me $35,000 to $50,000 a year. That was a mistake. I had to start from scratch. Who's going to give a thirty-five to forty-year-old that kind of money? I joined a black millionaire in LA, Thomas Stones, who said he didn't want me to fail like most other black athletes. He gave me my own office, and taught me how to put together small business loans and tax shelters. Soon I became his right hand man. I learned I could acquire money for people, and that gave me a different dimension than most pampered ball players.

"I'm still using that skill today. Plus I've become a psychologist. You have to be a shrink to sell cars. I make people feel like they're worth a million dollars. Now I'm the complete salesman. But I want to turn all this loose for the Oakland Athletics. They're a young organization, they need someone to do a job for them in PR. I want to be that man; I'm no dummy.

"If that doesn't happen, then I'm destined to be a movie star. I've already been in *The Man From Uncle*, commercials, a bit part in Cassavetes's film, *A Woman Under The Influence*, and *Bingo Long Traveling All-Stars and Motor Kings*. It was obvious to me in Hollywood that I was twenty years behind people like James Earl Jones and Pryor. But I feel like I can be like them one day. In baseball you're stifled, you can't think of the future, or else it will take away from your game. It's a full-time job to concentrate on not being humiliated. But now I have all kinds of things to explore, I'm into progress."

After going into the bathroom to spray himself with cologne, he comes back, shaking his head. Not knowing what to wear on a date, he points to a closet and exclaims, "Having all these clothes, it's sometimes impossible to figure out what you want to wear. Man, I just don't know. But getting back to what I was saying. I do know that one day soon I'm going to launch my acting career again. Burt Reynolds, Redford, what's his name, Paul Newman, they better watch out. I'm waiting on superstar stature."

Big Gene Conley made that rare double play—he threw sweeping curves for the Red Sox and swept down rebounds for the Boston Celtics.

GENE CONLEY
The Kibbutz Kid, or The One That Got Away

The greatest baseball adventure of all time dwarfs such epic moments as Bobby Thompson's shot heard round the world, Hank Aaron's 715th home run, or Don Larsen's perfect game. It's the still-mystifying "Escape to Jerusalem," inspired by the game's own Houdini, Gene Conley.

Besides turning into a pro basketball player during the off-season—a trick only Dave DeBusschere has been able to perform—the six-foot nine-inch Conley managed to disappear for three days in 1962. Before one could say Jackie Robinson, Conley somehow convinced teammate Pumpsie Green to join him to go looking for their savior in Israel. They jumped off a Red Sox bus in the middle of a New York City traffic jam and checked into a swanky midtown hotel. Green soon got homesick, and caught up with the team two days later. But Conley persevered. He bought a plane ticket for Jerusalem.

He did get off the ground, metaphorically speaking (even if he forgot to get a passport). Conley visited most of New York's best known watering-holes, and as he puckishly says now, in his Foxboro, Massachusetts, paper products plant, "I was so tanked up I didn't have to fly."

Unfortunately, however, his caper was foiled at the last minute. Loose-lipped from too many highballs,

Conley spoke to every reporter and bartender in town about visiting the Wailing Wall, and word got back to Boston. If the Red Sox hadn't been so short-handed in pitching that year (Conley was 91-96 lifetime, after beginning his career with the Boston Braves, Milwaukee, and the Phillies), it's conceivable they would've let him go (management was already confused by watching him suit up with the Boston Celtics for three straight NBA championships, 1958-1960, averaging ten points a game, alongside the likes of Cousy, Sharman, and Russell). Instead they sent a troop of bloodhounds to nab Conley at the airport, and he was immediately branded a space cadet, a marked man who would be out of baseball one year later.

Far from being embarrassed by the incident, Conley glowingly relates every last detail, as if the prank was in the same league with pitching a no-hitter. And while his current business schedule is almost as frenetic as bouncing from a basketball court to a pitcher's mound, he takes the time to share one all-consuming wish. Still playing tricks on friends, he wants to be known as baseball's only Disappearing, Invisible, Shrinking Man.

"I had my fun, I was no lily on the pond. I know I was nuts sometimes, but why not? I had to be a little crazy to play both sports. Who cares? Pumpsie and I really left our mark. We made every front page in Boston, and even some of the papers in Europe. It was just an innocent three-day binge. Maybe now I'd think of my family more. Later I realized there's more to life than just me. But part of me would do it all over again. I wasn't a Spahn, so I had to be known for something.

"I'm not sure if the incident hurt me. Only the front office could answer that. Most likely they thought I was bad for the team. That I'd corrupt the youth by my craziness. I only know that I'm still adjusting to being out of sports. When my playing days were over I couldn't go to a ball game. I still can't. Maybe inside there's a feeling that I can do it better than the guys out there. Maybe. I don't know what the pain is. I just miss both of those games. Now I'm on the other side of the

Today, Gene Conley is still headed for the Promised Land.

fence, they've locked me out, and it's cold. They put you up in the seats, and want you to applaud the athletes. But I'm used to patting them on the ass. I guess life is over, in a way.

"Wow, I had so much. Just think of it, I played with the greatest names in both sports, Spahn, Cousy, Russell. It was tough physically, never having an off-season. But how could I get tired? I had three kids to feed. I wore number 17 as a Celtic. I got that shirt ready for Havlicek.

"But my work is sometimes as exciting. You just have to make business a game. You can make sure shipments get out on time, and that everyone is doing their job. What you're really doing is trying to stay afloat in the business world. It's hard on someone who gets in there late. You have to make it seem like you're fighting a batter. Because I was a pitcher, I'll always want to control the game. Even if it's a business deal.

"I'm just sorry I never made it to Israel. I was really depressed at the time, and completely exhausted. I told Pumpsie, and I still believe it, if we had been able to make it there, and found God, he would've hit .350, and I would've won twenty games. I'm sure of it. I've never gotten there. But you know what? Someday I will."

ELIJAH PUMPSIE GREEN
An Unlikely Jackie Robinson

Unlike Gene Conley, his partner in crime, Pumpsie Green is a quiet, self-effacing man, a reluctant hero who not only tagged along with his Boston teammate on a madcap binge in New York, but also followed Jackie Robinson's footsteps into baseball history.

Up until 1959, the Red Sox maintained the last Jim Crow color line in either league. Their message to blacks was simply Do Not Apply. But early that season, Boston fans protested. They picketed Fenway Park for days, clamoring for Pumpsie's call-up. Management had to bow to the pressure, and Green became the first black to dent the segregated team.

Perhaps unnerved by all the media coverage, he hit only .233. Unfortunately, his next four years with the Sox (and Mets) were equally forgettable. Serving only as a utility infielder, he averaged about sixty games a year, and customarily batted near .245. No longer a *cause celebre*, Pumpsie gave the Sox little choice. By 1962, he was usually found on the bench.

Distraught and feeling isolated because of his color, Pumpsie was an easy mark for Conley's version of Exodus. At first he scoffed at the idea of jumping ship, calling Conley a crazy fool. But as the temperature climbed in the midday sun, Pumpsie started to think of

*Once notorious for his own mischief,
Pumpsie Green now oversees discipline at
Berkeley High School in California.*

his misfortunes, and eventually allowed destiny to play its hand. In a year, he too was out of baseball.

Today, Green tries to avoid talking about the stunt, and takes little credit for breaking baseball's most stubborn color line. Now the dean of boys and an assistant baseball coach in a Berkeley, California high school, he only becomes animated when recalling the racism black players encountered in the late 1950s and early '60s. But even though he's still on the firing line, patrolling schoolyards and enforcing discipline in corridors, he rarely gets angry or loses his composure. Once again, Pumpsie has found his escape. Whenever conditions at the school get too turbulent, Pumpsie takes a day off and goes fishing with his sixty-six-year-old-mother.

"I never really idolized Jackie Robinson; that was just a name to me. I would've been just as happy to stay in the minors. To me the Pacific Coast League was big-time enough. When the fans picketed in Boston and I saw my name in the papers, I wished it hadn't happened. It was too much pressure on me, it was too tough on a rookie. I was terrified at times. Everywhere I went, it was the first Negro this and the first Negro that. Not only did I have to be some kind of pioneer, but I also had to go up against Early Wynn curveballs.

"I wasn't about to say a word about the black-white thing. I knew twenty-four guys went one way and me another. I didn't even ride on the same plane with the other players. But it wouldn't have been too smart for me to challenge it. Stars like Banks, Elston Howard, and others didn't say anything, so how could a rookie like me do it? But my having to find a separate hotel room or a different place to eat didn't happen a hundred years ago. Imagine, this was America only a short time ago."

Disturbed by the noise from a group of cheerleaders outside his office, Green hurriedly shuts a window before reaching for a nearly empty pack of cigarettes. Then, between long, mechanical puffs, he continues, "The worst thing about being black in those days was that I was the only target in a beanball war. I was the wrong color. Nothing could be going on, but clubs like Cleveland or Detroit, they figured they owed me one. Things didn't get better until Willie Tasby came to Boston. Then I at least had someone to go over the tracks with.

"I don't really want to get into it, but my being black also led to everything being exaggerated about my so-called disappearance. Conley and I were just in the dumps. We needed some time alone. We were just crying in each other's beer. I was in Washington soon thereafter. It was all just something the reporters invented.

"I could look back at this, or the other racial things, and get mad. I do sometimes, but mostly I consider myself lucky. I got to do what I had always dreamed about, to play in the big leagues. Sure, I wanted to hit hundreds of homers, and make it to the Hall of Fame. But let me ask you a question. How many guys get where I got? How many people live to see their deepest dreams come true? I did."

DOUG RADER
Going Bananas with the Grape Bubble Gum Kid

A brown, mushy, foul-smelling "decoration" on the top of Joe Pepitone's birthday cake; holes drilled in the back of the dugout to look up women's dresses; sandwiches filled with saliva; classes in the use of vibrators; boccie games in the bullpen; and skinny-dipping parties in hotel swimming pools.

Baseball players often do some very strange things.

Guys like Curt "Cuckoo" Blefary, Joe Pepitone, and Jim "Bulldog" Bouton were forever going berserk, rewriting the record book on mischief, ding-donging their way to unparalleled expressions of bad taste. What else could they do? Faced with those dog days of summer, when first place was already thirty-five games away, they had to improvise, make things interesting, or they wouldn't have been the Houston Astros—the space cadets nonpareil of baseball—who even had their own special song:

> Now, the Astros are a team that likes to go out
>   on the town,
> We like to drink and fight till curfew comes
>   around.
> Then it's time to make the trek,
> We better be back to buddy's check,
> It makes a fellow proud to be a Houston Astro.

Tarzan, watch out, here comes Doug Rader!

Now Edwards is our catcher and he's really
  number one,
Dave Bristol said he drinks too much and calls
  some long home runs,
But we think John will be alright,
If we keep him in his room at night.
It make a fellow proud to be a Houston Astro.
Now, our pitching staff's composed of guys who
  think they're pretty cool,
With a case of Scotch, a greenie, and an old
  beat-up whirlpool,
We make the other hitters laugh,
Then calmly break their bats in half,
It makes a fellow proud to be a Houston Astro.
Now, Harry Walker is the one that manages this
  crew,
He doesn't like it when we drink and fight and
  smoke and screw,
But when we win our game each day,
Then what the hell can Harry say?
It makes a fellow proud to be a Houston Astro.

Yes, Doug Rader was certainly one of the inspired. As a leader of this renegade bunch, he had a unique gift, an unmistakable talent, which deserves an honored place in baseball folklore. Whenever the occasion called for it, he could always make someone vomit.

Understandably proud of this skill, Rader strutted around third base like a peacock, or, as his deranged teammates called him, the Red Rooster. Too busy swaggering, he wasn't much at bending down or moving sideways for ground balls (usually a leader in errors with twenty to twenty-five a year, his fielding average hovered between .930 to .950). Nor was he a force at the plate, not with a .251 lifetime batting average, coupled with a hundred or more strikeouts every season. He would come up with fifteen to twenty home runs, but don't let that deceive you. Dougie boy was one bad ballplayer. He needed something, anything, to stay in the biggies. And that, ladies and gentlemen, was his self-described ability "to take charge, to keep things loose, to bring out the best in people, to do the unexpected, so I could help my team, by not being just another Humpty Dumpty ballplayer."

What modesty! What selflessness! What dedication! It doesn't do Rader justice. Only a glimmer of the man comes across through those few words. It's much more meaningful to describe how he performed under the stress of daily competition; what made him unique from other men; and why he truly was a team leader—the captain who always brought the Astros through a crisis.

Basically, he was educated. He learned the game inside and out. How? The Rooster sat on the bench during games and ate baseball cards. Fleer's, Topp's, it didn't matter. They were so chock-full of stats, player profiles, and batting or fielding tips that Rader chewed them, hoping to absorb some of the information—and some of his heroes' skills. He'd even advise children to do the same, if they asked him about becoming a ballplayer. "Wanna be a Hank Aaron or a Tom Seaver? Then get yourself five of their cards, and start chewing."

Rader thought this Mr. Sanitation Man routine would make the Astros forget their own mess, to get jacked up. How wrong he was. Instead of taking opponents to the cleaners, Rader's teammates were ready to lie down and die—gasping to the end, one loud EEEC-CHH.

Such Raderisms were to be expected. Any schoolteacher could tell you that redheads always were trouble. Doug was the kid in the back of a classroom who pulled girls' hair, or drove teachers crazy with flying paper clips. Of course, he never did nothin', and was always picked on. Sure. He wound up with black eyes, hot candy store goods, and spankings because he was innocent as a choirboy.

"When you're stealing hubcaps, getting your hands where they aren't supposed to be, and you're in and out of jail, you can't help but be a ballplayer," explains

Rader, grabbing a long piece of bamboo in the back of his Florida home, preparing for yet another prank. "I always wanted to be a Tahitian warlord, or if that wasn't possible, a pirate. I guess I had to settle for baseball. Too bad I wasn't around for the 1930s Gashouse Gang. Now those guys really had fun. I had my share, I sure did. But you should have seen me in college. Then it was really Animal House. I cooled down a lot after that."

Before cooling down too much, Rader called himself Lou Bardini, middleweight fighter, otherwise known as the Chicago Cobra. He punched, jabbed, threw rights, lefts—and was knocked unconscious eight seconds after his first fight began.

Recovering from the shortest fight career ever, he then became Dominic Bulganzio, ice hockey player extraordinaire. Steal that puck. Knock heads. Protect the goalie. Trigger the power play. Rader did all of that—in his dreams. At six-feet-two, 200 pounds, the Rooster had the physical gifts for the sport. But you guessed it, with all that blood flowing around, "I didn't want to be no fighting cock. What do you think I am, a dumb turkey?"

Baseball was more relaxed, gentlemanly. Rader wasn't worried here. He could be himself. So, along with having a few good years—twenty-five homers in 1970, and twenty-two in '72 (in the tough, distant reaches of the AstroDome)—he (a) repeatedly stashed extra lobster tails or other food in his sports coat ("in case I got hungry at night"), then wondered why his jacket had so many stains; (b) set fire to baseballs to warm up the dugout on cold nights; (c) scared unwanted company away from his home by getting undressed and parading at the front door of his house; (d) videotaped nude swimming relays in the Astros' hotel pool, for later broadcasting on the hotel's closed-circuit TV system.

It's probably fitting by now to ask is this man insane? That's a distinct possibility. In any case, an even bigger mystery looms. One which completely stretches the imagination. How did Doug Rader become a minor league manager, with a Triple A franchise, no less?

Recently hired as the skipper of the Texas Rangers, after he piloted the Hawaiian Islanders, Rader is back in the majors, on the verge of following the hallowed footsteps of a Casey Stengel, Connie Mack, or John McGraw. And if this wasn't enough to rattle the conservative baseball establishment, Rader's other big surprise is his performance. In three years of minor league managing he's been to the playoffs twice—an achievement that certainly led to his new job, and might possibly destroy the game we all knew and loved.

"I can handle the biggies now, I'm a changed man," boasts Rader, poking his head out from behind a palm tree. "I was always a born leader. I was the Astros' captain for years. I'm a winner. Even if I was goofy, I was never irresponsible. Now I've settled down, become a Dr. Jekyll and learned to be invisible. We have a chicken at the ballpark in Hawaii, and I'm certainly no crazier than him.

"I'm prepared to manage because the game taught me so much. You go through a grind with it, and you eventually get to the end of the road. You learn something through this. To be a good manager, a good leader of fat and sassy ballplayers, you have to scare the shit out of them and really know the game. I'm fairly large, and I've learned some secrets from a few topnotch managers. I don't know if they really understood me at the time. No one knew what I was up to. But Harry Walker, my manager at Houston, was so honest, he had the best heart of anyone I ever knew. I've forgiven him for trying to make me like him, a singles hitter. I always had the potential of a Mantle or an Aaron. I just want to treat my guys the way he treated me, with respect."

Afraid that he's becoming too serious, Rader gets ready to climb the palm tree or to do his Tarzan impersonation. But just as he plants one of his legs on the trunk, his nine-year-old son, Matt, and a few other children run over to him, wondering if he'll play touch football.

"Come on, you guys, don't you see I'm really busy, that I got to get some coconuts? Don't you fellas have a home? You're always around here. Take a hike, go get some catfish."

"Ah, please, one game, then you can go back to that silly stuff," answers one of the bolder children.

"It's always one game, one game."

Despite his feigned toughness, Rader needs little convincing. He reties his sneakers, starts loosening up, and, just before running off, says, "Confrontation, there's nothing like it. The odds were five to one against my staying in the majors eleven years. Well, I fooled them. Now I just have to get back there. Will that be a riot. In the meantime, these kids can be really tough. Whew! I need something to relax me. You don't have any grape bubble gum, do you?"

*Chocolate-covered frycakes are
a Mickey Lolich specialty.*

MICKEY LOLICH
Sugar 'n' Spice, 'n' Everything Not So Nice

Known for throwing goose eggs throughout his career, longtime Detroit pitching ace Mickey Lolich is now mixing up batters in a different way.

A newly trained baker, he's hand-soaking, powdering, and glazing thousands of doughnuts daily in his Rochester, Michigan shop.

"What a mess; that batch isn't round, those things look like a bunch of footballs," complains Lolich, nudging aside an assistant to knead a fresh batch of crullers. "I don't know what's going on today. First the coffee machine breaks down, now this. Footballs, whew! Come on, get more dough out of the freezer."

Insisting that he makes the "best doughnut in the Midwest," Lolich directs a squadron of his daughters (three) and other workers (all wearing baseball jerseys with the number "29") to appointed tasks. Some must serve coffee at a busy counter, while a few work in the back of the doughnut parlor, preparing batters. Meanwhile, the forty-three-year-old Lolich is a whirling dervish. He first stacks rows of doughnuts in an oven, then simultaneously coats other crullers with colored sprinkles, and samples a chocolate-covered frycake. Beaming at this point, he takes another bite, and says, "It's this creation that got me into the business in the first place. No one else around here was making them." (Despite the surroundings, or the folklore about his eating habits, the six-foot-one lefthander has stayed close to his playing weight of 225.)

Lolich is working extra hard these days because he's thinking of opening a second shop (and a third, and a fourth . . .), or, as he puts it, "dunking it up with a nearby franchise." But even if he becomes the McDonald's of the doughnut world, his forty types of maple bars, buttermilk sticks, and cinnamon twists will never compare with 217 career wins, 2,832 strikeouts, a 25-14 season (1971), and, most spectacularly of all, three victories in the 1968 World Series. Against the likes of St. Louis sluggers Lou Brock, Curt Flood, and Orlando Cepeda, Lolich was simply dazzling. He struck out twenty-seven men, had a 1.67 ERA, and while it's not listed in any record book, his lifting the team to victory provided a spiritual boost that the racially upset city of Detroit so sorely needed.

Now Lolich faces a different kind of pressure—finding the right water temperature for each kind of doughnut. Dipping his hands into a vat of gooey butter and wearing a long, blueberry-streaked apron, he jokingly remarks, "When I started here a few years ago, my doughnuts usually had four or five holes in them. I didn't want to be just a name on the front door. So I put on my jeans and apron and learned the recipes. The proper mix of ingredients is important, but an oven temperature is the key. Now this is pressure. The World Series was nothing compared to this. You have to know how long it takes for these cakes to rise, or else you can spoil the whole shebang. I guess sometimes I feel like a woman at home, fidgeting with the oven, waiting for her husband's dessert to rise.

"This business is certainly an adjustment. In a few years I might own five or six of these shops. But in the meantime everything has changed in my life, financially. You just have to accept the fact that you're living another life, that you're an average workingman. I still have my home, I can maintain it, sure. I just can't blow $100 a night on dinner, or buy a new car every year. If you're a ballplayer, you never worry about these things. You just go out and buy what you want. It's that simple. You don't think twice. Now that's impossible for me. Psychologically, it's tough.

"What makes things worse is losing your friends. The clubhouse talk, the beer-drinking with the guys, all that's gone. I could go down to the stadium, talk to the guys, but that's nothing. It's not the same thing as really belonging there. I can't even talk about baseball to the people who come in here. They wouldn't know what it meant to set up a Boog Powell, or what velocity on the ball meant. It's like being a chess master and going to the park to play checkers."

Keeping an eye on his assistant throughout the conversation, Lolich suddenly barks, "You're using too much dough. Cut out the holes and save what's left over." Unsatisfied by the teenager's next attempt, Lolich walks over to the cutting or rolling table, and demonstrates. In a few minutes he returns, looking worried.

"Don't think this business is all sugar and honey. It ain't. There are some real joys here. I really like to see people eating my frycakes and leaving the shop happy. But customers can be too demanding, and you can go broke if you don't watch the help. It's impossible these days to find reliable counter girls. Almost every day I have the feeling that I want to sell out.

"But believe it or not, I stay in this business because it's a lot like pitching. You have to decide what has to be done, and then do it. And don't think for a moment that making a strawberry topping is all that easy . . ."

Sorry, Stonehands, the ball's behind you!

HECTOR LOPEZ
Memories in a Car Trunk

Ooops! Ooops! Ooops!

A bungled ground ball, off a glove, or through his feet. Then a misjudged pop fly, lost in the sun, and a wild throw over an infielder's head into the stands.

Not too many players resemble octopuses or flub enough balls to lose, single-handedly, scores of games. Dick "Dr. Strangeglove" Stuart, Chuck "Iron Hands" Hiller, and Rod "Stone Glove" Kanehl have all competed for the honor of being the game's all-time worst fielder. None of them compare, however, to Hector Lopez, the Bungling Bronx Butcher.

It didn't matter where Kansas City put him, second base or third, Hector always managed to make routine fielding chances a spine-tingling adventure. Fans never knew what was going to happen: a bobbled grounder, running the wrong way for a pop-up, or a missed tag, as the Panamanian-born Lopez led the league in errors at third base three out of four years (1955-1958). He would've undoubtedly improved on this streak, if not for a multi-player KC-Yankee trade (including Ralph Terry, Norm Siebern, Tom Sturdivant, and Jerry Lumpe in 1959), which resulted in his being converted to a left-fielder. (Or at least the Yankees tried.) Then Hector could only play easy fly balls into extra-base hits, but he continued to have one of the worst fielding averages on the team (about .950 to .970 in each of his seven pin-striped years).

"The way I was with a glove, it was a real shock when the Yankees gave up three players for two (him and Terry)." recalls the fifty-four-year old Lopez, sitting by a pool in the park he manages on Long Island. "Coming to New York, that was it. Casey and Houk, they'd call me into the office to talk about plays I botched up. Neither of them could do anything with my fielding. And me, after a while I got like the reporters and the fans. My errors just made me laugh."

In spite of his fielding, Lopez helped the Yankees win five consecutive pennants, from 1960 to 1964. Always a team player, he bunted well, pushed runners across the bases by hitting to the opposite field, and was one of the Bombers' most important RBI men. While Berra, Skowron, and Maris got all the headlines, Hector averaged an RBI with every two hits. He was especially productive in the 1962-63 seasons, when 200 safeties netted 100 RBIs, most of them in clutch situations. These key hits made him a special favorite of New York fans. And if managers Houk or Berra used Elston Howard or Johnny Blanchard in left field, the crowd's response was always predictable. After the initial chorus of boos, Lopez's Legions would loudly chant, "We want Hector, we want Hector."

"Everything I learned about hitting I got from Lou Boudreau. He gave me the points. I never thought I'd make it as a player, or stick around too long. Lou changed all that. He taught me when to go to the opposite field, or how to hit behind a runner. Thank God I ran into him. Staying in the game helped me grow up. I became a real person. I wasn't afraid of talking with people anymore even with my bad English. And I learned how to overcome obstacles, tension, and to deal with challenges."

The ultimate test of surviving under pressure is the World Series. And it was here that Lopez shined. A .286 hitter in post-season competition, he enjoyed his greatest moment in the last game of the 1961 clash against the Reds. With Mantle and Berra out of that game because of injuries, Lopez carried the Yankees to victory, driving in five runs with a homer and triple. He now wears a 1961 Series ring, and while proudly rubbing it says, "No matter what happens to me in life, I'll never equal what I did against the Reds. That day was unbelievable. I made people forget Maris and Mantle. I was the number one Yankee. No one was talking about my glove. I was Superman for a little while."

Lopez had another good year in 1962, batting .275 with 48 RBIs in 106 games. But there would be no more heroics. Tom Tresh and Roger Repoz, two outfielders who didn't live up to their billing as the next Mickey Mantle, were platooned with Lopez in left field, and his batting average started to slip. By 1965, he was down to .261, with only thirty-nine RBIs, as the Yankees often limited him to pinch hitting. From then on Lopez admits, "The fun stopped; playing became just a way to make a living." He only hit .214 in 1966, and when the Yankees released him after the season a familiar pattern was repeated. Like a lot of players who refused to face the inevitable, Lopez returned to the minors, hoping to launch a comeback.

"I figured if I could go to Hawaii and have a nice year, someone might pick me up." Lopez's eyes twinkle when this is said, and it seems as if he's still daydreaming about his career, or another attempt at a comeback. Proudly recalling his .293 batting average with the Hawaii Islanders, he goes on to say, "When you play ball all your life, and it's your only ambition, it's pretty tough to give up. I didn't want to do anything else, and I wasn't trained to do anything different. You don't think about the future while you're playing. Baseball lulls you to sleep in a way. I only studded a little of mechanics in school, but if I had it to do over, I would've gone to school, and worked in the offseason. Anyway, it doesn't matter, I loved playing, and I wouldn't trade in my baseball days for anything. What a life it was, so great."

After two years in Triple A ball, one season of managing at Buffalo, and three years of scouting, Lopez was hired by the Hempstead Town Board as a recreation specialist (in 1972). He advised the town supervisor on various park department matters and spoke to teenagers about drug abuse. Never forgetting his true love, Lopez also worked for the Yankees, serving as a part-time scout, speaker, and, true to his earlier origins, a public relations utility man.

Now Lopez has his own team, as he supervises six teenage counselors at the Harold A. Walker park in West Hempstead. Two swimming pools, daily educational programs, gymnastics, and personnel problems preoccupy Lopez most of the time. And while he admits that "the neighborhood is mainly interested in basketball," he still manages to look for a future baseball prospect, and to give a youngster a few pointers.

"I like working with kids, especially if I can teach them a few playing fundamentals. The only way you're going to keep them away from drugs is to keep them busy. The streets here are full of trouble. They have to do something, running, swimming, whatever, if they're not going to get into a jam. Hopefully, baseball can do for them what it did for me.

"The togetherness, the feeling of a team, that's the big thing. Baseball makes you feel more than an individual, it makes you responsible to others. The Yankees didn't need coaches around. We knew we had to do it as a team. The spirit there was like nowhere else. It was beautiful to see men so close. It's impossible to get that feeling now. I've tried, oh, have I tried to feel those emotions again. It just hasn't happened, and away from baseball I guess it never will.

"I do like working with kids, though. Now I'm a teacher in all aspects of sports. That's rewarding. I never badmouth a kid. I try to build them up, even when they're doing strange things, like playing hockey."

Chuckling, Lopez hands a checkers set to a young boy, and moves towards the parking lot. After opening the trunk of his Cadillac, he takes out his old Yankee uniform and says, "I keep this close to me all the time. Every time I open the trunk I say to myself, 'I used to

Good-natured Hector is still a crowd-pleaser.

play ball for the greatest team.' If they called me now for a position in the organization I'd be ready. I'll be there. I can still move around.

"It's satisfying to be in the park, to see that the fields are kept in good shape, and that the kids don't get hurt. Even if it's babysitting sometimes, I don't mind. Watching kids laughing and having a good time is really important.

"But once you play baseball, the feelings for it, the longings, the desires, never die. The game stays with you. It's just like your first romance." Lopez then picks up the glove he used as a Yankee, pounds the pocket and sighs, "I miss the game so much. I can be out there on the softball field, or by the pool, and when a plane goes by, I'll say to myself, 'I should be on that flight. I should be heading to Chicago or Kansas City with the guys, I should be going somewhere for a game.'"

GENE WOODLING
But Where's the Camel?

The search for black gold is usually perilous. Rich oil fields are a fabulous prize, but they also carry a steep price in dollars, sweat, and lives. Most people don't just get lucky and stumble onto a strike. They have to struggle. Some must tramp through the dusty, wind-blown reaches of Texas, plunge into the Louisiana swamps, or brave the parched California Baja. Some are forced into even trickier adventures. Against a background of foreign wars, politics, or Byzantine schemes, they cross disputed deserts, court mysterious sheiks, and even risk jail or death.

Only a chosen few strike it rich a lot easier. They've been blessed. They've worn a Yankee uniform.

Epitomizing this luck of the pinstripe, 1950s Yankee outfielder Gene Woodling literally struck oil in his back yard. Casually strolling around his Ohio farm a few years ago, surveying sites for water wells, he started to fantasize about getting lucky. He knew someone at the Quaker State oil company, and later asked him to come over with a drilling team. In three weeks, after six holes were dug, Woodling hit the ultimate grand slam. Two of the holes tapped sources of oil—and now "Iron Mikes" pump out 126 barrels every six weeks. And at $35 a barrel, that's quite a score for someone who's watching the action from the sidelines.

*Lefty Gene Woodling is about to hit a homer—
or lose a friend (Gil McDougald).*

Besides chuckling "An oil well is good work if you can find it," or making thinly-veiled threats about challenging OPEC, Woodling has retired to a life of Florida fishing and "very part-time" scouting for the Cleveland Indians. Formerly a salesman for the Eaton Corporation, specializing in selling golf grips and auto accessories, he now pictures himself a country gentleman. Work is simply dismissed as "someone else's headache." His wife occasionally dents this image by getting him to do a few household chores. But except for visiting the barn to pet his prized collection of Appaloosa horses, Woodling is making up for all those sweaty, nerve-wracking days spent in Yankee Stadium's left-field Death Valley. He's thoroughly enjoying himself.

"Now I just like getting into my jeep and going out there to watch one of those Iron Mikes," confesses Woodling, his face glowing as if a court had just named him Howard Hughes's beneficiary. "It's great watching those things go up and down. It's money. Every time they move it's money. And more money. My advice for ballplayers is, simply, buy land. Why? Because players aren't qualified to go into the business world. If they go into land no one will steal it from them. My whole success has been land, and I've had the good fortune to punch holes in it. I'd recommend this to anyone. It's the life."

But not everyone is as lucky as Gene Woodling. On the way out of baseball, after a rather poor debut with the Indians and Pirates (from 1943 to the '46-'47 seasons, he went from a .320 average to .188 and .266), Woodling started to connect at exactly the right time. Playing for the San Francisco Seals in the Pacific Coast League (1948), Woodling hit a whopping .700 against the Oakland Oaks, who happened to be led by the man who would become the next manager of the Yankees, Casey Stengel. That statistic was never forgotten by Stengel, and the following season Woodling was playing next to DiMaggio and Hank Bauer.

For six years, until a trade sent him to the Orioles for Don Larsen and Bob Turley in 1955, Woodling was a vital part of the New York machine. At first, laboring under the shadows of other great Yankee left fielders, Johnny Lindell and Charlie Keller wasn't easy. But those memories were soon put to rest as Woodling himself became a star in the Yankee constellation. He tamed the Stadium's tricky sun porch (averaging only two or three errors a year), and replaced Tommy Henrich as the club's Old Reliable. His combined Yankee average was .286, while in five World Series he hit an outstanding .318, with twenty-one runs scored, and a .529 slugging percentage.

The Baltimore trade completely surprised him, but the real shocker came seven years later. After several productive seasons with the Indians, Orioles, and Washington Senators (from 1955 to 1961 his average was usually close to .300, with sixty to seventy RBIs), Woodling was reunited with Casey in 1962 on a team that was every player's nightmare—the Mets.

Now sixty-one, Woodling laughs when recalling that mishap-plagued year, and declares, "Casey was the best PR guy in baseball, maybe the best ever in sports. He had to be a genius to get so much attention for that team. Boy, were the Mets bad. I still can't believe the way we played. Either we were too old or too young; we just didn't make it. Yet they weren't an embarrassment for me. I was still in the big leagues. That's a pretty good deal for a forty-year old, even if my favorite memory of 1962 was my getting ready to go home.

"But thank goodness I was a ballplayer. If not for baseball, I would've been working in a Goodyear factory (Woodling was born in Akron, Ohio, a town dominated by the giant rubber company). I've always been lucky. My, just think of it, in my day there were only 500 major leaguers. And I was one of them. That's why I got jobs later on. I only hope the guys today appreciate what they have. There's nothing like baseball.

"Look what the game gave me. I was never a farm boy, and here I am with thirty-three acres, a barn, wonderful horses, and two Iron Mikes pumping oil night and day. What more could I ask for? I really didn't

Besides taking care of his oil wells, Gene is black gold around the house.

do a thing for that oil, and yet now I have a condominium right on the water in Clearwater Beach. I was never a DiMaggio or a Williams, but I still did alright. Damn alright. That says something about playing for seventeen years, or maybe that Yankee uniform."

Then, grabbing a handful of travel brochures and smiling contentedly, Woodling continues, "Next year me and my wife are going to take a two month trip across the West. Then the following year we're going to see all of Europe. I'm quite a bug on American history, but I also want to see what foreign cultures are like. I want to sleep in a few of those Swiss palaces, and know what it's like to live like a king. Right now, you could say, my second life is just beginning."

MEL STOTTLEMYRE
Croquet, Anyone?

Except for Howard Cosell, all the big names in sports are there. Hockey sensation Wayne Gretzky turns up with models of his golden sticks. Running back Tony Dorsett has a display of Dallas Cowboy jerseys, warm-up outfits, and even a football or two. John McEnroe serves up a variety of tennis gear. As for baseball, there are sluggers from Winfield to Brett to Schmidt.

A star himself during the 1960s, Yankee pitcher Mel Stottlemyre has lined up all these big-name items for his Yakima, Washington sporting goods store. The super-market-sized shop is the Alice's Restaurant of the jock world. Athletes of every age, size, or disposition can get anything they want here, from barbells to Ping-Pong balls, from boxing gloves to croquet mallets. Since he's a minor league pitching coach for the Seattle Mariners during the summer, Mel isn't always around to service these customers. Still, the Yankee stopper's presence is always felt. Next to posters of modern-day greats, like Reggie and Doctor J, the walls are crammed with photos of Stot's most memorable moments.

Signed out of high school for what he laughingly calls "the worst deal ever made (a plane ticket and a few thousand dollars)," Stottlemyre joined the Yankees in 1964. By posting a 9-3 record with a 2.06 ERA, he helped lead the team to the World Series, and almost

Mel Stottlemyre, a man for all seasons.

beat out Tony Oliva for the Rookie of the Year award. In that Series against the Cardinals, he demonstrated so much poise in winning his first start that manager Yogi Berra later called upon him to pitch the decisive seventh game. Homers by Lou Brock and Ken Boyer knocked him out by the fourth inning, but Stottlemyre still says, "My achievements that year were the most satisfying of my life. I was only a rookie, and yet people had the confidence in me to win the greatest prize in baseball."

The lanky right-hander then went on to win twenty games in 1965 (with only nine losses and a 2.63 ERA), and to establish himself as the club's most important pitcher. The Yankees slipped to the bottom of the standings in the mid-1960s, but Stot didn't let the weak fielding or hitting of a Horace Clarke or Jake Gibbs upset him. Relying mainly on a sinker or slider, he consistently registered fifteen to twenty wins, and kept his ERA below 3.0 (along with a 164-139 lifetime record, he had three twenty-game seasons, and a career 2.97 ERA).

Recalling that he was the highest-paid Yankee by the early 1970s (at $95,000 a year), Stottlemyre shrugs off the club's misfortunes and says, "The guys weren't spoiled by their winning all the time. We gave it all we had, so it wasn't the end of the world finishing fifth or sixth. I guess we just didn't have the firepower in those years. I did the best I could." Then, smiling boyishly, he adds, "I'm only disappointed that I didn't reach my rainbow. I always wanted to make $100,000 and win a World Series. Maybe if I had stuck around a few more years I would've."

Those goals became impossible in 1974, when Stottlemyre suddenly developed arm trouble. Doctors initially diagnosed the problem as tendinitis, and Stot was temporarily placed on the disabled list. Only later, after two months of inactivity, was it discovered that the thirty-three-year-old pitcher had a torn rotator cuff—and was finished.

Embittered by bad doctoring, and by the way club officials subsequently treated him, Stottlemyre admits,

"I didn't want anyone to mention the word Yankees for years. I really thought I had been shuffled around pretty badly." That anger has since cooled, partially because of his involvement with the Mariners. But Stottlemyre has also been distracted lately by a family tragedy. His ten-year-old son, Jason, recently died of leukemia, and this has "given me a new perspective on what's important, and maybe the maturity to laugh at the small things that go wrong in life."

Indicative of this more relaxed attitude, Stot stands near a wall-sized cartoon in his shop that reads, "The quickest way to Yakima from New York is a sore arm and a 7.9 ERA," and he says, "It was super being a Yankee. It certainly hurt when they wanted to cut my salary in 1975. I didn't expect that, and I really thought I'd become a coach with them after my arm didn't respond that spring. I always thought I'd be a Yankee forever.

"But I don't have a single regret now. My entire system of values has changed, and everything's worked out for the best. It's only a little tough to see my older sons rooting for the Yankees against the Mariners. I can understand it, though. The club was such an important, overwhelming part of our lives. It was everything.

"That experience with the front office also helped me in later life. Now I want to be as honest as I can with players. I want them to really confide in me. I'm not going to get rich coaching, but I can help kids. A coach can turn their whole game around and be a very dominant influence in their lives. Baseball is often a tough game, and I think I'm making it easier for them.

"It's only difficult being in two places at the same time. All the traveling I'm doing these days isn't exactly helping the store. But no way am I going to give up either of them. The store's something I always wanted. I used to think of having it when I was out on the field. I'm an outdoor person, I enjoy coming here in the winter. I can meet people interested in sports, and it's a sure way to stay active. Sports is the most satisfying thing in life. Besides, the store is all mine. For someone with no business experience at all, I'm doing okay.

"Why, just look at all those people," continues Stottlemyre, pointing to a group of teenagers waiting to try on athletic shoes. He then walks over to the crowd, pats some of the shoppers on the back, and takes a few boxes off a shelf. Though unperturbed by the boys shouting to be waited upon, he finally says, "The store's great, but nothing competes with being a player. I can't describe the feeling, the magic of striking out a Tony Oliva, or what it means to fool a Kaline with a pitch. I think of these moments all the time. Now I'm looking forward to seeing my sons get into baseball."

Ouch! Baseball's Merry Pranksters, the O'Brien twins, are up to their old tricks.

JOHNNY AND
EDDIE O'BRIEN
Double Jeopardy

Give one of these wackos a harp. Or an exploding cigar, a water-squirting flower; anything at all that smacks of hanky-panky. Twins Eddie and Johnny are the Marx Brothers of baseball.

Who else with sub-.250 batting averages would hang a picture of Ted Williams on an office wall, put two photos of themselves next to it, and label the collage "The World's Three Greatest Hitters?"

No one.

Forget calling them the O'Briens. They are the M & M Boys, the mischief and mayhem pair that's spiritually tied to other misbegottens, the 1962 Mets. This latter group got the publicity. But it was the O'Briens who set the standards for running the wrong way on pop flies, missing signals, and stumbling on the basepaths. Admittedly, the last problem wasn't that significant. The twins rarely got to first base.

Johnny, the more powerful of the pair, usually struggled to hit .250, and had four homers in six major league years (mostly with the Pirates at various infield positions, before being optioned to St. Louis and Milwaukee). He did have a .299 percentage in 1955, but the following year he was the same old Johnny again, batting .173. Poor Eddie, meanwhile, had it even tougher. He was so weak with the stick (zero homers and a .236

lifetime batting average for five years) the Pirates constantly repositioned him—from short to the outfield to third to second to pitcher—hoping to find a place where he'd do the least damage.

Further complicating this comedy of errors, the brothers were exact lookalikes. That drove managers (and everyone else) bananas. Johnny (or his brother) could pull off a prank, and quickly alibi, "Hey, that wasn't me, that was Eddie."

Proudly recalling how this trick fooled the bubblegum people at Topp's, Johnny exclaims, grinning mischievously, "I'll never forget that one. I was in no condition to get my picture taken, so Eddie came to my rescue. While Topp's thought they were getting me for a card, they really got a double dose of Eddie. We did that kind of thing lots of times. In spring training one of us would want to get some sun. We'd only have to do some fast juggling, and one of us at the ballpark was usually enough. If both of us were there at the same time, it would've been certain disaster for the Pirates."

Ironically, Johnny now discourages certain shenanigans in his role as head of security at the Kingdome in Seattle. A veritable Groucho, chomping on an ever-present cigar, he was an elected King County commissioner before taking over the stadium post. While saying, "I didn't run for governor because I was mortally in fear of being elected," forty-three-year-old elder O'Brien (by four minutes) has realized that policing the Kingdome's 232 yearly events "isn't duck soup, or even chicken noodle." Yet he's still good-humored, joking, "I'm the real mover and shaker, I've got all the keys to the King-dom. $60 million, that's what I paid for that crazy bubble. I only wish I could've played there. I'd never have missed a ball."

Eddie, too, has prospered. A long, long way from his $7,000 playing years, he's an energy consultant to oil riggers and shipping magnates in Alaska. His job is to search out properties, purchase them before they're gobbled up by other companies, and then develop the land for exploration. The bottom line is wheeling and dealing in hundreds of millions, dog-sledding around the Yukon, traveling around the world to woo prospective investors, and dreaming about "a luscious Swiss bank account."

Chortling, "I'm not making errors anymore," Eddie happily describes other details of this lifestyle, and adds, "Not bad, eh? I can't believe it myself sometimes. Especially when I remember I was a baseball coach; yup, a baseball coach for fifteen straight years."

"Yeah, and what a bum he was," interrupts Johnny, flashing a wink, as if anyone would take him seriously anyway. "Eeeech! Those teams were worse than us. If that's the ticket to those oil fields, I'm leaving this crazy place and becoming a coach. Why should I have to deal with those crazy Rolling Stones, or any other concert? I'm leaving now."

"Come on Johnny, shut up. You had your chance. Go out and trip over second base."

"Hey, none of those cracks. I was the baserunner. Look, junior . . ."

Smiling like a newly-appointed chairman of the board, Eddie doesn't divulge the secret of his success until Johnny quiets down. Instead, he counters with a few wisecracks about Johnny's hairdo, and then finally explains, "Both of us were lucky. We had a father who always talked about our going to college, and we also got to know Branch Rickey (the Pirates' owner). He set us straight. No matter how good you are, he said, baseball's only one phase of your life. By thirty, thirty-five, your career's over. We both realized this early on, and planned accordingly. I got a commercial sciences degree, and Johnny, oh, I got him through school."

"Yeah, unlike most players, we were never in any dreamland," chimes in Johnny, faking a left jab to his brother's cheek. "Joke all you want about our baseball careers, and they were a joke. But at the time you're concentrating one hundred percent. It's not so easy getting ready for another career. Rickey knew that. He really knew what was going on in the world. He was so smart. He was really a barrel of a man. What common sense. Some of it had to rub off on us.

"I still remember the time Eddie was at short and I was at second base. Every time we made a double play or did the pivot in practice, Rickey was there with a bullhorn, yelling 'That's beautiful, that's my Pee Wee Reese.' Well, Eddie started firing the ball at me, and starting to take Rickey a little too seriously. That ball was nearly taking my belly button off. I didn't know what was going on; I wasn't out there for anything but a good time. So I went over to Rickey and told him, 'That may be Pee Wee Reese, but he's killing Jackie Robinson.' "

WILLIE McCOVEY
"Just Three Feet Higher"

Few baseball players make Charlie Brown cry. The *Peanuts* cartoon character is usually too busy with Lucy to care about the national pastime. Besides, if one of his heroes struck out, or disappointed him in some other way, Charlie wouldn't resort to tears. He'd simply borrow Linus's security blanket.

Only once has there been a Great Breakdown. In 1962, Charlie turned into a Niagara Falls, when "cruel, cruel" Willie McCovey let him down.

It was the seventh game of the World Series, between the Giants and Yankees, with New York leading 1-0 in the bottom of the ninth. Two men were on base, with two out, but before McCovey got a chance to hit, Yankee manager Ralph Houk asked pitcher Ralph Terry what he wanted to do—pitch to Big Mac or to Willie Mays. "Let's settle it right here," said Terry; and soon thereafter, McCovey hit a wicked line drive towards right field.

Poor Charlie Brown. The ball never got past the infield. Second baseman Bobby Richardson speared it, and the notorious Bronx Bombers had won again. There was no joy in Mudville. And a few days later, Charlie was crying in his comic strip, "Oh, Willie, Willie, why couldn't you've hit that ball three feet higher?"

It will certainly be sad if Stretch McCovey is only

Willie McCovey earns his nickname, Stretch.

remembered for that Series-ending frozen rope. He accomplished too many other things, to be known simply as a tear jerker. The Giants' slugging first baseman hit 521 lifetime homers, won three home run titles and tied for a fourth, was the NL's Rookie of the Year in 1959, and in 1969 he was named Most Valuable Player, after recording forty-five homers, 126 RBIs, and a .320 batting average.

He always played in the shadow of Willis Mays, but this six-foot four-inch, 200-pound powerhouse owned the National League's right-field seats. From 1963 to 1970 his home run totals only dipped below thirty-one once (eighteen in 1964), while in those other years he slammed forty-four, thirty-nine, thirty-six, thirty-one, thirty-six, forty-five, and thirty-nine. When the Giants unloaded some of their high-salaried stars in the mid-'70s, McCovey was traded to the San Diego Padres for Mike Caldwell. He kept hitting home runs, however, and eventually made it back to the Giants (in 1977), to slug twenty-eight homers at age thirty-nine.

Now a potential Hall of Famer, McCovey continues to rack up big numbers, not far from the Giants' Candlestick Park. A vice-president with the Ramallah Linen Company, a bedding products manufacturer five minutes from the ballpark, he visits wool mills, calls on customers, and has helped negotiate million-dollar-plus deals with Cannon and Macy's. His name could have gotten him a cushy PR job with any company in the Bay Area, which would mean "my only putting on a striped suit, chit-chatting with a few people, and taking it easy." But McCovey wants to stay "close to the action that's always part of an important business decision"—making contacts with prospective buyers, or lending support to Ramallah's sales staff.

Sitting in his small, stone-walled office, next to a sixty-pound, ten-foot bat, photos of various home run swings, and a blown-up version of Charlie Brown's tearful cartoon, Big Mac says, "Even though the camaraderie here isn't exactly the same as I had with the Giants (we did more crazy things playing ball), there's a family closeness that makes me happy. Ramallah is run by six Arab brothers, and I'm the seventh. To them, it doesn't matter if I get to the Hall of Fame, or if I got a hit or not. They've made me a part of the family, and so I've been real lucky in life."

McCovey's soft, measured speaking tone is hardly flamboyant, so it's understandable why he was always lost in the glitter surrounding the Say Hey Kid (Willie Mays). He's plain shy. Even as a child, growing up in a poor section of Mobile, Alabama, McCovey was a self-described loner. He'd only mingle with other teenagers on the ballfield. Baseball was so important to him he ignored his father's objections and left home (and a job in a bakery as a dough roller) for a Giants' tryout camp. While hitting was never a problem, it was difficult for him to adjust to the social niceties of big league life. Friend Leon "Daddy Wags" Wagner recalls, "The kid just wouldn't talk. I had to take Big Mac under my wing, show him the ropes, and get him to open his mouth. I showed him what it meant to be in public, to be a star."

Still somewhat withdrawn, McCovey has lived quietly in a big house outside San Francisco since retiring in 1980. He makes public appearances for the Giants and travels a lot for Ramallah. But he prefers being at home with his dog Homer, fooling around in the backyard or listening to music.

"I got a sad, choking feeling the day I retired. I knew everything would be for the last time. But in a way it's kinda good not to have been forced out. You can hold your head up higher when you go out that way. I don't feel like I left anything undone. I reached my goals. For me to play any longer would just have been icing on the cake. The most important thing for me was to reach my 500th homer. That made me part of an exclusive club. Mantle, Mays, Aaron; those guys will never be forgotten, and neither will I.

"Fortunately, getting to that plateau means lots of great moments. I don't have to live off one specific moment, or accomplishment. I guess, though, the World

Naturally, the slugger's dog is named Homer.

Series is an ultimate goal. I kind of feel sorry for guys who never get there. Right away I think of Ernie Banks. He was such a great player, he did everything for years. But the sad thing is, he doesn't know what the World Series is all about. You get a completely different feeling playing for the championship, and for me to play against the Yankees makes it even more special.

"There isn't a day that goes by that someone doesn't mention the World Series ball I hit to Richardson. What can I say? I hit that ball as hard as I could. I wasn't thinking about anything when I connected, but when you hit it good, you assume it's going to be a hit. I didn't have time to get excited. Later on I was sitting in front of my locker, wondering what happened. I was feeling sad, but at the time I really thought I was going to be able to redeem myself. Everyone on the team thought we'd dominate the league for ten years. I never thought we'd never get back (to the Series). I guess I would've felt sadder if I knew that was it.

"I'm just glad that I made it to the Series, that I got involved with sports in the first place. I wasn't a bad kid, but I could've gone a certain route if not for athletics. A lot of kids in my old neighborhood eventually got into trouble. Baseball, though, gave me a lot of things I would never have gotten otherwise. Respect from people all over the world; presidents and prime ministers have told me that they're fans of mine. That never would've happened if I had wound up working on the railroad, or a bakery in Mobile."

Responding to a few yelps from Homer, McCovey flings a huge bone at him and then walks off into the backyard. Still in excellent physical shape, he frolics with the dog for about half an hour. He only slows up to look at the surrounding hills, and to say, "I'm not lying awake at nights thinking of making a comeback. Yet I feel I could still play. That's a good feeling. I'm not chomping at the bit the get back there. It's just that baseball is something I've done all my life. If I didn't miss it, there'd be something wrong with me.

"Every time I come near Candlestick I feel like telling

(Giant manager) Frank Robinson I could still bring in a guy from third with a sac fly. I'd like to put that idea into his head. I would really have to get into shape, but if they called me to play, I'd jump at the chance."

The young Mudcat Grant wasn't the only one throwing curves . . .

JIM "MUDCAT" GRANT
Frank Sinatra, Move Over

As the cabaret lights dim, Mr. Soul pushes aside a curtain and jumps onstage. Not waiting for the applause to die down, he begins to do his thing. The effect is immediate. Couples hold hands, embrace, or look longingly at one another. They're responding to a soft, rich voice that is vintage Johnny Mathis:

> *You send me, well, well,*
> *You send me, you, you, you do,*
> *Well, well, well, you thrill me,*
> *You, oh, you thrill me,*
> *Honest you do, honest you do,*
> *Oh, oh, oh, honest you do . . .*

Adding to the spell, the singer shuffles between tables, smiling engagingly at misty-eyed females in the Cleveland club. He occasionally caresses a neck, or blows a flirtatious kiss. Then, taking his cues from a chorus onstage, a group of seven shimmying beauties called the Kittens, he belts out another song.

> *Blue moon, you saw me*
> *standing alone,*
> *Blue moon, you . . .*

James "Mudcat" Grant always was a performer. Blessed with a fourteen-karat voice and an equally golden right arm, he had a flair for winning routines. During the day, he'd blaze his heater past opposing batters, while at night (unquestionably his favorite time), either Cleveland or Minnesota crowds would warm to his sweet notes. The quick uniform changes never ruffled him. Not Mudcat. Raised in the muddy swamps of central Florida, he was thick-skinned as an alligator. It didn't matter that most of his baseball engagements were with second-division clubs. While his fastball sang, he watched batters cry.

Perfecting this talent wasn't easy. Like most artists, Mudcat had to start at the bottom—and he almost quit in desperation. Assigned to minor league teams in places such as Keokuk, Iowa, or Fargo, North Dakota (during the mid-1950s), Grant got more than a pitching education. As a black man, he had to learn how to deal with bigotry, often the violent kind that barred him from restaurants, hotels, bars, and certain water fountains.

"Believe me, the racial thing was a brutal psychological war between me and the people out to bury me," sighs Grant, leaning against a piano in the basement of his Shaker Heights, Ohio home. He grimaces, disgustedly. "From the time the Keokuk team photographer said, 'You black boys do strange things to the lighting,' I was ready to explode. I thought once I signed a pro contract I'd be able to eat where I wanted, or live peacefully like any other human being. It wasn't to be. I would've fought back if not for Larry Doby or Satchel Paige. They told me to cool it, to make sure no one kept me from making a living or ended my career.

"I guess I compensated, and moved on. There was a time I was outside a bar with (Don) Newcombe. Someone had told him we couldn't go in there. He pushed me right through the door. We sat in there for twenty minutes, without the cash register or jukebox making a sound. Newk finally asked me if I had had enough. So we left. What did blacks do to deserve this kind of treatment? I could've wound up pacing the floor like a lot of players, but I didn't let anyone destroy me. I waged that psychological war successfully."

Mudcat also resorted to force: his fastball. After the minors and three mediocre seasons with the Indians, he flirted with greatness in 1961, combining a 15-9 record with 146 strikeouts. Three more years of lacklustre pitching followed (34-37, with a 3.95 ERA). But in 1965, Grant suddenly looked like the pitching equivalent of Frank Sinatra, as he became the first black American League hurler to win twenty games (21-7, with a league-leading six shutouts). Besides giving Sandy Koufax a battle for the Cy Young award (unlike today, NL and AL pitchers competed for one award), he also carried the Twins to the World Series.

Here, he was spectacular. When Twins' big bats went silent, it fell on Grant's shoulders to keep them in the Series. Matched against the Dodgers' Don Drysdale in the opener, he had a laugher, as the Twins scored eight runs. But then Killebrew, Oliva, and Co. fell asleep at the plate, and with Minnesota trailing LA three games to two, Grant started the crucial sixth game. He was really a virtuoso that day. Limiting the Dodgers to one run and six hits, he lowered his Series ERA to 2.74—and also helped his own cause with a three-run homer. The Twins had their one more tomorrow, and while they'd bow to Koufax's three-hitter, 2-0, in the final game, Grant had done all that was possible. He now deserved star billing.

A happy-go-lucky free spirit, Grant exploited his new acclaim to the fullest. Not for money. That wasn't a priority. More importantly, he wanted to be recognized as another Johnny Mathis or Lou Rawls. So, flashing a big smile, some sweet talking, and a few fast steps backstage, he squeezed himself into a new rotation: the late-night TV talk show circuit. Appearing on the Johnny Carson and Mike Douglas shows along with his all-girl troupe, Mudcat got needed national exposure, and soon became a nightclub regular. The blues never sounded so fine.

"I was a singer first, then a ballplayer," raves Mudcat,

wearing a black shirt with a white-stitched cat's face on the collar. "People said I couldn't make it in both worlds. What nonsense. I liked enjoying myself. I don't go where I'm supposed to go, or just date who I'm supposed to date. I'm a free man. I can't say too much about this, because there's a cloud hanging over most black ballplayers, and one day I might want to get back into baseball. But my freedom became an inspiration to a lot of folks, so I had to keep myself in the race. I had to hang in there, for my self-respect, and for others'."

A 21-7 pitcher can sing his own tunes. Owners don't care about philosophy, they're too interested in winning. Their mood changes, however, when fastballs start disappearing over outfield fences. Then they clamp down. When Mudcat slipped to 13-13 in 1966, and 5-6 the next year, conservative Twins' owner Calvin Griffith laid down some new rules. It was lights-out time: far fewer nightclub appearances, and, most especially, no more dates with white women.

Grant naturally balked. Upset over his "being treated like a little boy," he voiced his feelings, and was soon traded to the Dodgers. That certainly complicated Grant's nightclub act. For Mudcat was now on a merry-go-round. One year he'd be in LA (6-4), then it was suddenly on to Montreal (1-6), St. Louis (7-5), Oakland (6-2), Pittsburgh (7-4), and back to Oakland (1-0). Overall, it was six teams in four years. He turned himself into a relief pitcher, with better than average success (forty-four saves) but his music had to suffer. He didn't play any town long enough to get a gig.

Tired of one-night stands, Grant retired in 1972. He remained inactive for a year. Then the Indians hired him as a broadcaster. Grant did the color commentary for five years, and while he again became a Cleveland celebrity (his singing group was renamed the Plum City Band), future problems were already brewing. Or, as Grant explains, "Broadcasting is a lot of fun, but it's not like baseball. You don't control you own destiny. Ballplayers in the TV booth are like streetcars, you come and go."

A successful public relations man, today Mudcat's got no reason to sing the blues.

Grant left Cleveland amicably in 1977 for a similar position with the Oakland As. Almost immediately, he ran into trouble. Confronted with another strong personality, his TV partner Harmon Killebrew, Grant competed with him to be the top banana. "We were just incompatible," says Grant, "and our different styles doomed the entire thing from the start." Lasting only one year in Oakland, Grant then went back to Cleveland and directed the team's community affairs, or public relations office. That, too, ended in controversy.

"Gabe Paul (the Indians general manager) and me were always yelling at each other," says Grant, who's now doing PR for a Cleveland Budweiser beer distributor. "He was paying me $12,000, and finally I was set to take him to court. That salary was too low, it was discriminatory. Blacks have rights too, we should be entitled to live. Well, eventually Gabe and I patched things up. Sometimes it's more important to go on. If I had pursued the case, and won, in the long run I'd be losing."

The Kittens persuaded Mudcat to go on a nightclub tour during the squabble, and that led to his meeting an Anheuser-Busch executive. The two men got friendly, Grant was taken to a cocktail party, and now, along with "Blue Moon" or "You Send Me," his other favorite lyric is "this Bud's for you." At long last, Mudcat seems satisfied. He has his long-sought freedom. The company lets him make decisions concerning promotional campaigns, plus they underscore their faith in him with a sizable budget. And while Grant often looks establishment in his pinstriped suits, he's still the flamboyant showman.

"My greatest hit here has been my selecting a Miss Budweiser. Nothing gets a product sold like a beautiful woman," says Mudcat, flashing a smile that's as bright as his old number, thirty-three, on the gold glove charm around his neck. "Did I interview her, wow. I interviewed and interviewed. I've livened things up. I love this job. I'm in contact with people, and my boss wants my advice. He doesn't want a pretty face, or just an ex-ballplayer with a name. They make me feel important, and that's like being a kid in a house full of Christmas toys.

"Now I have what I want. Respect. I have no regrets at all. And baseball got me here. The racial problems, my inner struggles, they don't matter anymore. The game was a great vehicle to the future. My whole life has been geared to success, and to get that you need standards. I got those from baseball, and I'm still applying them in business. Mental defeats and heartaches have to be overcome all the time in this world, and baseball taught me how."

Seated now at the piano, Grant thumbs through a few songs, and eventually sings a medley of Lou Rawls tunes. Throughout the impromptu performance, his voice and eyes are choked with emotion. "I've had a lot of tough times as a southern black. But my hurts are not getting in the way of my surviving. My hurts let me sing the blues. Things are okay now. I just hate to think what Jackie Robinson went through.

"Anyway, things must be getting better. A kid who wasn't allowed to drink from water fountains can now live in Shaker Heights. Most likely, as a black, I'll be knocked down again. That's the way things are. But I look at myself as a cork. You push it in water, it goes down, and comes right back up."

The Sam Spade of relief
pitchers, Elroy Face made hitting
a total mystery.

ELROY FACE
One Flew Over the Cuckoo's Nest

Pittsburgh's Mayview State Hospital for the criminally insane is a carpenter's nightmare. Doors get pulled off their hinges; cabinets are smashed apart; bedposts are pried loose and rammed through windows; tools disappear. It's dangerous working there.

None of this bothers Elroy Face. He's used to ticklish situations. Considered by many to be the best relief pitcher in history, the Pirate righthander (with Pittsburgh from 1953-1968) confronted all types of jams in his career. Relying mainly on a forkball, he squelched so many rallies in 1959, en route to his record winning percentage of .947 (18-1), that manager Danny Murtaugh tagged him Sam Spade. That nickname summed up Face's talent for solving problems on the mound. The five-foot-eight, herky-jerky reliever combined a 104-95 lifetime record, with a remarkable 193 saves (that's fourth among all relievers, behind Rollie Fingers, Sparky Lyle, and Hoyt Wilhelm).

Yet that ability to put out the fire is best illustrated by Face's role in the 1960 World Series between Pittsburgh and the Yankees. Not only did he save three of the four Pirate victories, but in two of those games he totally silenced the bats of Mantle, Maris, Berra, and Skowron. Keeping them off stride with the forkball and a variety of deliveries, Face didn't allow a hit in either the fourth or fifth games, retiring eight straight batters in both contests. Face was never so intimidating again, fading to 6-12 with only seventeen saves the next year, and a 3-9 record (sixteen saves) in 1963. (Eventually winding up with the Tigers, in 1968, and Expos, Face was 38-38, with an average of fourteen saves a year from 1962-69.) Yet nothing can diminish his Yankee-taming in 1960, for as Danny Murtaugh said, "That guy, forget the Sam Spade stuff; no detective was ever that good."

Now, Face merits a new nickname—Mr. Fixit. As the chief foreman of the hospital's maintenance crew, Face supervises repairs against a backdrop of constant bedlam. Never afraid of what's happening around him, he poignantly says, "Many of the people in here are saner than a lot of folks outside." He speaks from experience. Before passing a civil service test for the hospital position in 1978, he owned a bar and motel, which exposed him to what he calls "the sickest, most destructive behavior imaginable. Instead of giving people booze, I finally had to do something constructive." Trained in carpentry by his father, Face decided to work for the hospital, instead of a private construction company, because the pension plan was better, and "maybe I'm a little crazy too."

Nervously drawing on a cigarette while gluing Formica paneling to a piece of plywood, Face would rather concentrate on his work than talk about the past. A soft-spoken, shy individual, he likes the solitude of rustic fishing trips and puttering around the house, and he rarely horses around with fellow workers. They can constantly try to interrupt him with demands for a tape measure, a cigarette, or just a good-natured crack about him being "our Mr. Formica man." Yet Face just keeps on working, sanding the plywood until it has a rich, soft finish.

"I think of myself as an artist. I've always been a perfectionist. I have to excel. I don't look at this work as just fixing cabinets or door hinges. The taxpayers are paying a lot for this, and they should get their money's worth. The work load here is amazing. We never have a

Now a carpenter in an insane asylum, Elroy is still the master craftsman.

free moment. But that doesn't mean the work should be second-rate. Besides, I like it. I use a hammer and chisel to get my frustrations out. It's better than hitting people.

"When I finish a cabinet or something I like to stand back and look at it, the same way DaVinci did. Why not? Work like this gives me a religious type of satisfaction. I feel so close to what I'm doing. I was never happy in the bar business (Elroy Face's Bullpen, in downtown Pittsburgh). That just played on people's sicknesses. Plus I never made any money. Now I'm doing okay all around. I have a better idea of what I'm doing here than I ever did on the mound.

"That's not to say I didn't enjoy getting Mays or Aaron out. I think I'm the greatest relief pitcher of all time. Not too many guys get three saves in a World Series, or last sixteen years. And I'd probably have forty, fifty more saves if they kept stats in the 50s the way they do today (the requirements for earning a save have eased over the last few years). At times I feel bad about not being born twenty years later, what with these guys making a million a year. (Rich or Goose) Gossage and Fingers are good, I like watching them. But I'm better. Like I told Tom Johnson (one of the Pirate owners), if I was pitching today I'd own the club."

Summoned to a telephone by one of his assistants, Face rushes over to a desk and jots down the details of a current crisis. He then moves over to a locker, plainly marked "Face," to strap a set of tools around his khaki uniform. Upon returning, he jokes, "It's just like the old days. I'm always coming to the rescue. I just wish I didn't have to leave this sanding; it took me a hell of a long time getting this stain ready. But I gotta keep movin' all the time, or else my bosses think we're on vacation down here."

Before rushing off, Face adds, more seriously, "I've been on the Hall of Fame ballot now six or seven times. I don't know what my chances are. Who knows what the writers think of me? Maybe I got a few of them angry in my time. I wasn't always that talkative. But if I'm going to make it, I only have one wish. I want it to happen soon. My father's now seventy-nine, my mom seventy-eight. He taught me everything I know about carpentry, and it would give him one last kick to see me make it there. If he's not around, well, I don't care what happens. If he dies, and doesn't get to go to the ceremonies, then the Hall of Fame isn't so important."

Okay with the glove, Specs Torgesen was better known for his other mitts.

EARL TORGESON
Shadow Boxing

His fighting spirit is gone. Baseball's Raging Bull won't even put up his fists. Once a relentless heavyweight who proudly defended himself or his teammates, Earl Torgeson tried his hand at politics, took a series of low blows, and hasn't been the same since. He's now in retreat, a shaken and unhappy man.

That's not the Earl of Snohomish umpires invariably exiled to the showers. The old Torgy just had to be looked at the wrong way and fists flew, benches emptied, bodies littered the field. No one fooled with him. The muscular first baseman backed up his temper with the meanest left jab in the big leagues. By conservative estimates, he had about fifty main eventers, twenty-five torn jerseys, and an equal number of broken bones after fifteen years in the ring. Oh yes, he also scored dozens of KOs.

When Torgy wasn't playing the enforcer, he packed a more traditional wallop. The six-foot-three 180-pounder usually hit close to .275, had seventy to eighty RBIs, with fifteen to twenty homers. His best season was with the old Boston Braves in 1950, when he batted .290, along with twenty-three homers and eighty-seven RBIs (he'd later play for the White Sox, Tigers, Phillies, and Yankees). And as for post-season play, Torgeson was the leading hitter in the 1948 World Series, slugging a hefty .389 against Cleveland Hall of Famers Feller and Lemon.

Torgeson's stats would presumably be even better had he concentrated more on playing, and less on breaking noses. Three-day suspensions hardly helped his timing. Nor were cracked ribs or other injuries from fights good for swinging. Combined with head-hunting expeditions by opposing pitchers, all these extracurricular activities diminished Torgeson's value as a player, and often sapped his morale.

As the fifty-nine-year-old Snohomish, Washington native admits, "If I had to do it over again I wouldn't have been such a character. I'd just concentrate on playing baseball. Maybe all those fights were a way of revving myself up. I don't know; I just regret the fact that I'm labeled a bad boy. I don't want to have that image with the public. I guess I got that desperate need to win from my mother. I always saw people letting her win at bridge because she was so tough. She never gave anyone an inch."

Wearing steel-plated glasses as a player, and capable of unloading equally hard combinations, Specs didn't lose too many confrontations either. He may now regret some of this action, but that's difficult to tell by looking at him. Grinning like a mischievous Huckleberry Finn, he punctuates descriptions of his more memorable bouts with either a quick left-handed jab or a hearty laugh. He's so enthusiastic it's only surprising that he doesn't compare himself to Muhammad Ali.

"I was eighteen and playing in the Coast League. Something was said by a second baseman, I can't remember his name. He kicked my glove, and the next inning I threw his glove into the outfield. When he kicked my glove again, I not only threw his glove into the stands, but I also kicked him in after it.

"But my greatest fight was with (Warren) Spahn, after I joined the Phillies (1953). He drilled me pretty good one day.

There was always someone who wanted to clean my

clock. They'd go after my head all the time. Well, I waited for Spahn to say something the next time up, and when he did I went to the mound. I had a real good headlock on him. It was a retaliation thing. I had to act. If someone was making me a target, I couldn't sit still."

Today he'll recall his past exploits with a certain gusto. But when the present is discussed, Torgeson seems almost mournful, speaking in mere whispers. His eyes also have a strained quality. They look confused. It's a haunting expression, one which resembles a fighter's vacant stare after he's taken too many blows.

Torgeson has been battered in an arena far more ferocious than any baseball diamond. It's called "politics." A Snohomish county park director for two years (1967-68), Torgeson out-fought two rivals to get elected county commissioner in 1972. He immediately campaigned in Washington D.C. for a larger slice of revenue-sharing funds, revamped the organizational structure of his office, and, in the process, made lots of enemies.

The counterattack against him began with a blackmailing scheme, by someone who posed as his illegitimate son. That plot was quickly foiled, as Torgeson refused to do business with him and called in the police. But the assaults continued, with much bloodier results.

Using several local newspapers as a forum, critics charged Torgeson with illegally purchasing timber properties, or using his political office for financial gain. Other allegations, concerning the use of county employees and the disappearance of gravel supplies, were also raised during his 1976 reelection campaign, and these attacks eventually influenced voters. But Torgeson lost more than the election (by only 500 votes). He was also indicted by a grand jury on a variety of conflict of interest charges (1976), and had to spend the next few years defending himself in court.

Now Torgeson feels his name has been tarnished forever, that all of his accomplishments, both in baseball and in public service, have been destroyed. And despite

*Torgy always spoke softly—
and carried a big stick.*

being convinced that his opponents "did a hatchet job on me, to get their hands on the county's $24 million-plus budget," he's near tears when discussing the scandal.

"I did so much in office, I was able to unify all the road districts, get so many projects started, and really change the philosophy of the position. But look what happened, what I get for all that. I guess I was too threatening for a lot of people. They needed a fall guy, and I was the patsy. My head had to roll. It was said I was selling timber for profit. Hell. Nothing, nothing, nothing at all was proved, and nothing, nothing whatsoever was done wrong. It was a joke; they just needed a target. Sensationalism, that's all it was, and I paid. I'm still suffering, and it's going to be this way for a long time.

"Politics, boy, I don't know if competitive is a strong enough word for what I'm going through. I was able to get the indictment thrown out, after spending $25,000 in legal fees, but the thing is still not over. Just imagine the headlines in those days, those Hearst newspapers yelling that thousands of dollars in timber and gravel were missing. I still hear remarks about it. They'll always bother me. I don't think I'll ever get over what happened. The stigma will always be there. And so will my pain."

Deciding to get away from "that world where you have so many enemies you have to keep your back to the wall," Torgeson moved with his family to a small house in the woods outside Everett, Washington. He does make public appearances, judging beauty contests and log-rolling exhibitions. But his long-held commitment to public service has ended. Once devoted to saving park lands, building playgrounds, and taking polluting factories to court, he's now approaching land development from a different direction. Working for a lumber company for the last five years, he purchases timber properties, supervises logging operations, and then gets the land ready for multi-tract housing. And while sales commissions are helping him recoup his legal expenses, Torgeson is still frustrated. The money hasn't brought back his good name.

"I feel like half a man sometimes; people are always taking whacks at me, and I can't even fight back. The one thing that hurts me the most is the beating I took from the prosecuting attorney and from the press. I wish I could be a factor in the success of this (lumber) company. But the political thing still limits me around here. It's virtually impossible to erase the stigma. I can't do anything about the talk that comes out of the shadows, the ugly gossip. I'd be punching at thin air. People don't know what really happened. I want to grab them on the street and tell them the truth.

"If I had it all to do over again, I'd learn to compromise, not to go after everyone all the time, and I would've certainly stayed in baseball. I was once asked to manage Hawaii (Pacific Coast League). I'm sorry I didn't. Bill Veeck asked me then, 'When are you going to wise up? Why don't you get your own team?' I was a wise guy, I said, 'I'd only manage if you got some real players.' He wanted me to manage at San Diego (then a minor league team) and it was a bona fide stepping stone. I really regret not taking that spot. My whole life would've been better.

"Instead I prepared myself for managing by spending two years in Nicaragua, in winter ball (Torgeson managed in the minor leagues for years, from 1966 to 1970.). Talk about fights, it got nasty down there. There were four political factions in the league, Somoza had a team, while my club was the Boer team of the lower-class people. Things were really heating up in those days. It was very intriguing. Sometimes you had to lose a game to avert a civil war."

Leaning forward in an office chair and looking glumly at his clenched fists, he concludes, "Baseball prepared me for some of the disappointments. The game teaches you that there's going to be good and bad years. I learned to adapt from (Ralph) Houk; he taught me that life isn't a pat hand. But life was certainly simpler back then. I could adjust better. Playing ball, that was, well, at least you knew who your friends were. It's not that I would like to do it all over again. No, it just can't be. But gee, now, all these disappointments. You can fantasize about being back in baseball, can't you?"

*Painting signs has made Jim Landis
a business success, but he sorely misses
his old friend, Nellie Fox.*

JIM LANDIS
Ode to a Friend

They were Larceny Incorporated on the basepaths. The Go-Go White Sox, speedsters who ran-ran-ran to steal the 1959 pennant. No base was safe from the flying feet or daring head-first sprints of an Aparicio, Rivera, or Jim Landis. Their quickness also translated into defense, and as their league-leading fielding averages point out, the almost hit-proof combination of Aparicio, Landis, Al Smith, and the late Nellie Fox sometimes seemed like the Berlin Wall.

Today, center fielder Landis is still a defensive specialist—a sign-maker who designs posters to protect factory workers from industrial accidents. And while business has been thriving lately, thanks to safety regulations formulated by OSHA (the Occupational Safety Hazards Administration) the forty-four-year-old, .247 lifetime hitter often relaxes under a wall photo of the 1959 team, reflecting on his eleven years in the big leagues. It's then that he thinks of manager Al Lopez ("the greatest psychiatrist I've ever known, he knew how to create the unity on our team"), the dumb mistakes the Sox made in losing the World Series to the Dodgers, four games to two, and especially his closest friend, famed second baseman Nellie Fox.

Head bowed, his hands cupped tightly on his chin, Landis first finds it difficult to speak about Fox, who died in 1975 at age forty-eight. Taking a cigarette out of his paint-covered overalls, he finally stammers, "I don't know who I miss more, Nellie or my father. I was closer to Nellie than guys I've run with since I'm six years old. He was a hell of a ballplayer, but even more, what a man. I'll never forget, when I was just up from the minors I was in awe of the whole scene. There they were, my heroes, Musial, Mantle, and pitchers like (Herb) Score. Facing him was quite an ordeal. But Fox took me in hand and cared for me. He was like a father. He settled me down after I'd get upset for messing up. Whenever things were going wrong, on or off the field, Nellie was there for me. If not for him I don't know what would've happened. I owe him so much.

"You should have seen him in the World Series. He was great. He had something like a .390 batting average (.375), and was inspirational to all of us. He still is when I'm overworked here, or tense. I just have to think of him, the good times we had together, and I start smiling. Business has been really booming, factories have to go along with these Federal regs. Nellie would be happy to know I'm doing real well.

"I visited his place once. It was the greatest sight you could see, him in jeans, running around in a jeep, back there in Pennsylvania. Everything was so nice, the people around there loved him. You had to. He was so down-to-earth. So natural. He had the same togetherness with people there that we had on our team. A few years later, we saw each other at an Old Timers game. He was complaining about chest pains, but I didn't think much about it. I couldn't imagine anything happening to him. But it was cancer, and by then it was nearly all over. God. Once I got the news he died, it took me three days to call his family. I was so upset. I just couldn't do anything."

Fighting off a tear, Landis stares at a row of deserted machines. He then holds up two fingers about an inch apart, shakes them back and forth, and in a barely audible voice says, "This is your life right here. Life flies. It goes, goes, and that's it. You have to really live to the fullest. There are no second chances. I'm pretty happy. I've had a good business for fourteen years, sent my kids to college, and my wife, she's the greatest. But life flies, look at Nellie. Everything was so quick. Boom. Gone. I think his death *was* worse than my dad's."

*Irv Noren's about to light
that cigar; he just scored with
another winner.*

IRV NOREN
Fifty Dollars on the Nose

Chewing a cigar butt while studying a racing form in front of a ten-dollar window, Irv Noren looks like a character straight out of a John Garfield gangster movie.

"Hey Benny, who do you like in the third?" shouts the mid-1950s Yankee left fielder (who also played with five other teams), to one of his tough-looking Santa Anita friends. "Stardust really came on the last time out. I really think he can carry the weight, no matter what the distance."

Not waiting for Benny's reply, Noren takes a pencil from behind his ear, and marks the form. Then the man once heralded as another DiMaggio lays down fifty dollars at the teller's window and heads for the paddock area. On the way, all sorts of racing people—stewards, stableboys, a few jocks, even the famed trainer Laz Barrera—say hello. Unlike his days at Yankee Stadium, when easy fly balls were fumbled into extra-base hits, Noren feels at home here.

Along with owning a trophy shop ("just in case I do anything spectacular at the last minute"), the fifty-nine-year-old Noren has eighteen horses, all with names like Bunt-N-Run, Glove Man, Squeeze Play, and Nickle Curve. Preoccupied with finding a Spectacular Bid or an Affirmed, he first got interested in racing as a Yankee, when roommate Mickey Mantle took him to New York tracks. That connection helped him meet the right people. But the best hay for the Noren stable was three World Series. While embarrassed by a .148 fall classic average (.278 lifetime, with a lowly sixty-five homers in eleven years), paychecks from those games provided him with early seed money. He was able to parlay one thoroughbred into another, and now, after receiving three more Series winning shares as a coach with Oakland, Irv Noren has several potential stakes winners.

"Those Yankee pinstripes, were they something. The money kept rolling in. Not only was I making $25,000 a year, the same as Bauer and Woodling, but I was also being kept in big cigars with those Series checks. It was easy for me to go to the track. I had the money. Baseball made everything possible. Without it I'd never have my Sundance Ranch, the trophy shop, the horses, nothing. Today I got close to $750,000 tied up in horses. About the only thing I regret is that they compared me to DiMaggio. No way I was going to step into his shoes. That just wasn't right of them, it was too much pressure.

"I did enjoy being with Mickey. We'd walk every day to the Stage Deli for breakfast and talk to Danny Kaye, Jackie Leonard, all kinds of movie stars. You could just sit around there, and you'd meet the world. If you were a Yankee you had to love New York, the way you were treated at Danny's Hideaway or the Copa. Mickey, though, was a bashful kid. I miss not being with him. I drove him home once to Commerce after the '54 season, and on the way he had to listen to that cowboy music. Some of those songs were so damn emotional, there was Mickey, sitting there crying.

"I think about those days sitting at the track, or especially at the shop, looking at all those baseball trophies. But right now I'm so involved with horses I don't have a lot of time to relax. Racing is the same kind of challenge as baseball. I have to win. I'll tell you, I had a horse win at Bay Meadows, and it was the biggest thrill I've ever had. I played in the World Series, coached in the Series, played in an All-Star Game, but being in the winner's circle is something else. Going down to that circle with that sucker beats everything, a homer, a grand slam, anything.

"But it's such a risky business. I've spent so much money on Glove Man. One day he could even be worth millions. Knock on wood. Then again, he could go into a turn and break his leg. The percentage of horses breaking down is so high. I just need one winner. That's my dream."

Before laying the odds on his finding another Affirmed, Noren strides back towards the grandstand to watch the third race with his pals. Despite their yelling, Stardust finishes next to last. That prompts a torrent of four-letter words from Benny. He then gives Noren a dirty look and walks away.

Noren shakes his head. "You know, some things never change. I'm still getting it. When I came up with the Yankees everyone thought I was Jewish (he's Swedish). I'd get all this kidding from the bleachers everytime the team messed up. I'd hear them yelling, 'Irv, what happened, Irv. No chicken soup today, Irv?' Everything's still Irv's fault." Then, chuckling, Irv winks and adds, "Oh well. There's always the next race."

FELIPE ALOU
The Monopoly

The Great Debate remains unsettled. What was the greatest triple play in baseball history?

It could've been the DiMaggio brothers—Vince, Dom, and Joseph. All three men roamed the outfield with speed and effortless grace. Their collective .290 batting average wasn't too bad, either. The DiMaggios were certainly spectacular. But some diamond lovers will vote for another brotherly act.

The Alous—Felipe, Matty, and Jesus, the famed combination that was once called "the Dominican Republic's Gross National Product."

A veritable monopoly, this terrific trio dominated the San Francisco Giant outfield in the early 1960s. Two of the brothers frequently patrolled Candlestick's outer reaches together. In fact, the Alous made baseball history in one 1963 game, when the outfield became a total family affair. This wasn't a publicity stunt. The speedy Alous were defensive wizards. They only made ten or fifteen errors a year—between them—and sometimes that figure included winter ball.

They didn't only jump fences. Each Alou also dented them. With regularity. Their combined lifetime batting average was .291, and they totaled thirteen seasons of .300 hitting. Matty registered the clan's highest average, a blistering .342 in 1966, to win the National League batting crown. But interestingly, Felipe finished right behind him, with a .327 mark (plus he led the league in hits, 218, runs scored, 122, and total bases, 355). Then an Atlanta Brave, Felipe (the eldest of the three) also flexed his muscles in another way. Not just a singles hitter, he clubbed thirty-one homers (206 lifetime).

"The three of us were always competitive. We had to be to get out of the Dominican Republic," explains Felipe, standing near a batting cage at the Montreal Expos' training camp in Palm Beach, Florida. "We wanted to do something to change our country's image. Plus baseball was the only way we could get the hell away from Rafael Trujillo. Each of us felt that if we did well, people would think about other things besides the dictatorship."

Still reaching for glory, Felipe's now managing an Expos farm team, the Wichita Aeros. His brothers have also stayed close to baseball. They're coaching amateur teams in Santo Domingo. Felipe joins them each winter, but he isn't content with being a local hero. His eyes are on the biggest prize possible. He wants to lead a major league team.

"Once you get baseball fever, forget it, that's the only thing you want to do in life," continues Felipe, looking trim and as speedy as ever at 195 pounds. "Baseball was first our road out of poverty. Then the world got to know the real human side of the Dominican Republic through the Alou Brothers. That makes baseball more than a sport. It's a way for people to get closer together, to go beyond politics and see the truth."

Felipe caught the fever as a child, when he saw Jackie Robinson playing in an exhibition game. The son of a poor construction worker, who now admits "the family didn't eat right, we went hungry many nights," Alou competed in track and field events to raise money for college. He wanted to be a doctor, but when his savings ran out he had to turn to his other love—baseball.

"When I saw Jackie playing next to Snider, I said to myself, gee, I want to be a good ballplayer. I never thought of the majors, I always had my heart set on being a doctor. Later on, though, my folks just didn't have the money to get me through school. So I did what came naturally. I grabbed a bat. I could always outhit the kids in the neighborhood, and you should have seen me run in those days."

Signed by the Giants in 1955, Felipe became the club's leadoff batter three years later. He didn't have a Cinderella debut (San Francisco's icy winds were an adjustment), hitting only .253, with four homers. But the Giants didn't panic. With him, Mays, and Willie Kirkland in the outfield, the newly-transplanted club moved like Mercury—and sprinted from sixth to third place.

Felipe didn't hit, in fact, until 1961. He batted .289 that year, with eighteen homers and nineteen doubles. Perhaps spurred by Matty's joining the team, or their friendly rivalry (his younger brother hit .310 in 1961), Felipe got hot and laced the ball repeatedly. For the next eight seasons, he was the D.R.'s Sultan of Swat—averaging .293, with 139 homers.

During this period (1962), Felipe and Matty also led the Giants to a pennant (the club's only one since 1954). Despite rumblings in the clubhouse (reportedly derogatory remarks were made about a few of the Latin ballplayers), both men concentrated on beating out the Dodgers. Instead of bitching (Felipe still won't talk about what went on), they tagged opposing pitchers. Each of them hit over .300 in September—and in celebration of their final stats—Matty hit .292, while Felipe had twenty-five homers, a .317 average, and ninety-eight RBIs—San Francisco newspapers called them "the real Bay Area Earthquake."

"All three of us had to be pretty good, otherwise we wouldn't have gotten to play," says Felipe, taking a few practice swings with a fungo bat. "We belonged to an era when there were only eight clubs in each league. There was no excess then, there was no dilution of talent. Either you were good or you didn't make it. We all stayed around for at least fourteen years. That says a lot. We all knew and did our job. That's why the Dominican Republic should be proud of us. We cared."

Felipe certainly did his job, no matter where he played. Sent to the Braves in 1964, he gave them five years of solid .280-to-.325 hitting. Then it was on to Oakland, and the Yankees from 1970 to '72, and again he produced. His batting average dipped somewhat with the As, but, in typical Alou fashion, he hit .289 for the Bronx pinstripers in 1971. That, however, was Felipe's last hurrah. The following season he slipped to .278, and then New York waived him to the Expos at the end of the 1973 season (his average for the entire year was .232). He had a brief encore with the Braves in '74 (three games), but as Alou recalls, "I knew it was over a few years earlier, but I loved the uniform so much I just couldn't take it off. It meant everything in life to me. It still does."

That feeling is growing stronger. Alou has a bad case of the fever. Besides managing the Aeros during the summer, he returns to the Dominican Republic each winter and heads another team. Competition is described as his "greatest joy in life," and while personal triumphs are satisfying (Alou calls winning the D.R. league pennant in 1981 "my biggest baseball thrill"), they aren't his main priority. More importantly, he wants his leadership to serve as a role model for other Latins, so that they'll be inspired to "rebuild their countries."

Sitting in the Expos' dugout after giving phenom Terry Francona a few batting tips, he says, "I knew I had to make some adjustment from player to manager, and that I had to get over the obstacle of my Latin accent. There was a time when that was a real problem. Now the average player doesn't think of race. Now they only think if I have it to lead them to victory. It's my responsibility to develop players for the organization, and if I win people won't be able to think that Latins are only dum-dums.

"I would've made a good doctor, but my being a good manager is just as important. The people in my country can see what I'm doing, and maybe that will change their feelings about themselves. Too many of them think they're inferior. They need new self-confidence more than they need doctors."

Alou's olive face now takes on a new glow. He's been watching a few of his former players who are now trying out for the Expos. "Managing has been fun so far. I won't jump to a major league club just to do it. I want a club that has a chance to win. That way they won't pick out the Latin manager as a scapegoat. I know all managers get fired, and I've already had my share of losing streaks. But I've proven my point. I've shown GMs that I can win, with the right respect for players.

"That approach may lead to a pennant one day. But I don't want to be a national hero for that. I want to do other things to help my country. I hope I can influence people to invest in the Dominican Republic. Or to go down there and serve the people. We need so much, especially the young people. They need jobs, hopes, dreams, and one day I'm sure I'm going to help them."

GUS TRIANDOS

Step 'n Fetchit, Molasses, and Slo-Mo

Aesop's fable had it all wrong. The tortoise is not slow. Not when it's compared to the world's most sluggish creature, Gus Triandos.

The Oriole catcher (also with four other teams) wasn't just slow. Watching grass grow was speedier than following his lead-footed jogs towards first base. He could line sure doubles into right field and still be thrown out at first. Or, even more remarkably, his home run trot was so elephantine, fans could take a quick nap or eat a dozen hotdogs.

Incredibly enough, Gus hasn't changed at all. Though the pace of modern life has stepped up with computers, microprocessors, and new video systems, Triandos is still counting the seconds as they go by: "one Mississippi, two Mississippi, three Mississippi . . ." Unaffected by his Greek ancestors, old Gus doesn't have any Olympian fire. Instead, he likes to sit in his ten-by-fourteen-foot office all day, sip countless glasses of vodka, and partake of another Mediterranean custom, the siesta, especially a long one. Ironically, this man runs a mail delivery service.

"I'm satisfied with only having this little business. I don't want to pound and pound at something like most businessmen," admits Triandos, perched on a small bed in his San Jose, California office. "This place is my

Gus Triandos is talking about his running skills, but somehow good friend Roy Sievers isn't taking him too seriously.

sanctuary. I like to come here and unwind, or have people over for drinks. What can I get you, a Scotch, a vodka?

"If I was smarter maybe I'd have a bigger operation, but I don't really want anything more than this. I don't care if I'm never going to get rich. I don't want the heavy pressure that goes with it. At some point in your life you stop being a high school hero."

Calling his relaxed lifestyle "hog heaven," Triandos has a distinct strategy for finding new customers. He avoids them. He doesn't put his company's name on delivery vans, will invariably switch off his phone during the morning or afternoon, and, rather than advertise, he'll talk it up with the boys at a local saloon. Somehow he's kept his service rolling for five years. And just in case you were wondering what it's called, as Gus relates, "I was really stumped for a while. I didn't know what to name it. Then I remembered that (Bob) Turley had called our insurance agency Diamond Associates. Then this name, Diamond Mail Service, came to me real fast."

Bullet Bob Turley and Speedy Gonzalez go back a long way together, to the early 1950s, when they played for Uncle Sam on a U.S. Army team. The khaki version of TNT, Turley fired off strikes, and the gung-ho Triandos risked life and limb to catch these blazing pellets. In those days, taking foul tips on fingers, squatting, or blocking fast-charging spikes wasn't a problem. Gus was 55 pounds lighter in the Army (he's 260 now), and his teammates called him "the dancing Greek."

But when you play in a place like Twin Falls, Idaho, there are only two things to do—eat and drink. Suddenly becoming a stereotypical roly-poly catcher, Gus recalls that "playing in the minors was for fun, we were always having a good time. It was different in the majors. There, you played to survive."

In Triandos's case, though, it was called hanging on by the skin of your teeth. Called up by the Yankees in 1953, Gus only had one obstacle to overcome. Its name was Yogi Berra. No one could dislodge this Yankee great, let alone Triandos, who would eventually hit .244 lifetime, with 167 homers (in 1957 and '58, he did have 30 and 25 homers respectively). Besides, how many catchers with big paunches, dented noses, and fatty jowls could the team carry at once? The answer was simple. Gus had to go.

"I was overmatched on the Yankees," says Triandos, still on the bed, armed now with a bottle of vodka. "The park was too tough on right-handers. And I was always so damn slow. Stengel didn't like guys like me. I would've showed him if I was there longer (than two years). Anyway, who was going to replace Yogi? He's the most durable catcher that ever lived."

The big trade occurred in 1955. And, in a curious twist of fate, Triandos and Turley again crossed each other's paths. Only this time the two men went in opposite directions: Gus was traded to Baltimore with Gene Woodling, Harry Byrd, Al Smith, and Don Leppert for Turley, Billy Hunter, and Mr. Perfection, Don Larsen.

Baltimore's Memorial Stadium was another tough park for righties, but Gus showed some surprising power. After hitting twelve homers in his first Oriole season, he belted twenty-one in 1956 (with eighty-eight RBIs), and then nineteen the following year. Over those three seasons he averaged .270 and was a workhorse behind the plate (only missing about fifteen or twenty games a year).

But Gus's greatest year had to be 1958—or the Season of the Steal. That's right, the snail actually swiped a base. Even though he calls his only base-stealing attempt a fluke success (and it was, since Gus tumbled into second after the Yankees built a big lead in a late-season game and didn't try to throw him out), this theft gives him a 1.000 career percentage. And the right to say, "Willie Mays, Lou Brock, Maury Wills, eat your heart out."

It's possible that the steal went to Triandos's head. After that it was mostly downhill. In 1959, even though he hit twenty-five homers, his batting average dropped to a woeful .216. The next few seasons were also disas-

*No, this isn't Robert DeNiro,
it's only Gus—at work.*

ters. Triandos's home run output sank to twelve or fourteen a year; and from 1960-62, he could only muster stats like .244 or .159.

The great young Oriole pitching staff, nicknamed the "Kiddie Korps," had been centered around him. No one ever questioned his defensive talents or ability to handle the likes of Chuck Estrada, Steve Barber, or Milt Pappas. But Baltimore needed more hitting, and by 1963 Johnny Orsino did most of the catching. Gus soon got his walking papers. He was sent to Detroit (batted .239), then went to the Phillies, and finally wound up hitting .181 for the Astros in 1965.

"I think catching Hoyt Wilhelm and his knucklers ruined my career," says Triandos. "The more I caught him, the worse I got. I was always worried that one of his pitches would get by me and runs would score. Maybe I was too anxious about screwing up. In any case, I let it get to me. There was a great deal of umcomfortableness. I never enjoyed catching. It tears you apart. I guess I was too clumsy and slow to do anything else."

The fast-paced business world was also overwhelming. Gus spent six miserable years managing a San Francisco discount store. Then, thinking that he wanted to own his own business, he bought a liquor shop. That drove him "fruity." He couldn't get used to the routine, and felt tied down. Plus, as Gus now says, "The store made it easy for my wife to get on my ass all the time about my drinking."

Gus next tried scouting for the Dodgers, but that, too, ended in failure. He got fired for breaking a basic rule of any game: he fell asleep while his boss was telling a few jokes.

In 1978, after working as a furniture salesman for two years, Triandos bought his mail service. Ever since then, he's been in hog heaven.

"All that crapping around while you're in the game is great, but I've been even luckier; I'm my own boss," says Triandos, glancing at a *Playboy* centerfold calendar on a wall and smirking. "You hear all the time about the pressure in the World Series. Hell, that's nothin' (Gus never was in a Series). As a businessman you got to hock your butt.

"Fortunately, I haven't been close to bankruptcy. There have been moments I've been worried. In fact, I'm always worried. I'm a professional worrier. I guess it's my being Greek. But I don't need a lot. Big cars, fancy clothes, all that stuff isn't worth the heartache. Maybe if I was smarter I'd like to have a few more comforts, but it's not going to work that way. I'm just simple Gus."

He then stretches his legs out and sighs contentedly. "I was grumpy when I played, and the other guys would've been grumpy too, if they had my body. Now, though, I'm doing real nice. I only wish I could've been a better player. I was so painfully slow. I don't moon about it, but it was an embarrassment to me how slow I was. My teammates were always laughing at me. Christ's sake, that was real painful at times.

"Well, none of that matters now. I'm making enough money to be comfortable. I've got everything I need. My family's great, I have good friends at a few of the bars I go to. Then there's this office. I've got my bed, a refrigerator, a hot plate for my lunches. What more can a man ask for? Come on, how 'bout it? I'm making myself some lunch. Would you like some soup?"

Juan Pizarro doesn't have a ball in that glove, so what could it be?

JUAN PIZARRO
Here Comes the Coconut Cowboy

On the Strip, San Juan's version of Hollywood and Vine, the stream of beautiful, dark-haired señoritas is so unnerving, sidewalk cafe patrons forget their domino games, leap out of their seats, and, with mouths watering, start talking incoherently about coconuts.

Just to make sure they are seeing right, these fruit connoisseurs steady themselves with a large gulp of rum or Scotch. Only then will they whistle, loudly and provocatively. Nothing usually happens. So, defeated, the men either act out some macho drama or shout out to the heavens, "Oh, God, what coconuts. Oh man. Caramba!"

Uno, or Juan the Wonderful, just looks on, laughing. Whistling and wolf-calling isn't his style. The suave sweet-talker has a different approach. You can see him in action on his own turf, stretching from swank Condado Beach casinos to San Juan's choicest bars. A devout disciple of *mañana*, he knows how to celebrate. Always has. Once known as the fastest, craziest coconut-tree climber on the island, he's still swinging, connecting with the prettiest *chiquitas*.

Señor Pizarro has always confused scoring with play-boying, or pitching with hustling. In the old days, it didn't matter what team he was with—most notoriously, the Braves, Cubs, and White Sox—J. P. broke every rule, from partying before big games to drinking his meal money, to going AWOL at the nearest racetrack. No one was more unpredictable. One season (1961) he'd be brilliant, the model ballplayer, who hardly strained himself to go 14-7, helping to make the White Sox a contender. While the following year, his late-night carousing and skipping practices led to a 12-14 mark, numerous fines, and manager Al Lopez's turning gray.

"I enjoy life. I don't do anything half-assed, even if that means raising a lot of hell," boasts Pizarro, smiling roguishly, in between sips of a double Scotch highball. "I like the track, the casino, every day I have my drinks. If my old lady says anything, I kick her ass. I don't know how long I'm married, I've been too busy to remember things like that."

Swallowing the rest of his drink and increasingly eager to talk, he reaches into his pocket and starts talking about purchasing a gun. Indifferent to the amazement this causes, he casually continues, "The whole world out there is crazy. Even in Africa there's fourteen-year-olds with guns, holding up people. No one's going to mess with me. Today you get shot for fifteen cents, especially here in Puerto Rico. This place is crazy. When I was a kid I was bad, really bad. But my father slapped me, and I was an instant angel, for a while. I did go back to stealing, apples, oranges, coconuts, anything I could find. I was so busy being bad, I didn't start playing ball until I was fourteen.

"That's when the fun really started. I was the king among my friends. And I guess it ruined me for life. Baseball makes some people good. Me, it made me a sly devil. I had good hands from stealing coconuts, so I could play, and because of that I got my way with all the women. I don't know why I got married. Those days were so much fun. Well, getting back to the coconuts, the eating kind, I'd throw a rock up at a tree, knock one down, and catch it. At least I wasn't hurting anyone, and the stealing wasn't so bad. It made me a major leaguer."

Combining his sure-shot left arm with a burning desire not to be like his father (a trainer/gambler involved in cockfighting), Pizarro played a year of Puerto Rican semi-pro ball (1956), and then got a tryout with the Milwaukee Braves. He was immediately impressive, striking out stars like Eddie Matthews, Frank Torre, and Hank Aaron in spring training. But even though making the team in 1957 made him feel proud, or "like a kid with a new toy," Juan was still restless. Besides, he had to uphold his "wonderful" reputation. Especially with manager Fred Haney, who wondered so much about J. P.'s whereabouts he had to send out groups of players, or even the police, to scour the bars for the missing rookie.

When Pizarro wasn't partying—he overpowered batters with a blazing fastball. At ninety-five MPH, it was one of the fastest pellets in the league, especially when J. P. was in a groove. But since the Braves had an overabundance of pitching (along with the Spahn-Burdette-Buhl axis, they had Joey Jay, Carlton Willey, Bob Rush, etc.), Uno was really the fourth or fifth starter, if he pitched at all. In four years with Milwaukee, Pizarro won twenty-three, lost nineteen, had an aggregate 4.00 ERA, and, underscoring his limited value, the Braves never gave him a World Series start.

Manager Charlie Dressen got so disgusted with him, Pizarro was traded to the White Sox in 1960 for Gene Freese. Responding as if he had suddenly found religion, Pizarro turned in a 14-7 season with 188 strikeouts. Though his 1962 performance was hardly as visionary, he straightened himself out again in '63, masterfully combining a 16-8 mark with a 163 Ks and a 2.39 ERA. An All-Star Game berth sanctified his transformation. But Juan was even better in 1964, when he rose to star status, with a 19-9 record, 162 Ks, and a deft 2.56 ERA. Now Juan certainly deserved his "wonderful" tag, and was demonstrating why he'd wind up as the winningest Puerto Rican pitcher ever.

"I just never got a chance in Milwaukee," screeches Pizarro, pushing his empty glass to the side, disgustedly.

*Schaefer? Miller? Only the Coconut
Man knows for sure.*

"Because I was Latin they thought I was a trouble-maker. I had my moments, everyone does. But my pitching, that was *mucho* okay. Just look at my Chicago stats. Look. Look. The White Sox didn't give up on me, they didn't punish me, and I pitched my ass off for them. Too bad they only wanted to give me a $1,500 raise after I won those nineteen games. I had to fight like hell to get an $8,000 raise, or my lousy $27,000 in '65."

Holding out that spring, however, was costly. J. P. hurt his shoulder, and was never the same again. He pitched well enough in '65 to go 6-3, but he lost velocity on his fastball and dipped to 8-6 in '66. Disappointed in himself, he also feuded with manager Eddie Stanky, whom he calls "a stupid ass" for "sending me down the river, to the bullpen. If I saw him right now I'd shoot him."

Pizarro stayed in the bullpen with the Pirates in 1967, winning only eight games while losing ten. Then he drifted. With the Red Sox at the beginning of the '69 season, he played with two more teams that year (a combined 4-5 record), and was then sent to the Cubs. Not too inspired by his 4-5 struggling in 1972, they too gave up on him. Though J. P. was admittedly "fat, lazy and not giving a shit at this point," he was picked up by the Astros. But not for long. In 1974, Pizarro moved to the Mexican League (16-4), was later re-signed by the Pirates, and subsequently went to the Dominican Republic, still fantasizing about "coming back, or fighting off what was always inevitable, my going over the hill. Or not being able to climb those trees all that good."

Only now Pizarro admits, "I came to the end of the road a lot quicker because I loved to eat." Patting his stomach and smiling, he further says, "I think the rice, beans, and lamb chops ended my career. The chicken gumbo, and oh, those shrimps didn't help either. It was a good life being a player. I didn't have to get up at six in the morning and go to work. I could just lie around all day, get me some pizza, or corned beef sandwiches, and then think of getting to the ballpark, or fool around with some women. It was great, being on top of the world."

Retirement, however, posed problems. Needing money for filet mignon, prime ribs, and his customary champagne, J. P. had to develop a skill he never had in baseball—finesse. He couldn't go to just anybody for a job. After a few ill-fated attempts at coaching winter ball, he got close to people in San Juan's mayor's office (1978). Again the sharpshooter, he landed a government job, teaching baseball to children.

Recently installed as the program's "Señor Director," the forty-five-year-old Pizarro travels around the island in a big car, and palms the flesh wherever he goes. Constantly greeted by friends on the Strip, otherwise known as San Juan's fashionable Isla Verde section, he promises to buy a few of them drinks, and then says, "Everyone remembers Juan. I've always tried to be a good guy. With all this craziness in the world, I only hope I'm keeping a few of my kids away from guns. I love these kids. I was a lad too, and I know how hard it was to have a clean mind. I was an example of that for sure. Man, did I pull off some shit. But I got scared of really messing up. That's why I love what I'm doing. I don't want these kids murdering themselves.

"This job is enough for me. The money could be better, but I don't really care about that. The main thing is to just stay alive. If you do that you can make it. I don't want to go back to the States to look for gold. I could have $10,000 today, and tomorrow I'd be broke. If I have it, I got to spend it. That's in my blood.

"Yeah, I love to cel-e-brate. Yeah. Tonight I'm going to a party. With my wife, hell, no. I love these ballplayers who talk about their favorite moment, or what they did out there. What a lot of bullshit. I only remember the parties, the women, the hot times. Yeah. That's what I'm going to do tonight. I know, I know, you guys are all the same. What's my favorite moment. Well, it was after the Braves won the Series in '57. I had a dozen big glasses of champagne on the plane, and who knows how many more after we landed. I was drunk, d-r-u-n-k. Getting that high, that was something to remember. Not that other shit. Plus, that woman I was with that night. Man, that was really something to remember. Did I climb that coconut tree, brother, whew!"

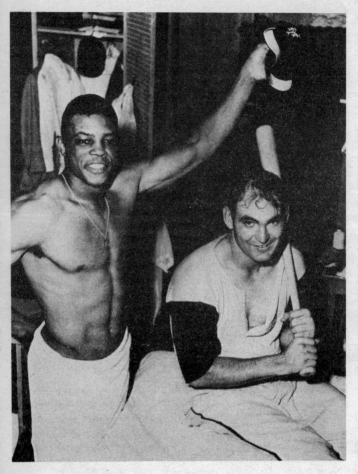

Willie Mays rarely took a back seat to any man, but in 1954 he had to take his hat off to Dusty Rhodes.

DUSTY RHODES
All Roads Lead to New York Harbor

James Lamar Rhodes, or Dusty, is still walking on water.

As the late Red Smith wrote in 1954, to describe Dusty's ownership of that year's World Series (three pinch hits, two game-winning blows, seven crucial RBIs), "A possibility developed that the Giants and Indians may not bother playing the fourth game of the World Series. There's talk of calling it off in order that James Lamar Rhodes of Rock Hill, South Carolina may give an exhibition of walking on water."

Rhodes wasn't in Cleveland long enough to perform any tricks on Lake Erie. His own hitting assured the New York Giants a short stay.

In Game One the scalping began when he hit a Chinese shot down the right field line, about 260 feet from home plate. The chopstick home run wasn't as artistic as Willie Mays's back-to-the-plate grab of Vic Wertz's towering drive, but Rhodes's tenth-inning, pinch-hit home run dramatically meant a 5-2 Giant win—and New York Mo-Men-Tum.

The heroics continued in Game Two. With the Tribe leading 1-0 and Mays on second base, manager Leo "The Lip" Durocher again tabbed Rhodes to hit for eventual Hall of Famer Monte Irvin. And again Dusty connected, singling to center to tie the score. Left in the game, the Giant outfielder later homered to give the "Jints" an insurance run.

Then, in Game Three, the .253 lifetime hitter dusted off the Indians one more time by driving in two runs with another pinch-hit single (again taking Irvin's place, and, for the third straight time, hitting the first pitch).

It was certainly Massacre City. The Giants crushed Feller, Mike Garcia, Larry Doby, and Co. in four straight—yet the show wasn't complete. Despite the greatest one-man act in Series history, Giant fans had to be disappointed. Rhodes never took on Lake Erie.

Only now is he making up for that omission. Dusty is a steerer, deckman, cook, and whatever else is needed on the *Peter Callahan*, a tugboat for the Manhattan Oil Transportation Company, which moves barges in and out of New York harbor. His daily routine doesn't seem all that romantic—up at five every morning, into the kitchen to feed two cats, a few Scotches at his wife's bar, maybe a quick game of pool, then onto the tug. But the fifty-six-year-old's walking talents are constantly being tested, every time he maneuvers a multi-million-dollar tanker into port.

"Hell, those Series hits were fun, they kinda made me a hero for a while, but bringing a boat in, with the wind at forty MPH, that's real excitement," insists Rhodes, nursing a drink in Ginger's, his wife's dockside Staten Island bar. The dingy shot-in-the-beer joint is not the quietest place to talk. A steady stream of seamen amble in, and either poke Rhodes with cue sticks or make crude jokes about his 1954 heroics. But Rhodes knows how to fight back—eighty-one stitches on his scalp prove that. He tells a few of the hecklers to f--- off, and then says, "Shit, this place is worst than a clubhouse. Dirty, jealous minds, that's sailors for you. But the life, it's the open air, and good, hard living.

"Like I was saying, baseball's tough. Wynn, Garcia, and Bob Feller, shit, they were mean son of a bitches. But they were nothin' compared to picking up a barge in the high seas. You can get hurt out there, even killed.

You could lose one of those babies. Geez, that's responsibility. Landing one of those mothers is a lot more satisfying than all the home runs, pinch hits, or my drinking and carousing."

Yet the Three Bs, brawling, bull-throwing, and boozing, are the Dusty Rhodes story. These talents, more than hitting, got him to the big leagues, and a reputation as the baddest, craziest man in baseball.

A country boy who spent his childhood in Mathews, Alabama, Dusty had to be resourceful to escape his father's cotton fields. There just weren't too many tryout camps in his neck of the woods. Most boys were fated to fight off boll weevils, not Bob Feller fastballs. But the fifteen-year-old Dusty was the same as the current model—wild-spirited and impulsive. Disgusted with farm chores or lectures about getting one more pint of milk from Bessie, Rhodes jumped on a freight train and ran off to Montgomery.

The crucial moment had arrived—Dusty now picked up a baseball glove for the first time. The discovery doesn't rank with Edison's electricity experiments, or Einstein's unleashing of the atom, but the move was still fateful—the Ty Cobb of World Series pinch-hitters was born, and in twelve years Cleveland would figuratively be reduced to a Hiroshima.

Hitting became a Rhodes staple out of necessity. He couldn't do much else running around barefooted. This money problem was only solved when a local dry cleaning shop proprietor put him to work, next to an ironing board and on their softball team. Rhodes was so grateful, he quickly got his own uniform filthy, diving after misjudged fly balls, or from hiding in a coal bin after thumping balls through windows.

Softball was, well, only softball. In those days (the late 1940s), the real men played hardball, while softballers were a lesser breed of athlete. Our Dusty has always gone after the real thing, and his ballplaying was no exception. He soon accepted an invitation from a friend to watch the big boys play, and when a few

Now a crewman aboard a New York City tugboat, Dusty's always ready—and eager for all kinds of adventures.

members of one team (the Gaels) failed to appear, Dusty found himself in the outfield. Three home runs later, his future was sealed.

Only one thing stood between Dusty and the biggies—World War II. Never one to shy away from a fight (those eighty-one stitches are from numerous brawls onboard ship, or battles with muggers), Rhodes wanted "to take on a bunch of Nazis single-handed." Uncle Sam quickly obliged. He sent the seventeen-year-old to the South Pacific, where Rhodes bounced around on LST 706 for two years.

Characteristically, Dusty laughs about "having more fights over grass skirts than with the Japanese." But upon returning home he faced a serious dilemma, or, in this case, a crossRhodes. How was he going to make a living?

"I didn't give baseball too much thought. I really didn't know what I aimed to do," recalls Rhodes, spitting a wad of chewing tobacco onto the floor. Pausing to yell a few obscenities at a long-time friend, he doesn't continue until another Scotch is put in front of him. "I was just bouncing around. Who knew what to do in those crazy days? I just went down to see my friends on the Gaels, and before I knew it they wanted me to take a few swings. A born hitter can never refuse such an invite.

"I did okay. No doubt about that. Yup, a few days later I came down again, got a couple good shots, and this guy comes up to me. He asked me, 'Hey, young fella, have you ever thought of playing pro ball?' I thought the guy was making a fool of me, and I got ready to punch him in the mouth. No one in those days fooled around with me. They still don't. Old Dusty is still a mean son of a bitch. Well, then this nut introduced himself. He was Bruce Hayes, a scout for the Nashville Vols of the Southern Association, and he told me to come see him if I was interested.

"Later on I told my friend about it, and he said I was a damn fool for not singing on the spot. What did I know? Well, the next day I went down to Hayes's hotel. I still thought the guy was giving me all this maroney and baloney. But I went. I said, 'How much money am I going to make, and cut this shit about how good I am.' He was flabbergasted. Especially when I started walking out of his room. He called me Dusty, I don't know why, I guess the town was dusty, or something. Then, when I stopped at the door, he said he'd give me $125 a month. Shit. I only laughed. But he gave me this contract, and told me to send it to him if I changed my mind. Hell, he had to be kidding, I thought. $125 a month. No way in hell did I ever think that I was going to take him up on it."

Rhodes stuffed the "lousy piece of paper" into his pocket, and along with a friend was soon headed for Miami. That trip can be entitled "The Misadventures of Wayward Youth." Hitch-hiking their way south, the two nineteen-year-olds got into all sorts of trouble, the most serious of which was getting arrested for vagrancy, spending a few nights in jail, and then persuading a judge to let them get out of town, or, as Dusty puts it, "I told the judge if he lets us out we wouldn't catch the next train. We'd be on the one that just left."

Broke and seemingly destined for his father's farm, Rhodes took the Big Leap—he signed and mailed his Vols contract. Then Rhodes cooled his heels. He got a job packing coffee in a grocery store, and had almost forgotten about playing baseball when word finally came (six months later, at the beginning of 1947). He was supposed to report to Hopkinsville, Kentucky (Class D ball), for spring training.

Yet Rhodes's rise to the majors was anything but meteoric. He spent five frustrating years in the minors, skipping from places like Hutchinson, Kansas to Macon, Georgia to Springfield, Massachusetts. At every stop Dusty hit over .300, but he also got a reputation for another type of heavy hitting—"being a twelve-o'clock-guy in a nine-o'clock town." Clubs or league presidents fined him for various incidents; managers shuffled him around before he could be a bad influence on other players; and at age twenty-four (1951) Rhodes was thinking "getting into baseball was the biggest mistake of my life."

Meanwhile, the New York Giants had a problem. The peerless Willie Mays was headed for the Army in 1952, and that left a gaping hole in the outfield. A gamble had to be taken—even if it meant calling up Rhodes, the reputed bad boy who had finally made it to Nashville.

Rhodes was hitting .354 with the Vols, but once in the short-fenced Polo Grounds, he pulled-pulled-pulled—and in his desperation for the long ball his batting average plunged-plunged-plunged, to .250, then to .233 in 1953. "I was swinging for too many homers, and I knew if things didn't improve I'd be back in the minors. Shit, I'd been there so long already, I had to do something. I had to meet the ball. My job as a pinch hitter or as a sub was to get on base, and the best way to do that was to forget my being some Babe Ruth. I didn't want to be so well known anyway."

Once Rhodes settled for making simple contact, the sting came back. In 1954, besides adding 110 points to his average, he delivered fifteen pinch-hits, which won thirteen ballgames. His Series marks are certainly better remembered (Rhodes set eleven individual records in the fall classic), but it's doubtful whether the Giants would've won the pennant without those pinch-hits, or his slugging a Ruthian .695.

Rhodes had another good season in 1955, batting .305, with eleven more pinch hits. Subsequently, however, his stats resembled the 1929 stock market crash—the bottom fell out. Playing left field more regularly than ever before (111 games), he slumped to .217. Then, showing that this performance was no fluke, Rhodes barely hit his weight: .205 in 1957 and .188 in '59. The Giants were then embarking on a new adventure in San Francisco, and suddenly Dusty became excess baggage.

Admitting "it was really tough to give it up, especially in the spring when the sun comes up and everyone is having a great time in Florida," Dusty played three more years in the Pacific Coast League. He never regained his 1954 stroke, however, and went from selling cars to working as a Pinkerton's guard at the 1964 World's Fair in New York. "I had to watch over the ticket takers, and you know what, we handled $28 million without losing a nickel. That job made me sweat more than the World Series."

At this point, his wife, Gloria, pops out from a room behind the bar, and shouts, "Hey, Dusty, who are you kidding? You've never sweated in your life. What are you telling these guys? How much have you been drinking?"

"Come on dear, that Pinkerton's thing wasn't easy. There were all sorts of characters running around."

"Look, just tell me one thing, did you feed the cats the way you're supposed to?"

Tough guy Dusty then blushes and makes some cooing noises about his cats back home. "You should see those little fellas. They're our babies. Since the kids left home that's all we have left. I bought a camera just to take their picture. They're so cute. I got to give them fresh salmon, filets, they're my babies. Shit, do I miss them when I'm out on the boat."

Dusty first left home for the open seas in 1966. Though he "didn't know a damn thing about boats," he then got a job on an oil tanker, docked in Miami. He had always liked to fish, and this "natural talent for the wide, open waters," helped him move up from engine oiler to deck hand in six months. Moby Dick and Billy Budd were clearly in his blood; so Rhodes took the ultimate plunge—he studied to become an able-bodied seaman—and eventually his odyssey was completed. A barefoot farm boy wound up in the wheelhouse of a tugboat, guiding $25 million tankers into port.

"It's sure funny how life works. How could I think about sea adventures? I didn't even know that boats existed," says Rhodes, steering the rest of his Scotch down the hatch. His weather-beaten face now takes on a reddish glow. Clearly enjoying this opportunity to reminisce, he continues, "I gotta like what I'm doing; I'm out in the fresh air, the sea is a constant challenge, and the guys on the boat, we're as close as players in a club-house.

"I don't feel lost any more not being in baseball. Those first few years were a horror show, sure. But I'm okay now. I do miss Leo (Durocher) and a few of the guys. Getting chewed out by him was okay. You never knew what he was going to say next. He was tough, a lot like Billy Martin, I suppose. He psyched us up in '54. If you didn't put out he'd beat the hell out of you. That's my type of man. You have to do your job in baseball, or on a ship, and if you don't, to hell with you.

"Now I want to retire and head out to the Great Northwest. That's always been my dream. You know, I've never had a vacation in my life. It's time. I want to have some fun. I like this boat thing, directing these babies into a pier is goddamn fun. In fact, I love having people listen to me. But I'm tired of the knocking around. I just want to sit on my ass next to a stream for a while."

Rhodes now moves away from the bar and stands near a window overlooking a few tugs. He gruffly yells a few more choice epithets at a passing seaman and says, "I'll miss this place, too, but it's getting like baseball at the end, there was nothing left for me to do. I was at the top, a hero, the only place I could go was down. Still, I loved the game. I was right up there for awhile, with Ruth, Gehrig, DiMaggio. I even had a nickname. You have to have a nickname to be remembered. Even today kids call me Dusty. They'll always call me that. That makes me feel real good inside. Real good."

JIM BUNNING
Welcome to the White House

Imagine the following scenario. It's 1984, and two ceremonies are taking place in two different cities. One is in
Washington, where a man is being sworn in as a United
States senator. While miles away, in Cooperstown, New
York, that same individual is part of an unprecedented
double play. He's becoming a member of another august
body, baseball's Hall of Fame.

A star for all seasons, Jim Bunning is turning fantasies
into reality. He was recently elected to the Kentucky
State Senate (from Campbell County in the northwestern part of the state), after serving as Ronald Rea-
gan's local campaign director in 1980. Just as he blew
smoke past the likes of Mays, Aaron, and Mantle, pitching no-hitters in both leagues (one with the Tigers, and
the other a perfect game for the Phillies against the
Mets), the fifty-two-year-old Bunning beat out a sixteen-year incumbent for the Senate seat—and immediately propelled himself into candidacy for national
office in 1984.

With his credentials, 1984 could easily be the same
year he's elected to the Hall of Fame. In the big leagues
from 1955-1971, Bunning had a 224-184 record, a
combined 3.27 ERA, and enough strikeouts (2855) to
place him fourth on the all-time list. And while his 100
or more wins in each league are a baseball oddity, he

wasn't just recording trivia. More importantly, the hard-throwing right-hander was able to make a smooth transition to a different league (traded from Detroit to Philadelphia in 1964), and won with another very mediocre team. So, even though Bunning modestly tries to shrug off the distinction, he must be considered as one of the most intimidating pitchers of his era. And if his accomplishments are finally recognized by Cooperstown (a league strikeout leader three times, he had years of 268, 252, and 253 Ks), it's conceivable the recognition factor might lead to the U.S. House of Representatives, the Senate, or even . . .

Already a successful Cincinnati stockbroker and agent for several major leaguers, he admits to following (ex-basketball player) Bill Bradley's Senate career, saying, "Athletes can serve the public too; they know what it means to play by rules of the game." But when talk drifts around to his own plans, Bunning's like any other good politician. He chuckles, then winks mysteriously.

"Politics is just like baseball, it's one on one. In committee meetings you have to convince people you have a legitimate point. Baseball was also a control thing for me. I had to dominate the batter. It didn't matter what the score was, if I handled the guy at the plate I thought I had won. It took me a long time to stop being a redass, to control my emotions. I finally did become a much better person to live with. That's when baseball became a lot more fun. Now I'm learning how to apply these lessons in the political world. I'm learning how to listen to people.

"It's really tough for a guy who's been pitching twenty-two years to mellow out, to be less competitive. I think it's impossible. Even when I couldn't get the ball up to the plate in 1971, I still had the competitive drive in me. So instead of struggling with an aging body or finding a wonder drug, I managed two teams for five years (Double and Triple A ball). Then I decided to stay out of baseball, and it took me almost a year to get over that psychological hump. The depression was terrible, but my wife was a real support. We got even closer when I started to get involved in politics. With her help, I found a whole new direction.

"Being in the Senate is even more exciting than a World Series against the Yankees. You stand up there and influence what happens to three and a half million people. You feel euphoria, like in a perfect game. Now I just want to make Northern Kentucky a better place to live. It has always been a step-child in the legislature. Our auto and appliance industries, along with a few steel plants, are really suffering. I won't feel contented until I do something for these workers.

"With this on my mind I never think of the Hall of Fame. I can't do anything about my numbers anyway, so I'm just sitting back, waiting. I'm pleased with what I accomplished. But if I had it to do over again, I'd have been studying law while I was playing. Baseball gave me a great image. People know that I play the game by the rules, that I have ethics. They also know I'm a competitor. And I'm grateful for that."

Interrupted by a secretary reminding him about a meeting with a group of Cincinnati businessmen, he hurriedly puts on a sports jacket, and, while running out the door says, "But baseball can hurt you, too. If I hadn't been so involved in the game I'd know more about debating, corporations, or the law. That way I wouldn't have to depend on my brother to help write my speeches."

BOB BUHL
Life Among the Seven Dwarfs

Does your faucet leak? Is the dishwasher on the fritz, or are other cranky appliances giving you problems? And what about refinishing the basement playroom? Do you have too many thumbs to give this a try?

Well, there's hope. Call him whatever you want, handyman, jack-of-all-trades, Bonnie Bob Buhl can fix anything from air conditioners to zippers. Just move into the Kissimmee, Florida trailer camp where he's the maintenance manager, and your worries will disappear. Bob loves to be a good neighbor. First offer him a cold beer, chitchat for a while, then turn to serious matters. The bathroom toilet, the pop that's gone out of your toaster, or the leaky roof. A descendant of a long family line of carpenters and general contractors, Bob will dip into his toolbox and come up with answers—just as he did during the glory years of the Milwaukee Braves (1956-60), when the pitching trio of Warren Spahn, Lew Burdette, and Bob Buhl dominated the National League.

Buhl was then the third man in the rotation, the nickle and dime curveball and slider specialist, who used guile instead of fastballs to record a 166-132 lifetime record. He never had a twenty-game season with either the Braves, the Cubs, or the Phils. But when the Braves won the pennant in 1957 and '58, or finished second in '56,

Bob Buhl could mow down those batters, but wife Joyce calls the signals when it comes to gardening.

'59, and '60, Buhl contributed as much as Spahn, Joe Adcock, Eddie Mathews, or any of the team's bigger-name stars. During this period, he posted marks like 18-8 in 1956, 18-7 (with a 2.74 ERA) the following year, and, after injuring his shoulder in 1958 (a 5-2 record), his stats rose to 15-9 and 16-9 the next two seasons. Equally important, he was also the Dodger Killer. The Bums were perennially pennant contenders, and, while they beat out the Braves twice in the late 1950s, Buhl owned them. In 1956, for example, he had eight starts against Snider, Furillo, and Company, and he won all of them.

"That had to be one of the biggest highlights in my career," says the fifty-five-year old right-hander, leaning against several cases of beer stacked outside the family trailer. Staring wistfully at his wife's gardenia bushes, he continues, "But just being in baseball, with the Braves, was enough of a thrill. My father drove a big semi, and when I knew I didn't want to do that, or be a contractor like my grandfather, my dream was to play ball. It was the competition; I loved being with guys who wanted to win. Those Braves, geez, all of them hated to lose, even at checkers."

Daddy, as his wife calls him, is now venting this competitive zeal at the trailer park's weekly bingo meeting. Even though losing still disturbs him (to the point of yelling at the number caller), he relishes the competition. Apart from the joy of being greeted with "Aren't you Bob Buhl, the baseball pitcher?" he can be sitting at the table, waiting for a number, when his thoughts suddenly turn to baseball. Or more specifically, his pitching in a big game.

"I was never disappointed once I got to the big leagues," says Buhl, grinning. "Besides the Braves being a close outfit, we were treated real good by the city. My first year with the team (1953) was also the first year for the club in Milwaukee (they had moved from Boston). So the city went all out. All our dairy products, Golden Guernsey, were free. We got free dry cleaning, and each player was given a car to use by a local Dodge dealer. We really owned the town, those first few years.

"Damn, the Braves were great. They gave me the ball every time we needed a big win. I remember in 1959, the Dodgers had beaten the Cubs in a day game, and we had to win at night to tie for the championship. It was (Juan) Pizarro's turn to pitch, but he said, 'Why me?' So who got the ball? I talked (manager) Fred Haney into letting me pitch, and I only gave the Phils one run that night. That was the end of the rainbow for me; I was playing for the entire season."

Able to keep batters off stride with his tricky array of change-ups and sliders, Buhl enjoyed many dramatic moments during the 1950s. He pitched in two All-Star Games, had the NL's best winning percentage (.714) in 1958, and after pitching a few shutouts at the end of the '59 season, narrowly missed winning the ERA title (with a 2.86). But once the Braves started to fade in the early '60s, Buhl lost his spot in the rotation to younger pitchers like Bob Shaw, Carlton Willey, and Toni Cloninger. His competitive spirit couldn't take this, so he eventually demanded to be traded. In 1962 his not seeing eye-to-eye with manager Birdie Tebbetts resulted in his going to the Cubs in exchange for Jackie Curtis, a left-hander with a 14-19 lifetime record.

Buhl had a few decent seasons in Wrigley Field, 15-14 in 1964 and 13-11 in '65, although commuting to Milwaukee to see his family left him "plain tuckered out." He was also troubled by the Cubs system of rotating managers. (Utilizing eight coaches, the short-lived experiment called for a different "manager" every month.) Understandably, Buhl found this confusing. So he complained again. And as a result, was traded to the Phillies for Ferguson Jenkins in 1966. One year later, feeling "drained, disgusted, and traveled out," he retired.

It was a major financial adjustment, to go from $40,000 to nothing. But Buhl happily resettled in Michigan, where he could enjoy fishing and hunting. Instead of looking for work, he spent two years at home, "getting to know my children for the first time." The bills, however, started to pile up. Forced to fall back on his only non-baseball skill—carpentry—he formed a partnership with another general contractor and built luxury homes, at $50,000 to $150,000 each. And again, baseball gave him an extra edge.

"I never had to advertise. People just wanted to tell their friends, 'Guess who's building my house? Bob Buhl, the Braves pitcher.' But besides that, the game gave me a thirst to win, so I had to do better work than the next guy. I had to build the best houses. Even when I attach a water pipe to one of these trailers, it's gotta be done perfectly. Nothing else makes it for me."

Convinced that he could be more creative in Florida (and also tired of Michigan's winters), Buhl became the director of maintenance at the RV (recreational vehicle) camp six years ago. He now supervises all construction, installs electrical wiring, keeps the swimming pool heated or its machinery functional, and will often help remodel someone's trailer. His own boss, the position gives him a new sense of freedom that's described as "the best thing to happen to me since being with Eddie (Mathews) and the rest of the Braves."

Relaxing after work with his wife Joyce, in their patio, Buhl cheerfully recalls, "Baseball was a good, clean life. Not everyone could put on a uniform in those days. I was a special person to be playing alongside Spahnie and Burdette. That has to make me feel proud.

"The thing I miss most is being with Eddie (Mathews). What a hell of a guy he is. He's so damn set in his ways, but he'd do anything for a person, especially for someone who's down, or the underdog. We'd always talk nights about hitting and pitching. He had his theory about how he'd try to hit me, and I had my own thoughts about how I'd pitch to him. Talking to him made me realize that batters didn't want to look like fools at the plate. They waited for the fastball. So that made me think, I have to develop other kinds of pitches. Or else I'd be the one looking stupid.

"Yeah, baseball really demanded a lot from you. It might look easy, but hell, it's a science sometimes. How easy could it be, when I'd have to get guys like Mays, Snider, or Kluszewski out. Wow. I never thought I'd get such an opportunity when I was a kid. I used to ride my bike in the winter, with my glove hooked onto the handlebars. There was always snow around, but I wanted to be ready, just in case one of my friends had a ball."

Bonnie Bob then moves his chair aside, and gets set to show off his pitching style. Before he can bring his right leg towards the "plate," a howl goes up in the background. Wife Joyce, worried that Bob will step too close to the gardenias or on their ceramic guardians, the Seven Dwarfs, jumps up, and shouts, "Watch out, watch out. Don't go near my honeys. Go over there, like a good boy. You can't hurt anything in the grass."

Bob, looking as sheepish as one of the dwarfs, just shrugs. "Oh well, at least I didn't have this kind of trouble with Mays. Compared to this, he was kid stuff."

ROGER MARIS
The Conspiracy Thickens

Agatha Christie couldn't have written a better script.

Suspense, intrigue, plus All-American heroes, villains, hints of foul play, back-stabbing, and double-dealing.

It was certainly a spine-tingler. Not just another baseball milestone or dry statistic for the record books. No, these events in 1961 had a special quality, a spellbinding effect that divided the nation into warring factions. One group clamored for the Babe's record to be broken while the other decried each passing home run as un-American, unpatriotic.

Roger Maris, meanwhile, tried to ignore these pressures as he closed in on Ruth's sixty-home run mark. But would-be challengers to the great Babe's record have always dubbed September the cruelest month of the season, and in Maris's case it was especially grueling. Besides chasing this almost mythical home run mark, the Yankee slugger had to contend with management. A few execs were distressed by the prospect of his breaking the record, and they hoped to sabotage him by exerting pressure on manager Ralph Houk to change the lineup. Although Maris continued to play, he still had to deal with commissioner Ford Frick. He was a more substantial threat. A self-described "savior of all that was holy with the game," Frick nearly compared Maris to an infidel, announcing that if Maris broke the record

There it goes, Roger Maris's record-breaking sixty-first home run.

during the 162-game season, as contrasted to Ruth's 154 games, an asterisk would be placed after his name in the record books.

None of these or cloak-and-dagger machinations eventually mattered. Much to the dismay of Yankee management, and some fans who pelted him with foreign objects, Maris kept slugging. He outhit the team's golden boy, Mickey Mantle, in the closing stages of the season (both men, or as the local press called them, the M&M Boys, had a shot at eclipsing Ruth's record), and on October 1st, 1961, getting a nonbreaking curve ball from Boston right-hander Tracy Stallard, he pulled number sixty-one into the right-field seats.

It was done. No more shadows had to be chased. No more reporters had to be ducked. A shy, overly modest man who escaped from the publicity by living in a small Queens apartment, Maris could now try to go back to the game he loved. "It started off as such a dream. My making it to Yankee Stadium, then being on equal terms with a legend. I never thought I'd ever get a chance to break such a record. Too bad it ended so badly. It would've been a helluva lot more fun if I had never hit those sixty-one home runs. All it brought me was headaches."

Maris's career began on a far more positive note ten years earlier in Fargo, North Dakota. The son of a Great Northern Railway worker, he drove so many balls into nearby wheat fields, his American Legion coach hailed him as another DiMaggio. Also impressed, a Cleveland Indians scout signed him up for a tryout. When that didn't pan out, Maris got another chance with the Cubs. But that, too, went nowhere, the Cubs telling him to give up baseball, because at 195 pounds he was too small.

Frustrated by the experience, Maris briefly considered a pro football career. He changed his mind a few months later, got another tryout with the Indians, and this time was assigned to the Fargo/Morehead Twins, a minor league club in the Cleveland organization. Here he met JoJo White, the manager he now credits for his making it to the big leagues.

"I wasn't really using all my strength as a hitter until I met JoJo," admits Maris, sitting under photos of other strong hitters, namely DiMaggio, Mantle, and Hank Bauer, in the office of his Gainesville, Florida beer distributorship. "I used to hit the ball where it was pitched, and at Fargo that first year, that only got me nine or ten home runs. But JoJo changed my style. He said I was too big for only scratching out singles or long doubles, that I had to start pulling the ball. The next year (1954), after I changed, I hit thirty-two homers. He also made me a good outfielder, and for what he did I'll always be grateful."

The Indians brought him up in 1957, and Maris led the league in homers and RBIs, before he broke a few ribs in a midseason headfirst slide. Then he became a gypsy. Cleveland traded him to Kansas City for Vic Power and Woodie Held, where he batted .273, with sixteen homers and 72 RBIs. But soon, it was on the road again. Known then as a Yankee farm team, the As sent him to New York for Marvelous Marv Throneberry, Don Larsen, and Hank Bauer. And the change worked wonders. In 1960 Maris gave fans a preview of what was to come, by erupting for thirty-nine homers, 112 RBIs, and a .283 batting average.

Without question, 1961 then became the year of the Rajah. Newspapers either extolled or criticized Maris. But however public opinion swung, the daily headlines, comparing Maris's home run pace to Ruth's, added up to near-hysterical excitement. It's true that Maris timed his big year to the American League's first season of expansion (to ten teams), and enjoyed the benefits of facing diluted pitching staffs. Nonetheless, his season-long battle with Ruth—and Mantle—for two home run crowns gave baseball a much needed shot of adrenalin. Fans came pouring through the turnstiles again, and, even more importantly, talk of a new Murderer's Row (the Yankees hit 240 homers that year, and all-time record), provided Americans an escape from the frightening storm clouds of the Cold War.

And while making history put tremendous pressure on Maris, he coolly says, "Everyone talks about the publicity, the drama of going after Ruth, or the excitement. But I didn't feel any differently. It was rather difficult coping with the pre- and post-game activities, the frenzy that was always a part of the clubhouse. Yet I didn't play a different game, or change my attitude when I was out on the field. Yeah, it was tough being Roger Maris then, and it's still difficult at times, being recognized in public. But I only got that chance at the record because pitchers couldn't circle around me. I was in some lineup. People forget that the 1961 Yankees were the greatest team ever."

Maris, now forty-nine, then looks around the office, at a few trophies or souvenirs, and his mood perceptibly changes. Sitting more erect in his chair, the lines in his sun-tanned face tightening, he angrily says, "I was still happy when the season ended. I never had a chance to look forward to the World Series, and God, was I miserable in it (a .105 batting average, with only two hits in nineteen at-bats). I was tired of the fanfare. I don't want to sound bitter, because I'm not. But I was never the best-liked Yankee who ever came through Yankee Stadium. I had so many people on my ass. People resented me for breaking Ruth's record, the press especially. They made me into a machine. The Yankees, too, played a part. Let's not kid anybody. They wanted Mantle to break the record, not me. They did everything possible to assure that. They wanted to reduce my chances. Even today I don't get the right credit for it."

Critics lashed out at him even more in 1962. Maris's stats fell off, to thirty-three homers, 100 RBIs (from 142), and a .256 batting average, so his enemies bitingly called 1961 a fluke, or went so far as to hang him in effigy in the right-field bleachers. Undisturbed by these outbursts, Maris pocketed thousands of dollars from various endorsements, and says, "By everyone's standards I had a bad year in '62. I disagree. I was still hitting the ball hard, I just wasn't getting the altitude. Most of them were sinking line drives; still, thirty-three homers insn't too shabby in any league."

World Series checks also served to soften the criticism. But once the Yankees started to stumble in the mid-'60s, the fans looked for scapegoats and Maris was an easy target. From hitting a highly-respectable .281 in 1964, he dipped to a tormenting .239 in '65, partly because of injuries and a deepening sense of estrangement from the fans. Maris just wasn't happy in New York anymore, and after a broken hand contributed to his having another miserable season in 1966 (he hit only .233), he told the Yankees to get a new right-fielder.

"Can you imagine what the press would have done to me if I had gone ahead and retired?" asks Maris, disgustedly. "It was partly the Yankees' fault. They kept me in uniform all year. Only at the end of the season did they tell me I needed a hand operation. So of course the press thought I was dogging it. But the sportswriters crucified me for six years, so I can see the headlines, 'Maris is a quitter, the great home run hitter is a sore loser.' If I had quit, my name would've been disgraced. All my achievements would've been ridiculed. The press even insinuated that I was the cause of the Yankee downfall. Things had gotten so bad in New York, I had to get out."

Before the 1967 season began, the Yankees convinced Maris not to retire, then traded him to St. Louis for third baseman Charley Smith. While Maris came back to hit .261, and .385 in the World Series (ten for twenty-six), the deal instantly touched off numerous rumors. The most dramatic one concerned Cardinal president August Busch. He supposedly talked Maris out of retirement by offering him a beer distributorship in return for a two-year contract. Maris now denies this, and is only willing to say, "As for how I got into this business, let's put it this way: I've always had a lot of friends in beer companies. My place wasn't a price for me to join the Cardinals. I'm just glad that I had a chance to show the

Mr. Swat is also a natural when it comes to selling Bud.

world that I was a winner (St. Louis won two pennants with him), and that I'm again with a number one outfit (Budweiser). Forget those rumors; most of our newspapers are communist anyway."

Maris finally retired after the 1968 season. He immediately settled in Gainesville, and his beer distributorship is now a prosperous, multi-million-dollar operation, which serves an eight-county area. Though Bud's more celebrated distributors tour the banquet circuit, Maris doesn't get involved in these promotional activities. Instead, he's leading a leisurely life, only showing up at the office sporadically, and playing lots of golf (a nine handicapper).

Before flying off for another Florida golf date with Mantle, Whitey Ford, and assorted Yankees, he walks through his 36,000-square-foot warehouse and says, "Getting out of baseball is usually a tough adjustment. It's really hard, excruciatingly so, for most guys. It didn't hit me that way, since I was happy to get out. The press gave me such a rough time I looked forward to a quieter life. And now I'm having a great time.

"But don't get me wrong. I'm not miffed. I have no qualms with baseball at all. I had my disappointments, but everyone has those in life. I'm just sorry that everyone harps on my cheapening Ruth's record. That's not true. You only hear about the extra games I had. Well, if you look at the records, Ruth hit number sixty in his 687th appearance. I hit mine in 684 appearances. Anyway, I know I have the record, and that's the only thing that counts."

Looking contentedly at the stacks of beer cases, he starts to talk about refrigeration, only to interrupt himself, and to say instead, "Baseball, or my breaking that record, led to this. It doesn't matter if there were problems in '61. Everything still worked out alright. Sure, New York was pulling for Mickey, he was the Yankees, and justifiably so. But no matter what people say, I'm going to be remembered too, along with Mickey and the Babe."

JIM RIVERA
But Where's Ingrid Bergman?

"Welcome to the Screwball Club."

Combining that greeting with a roguish wink and a heavy-handed martini, Joseph "Jungle Jim" Rivera has made his Captain's Cabin restaurant the hit of Angola, Indiana. The secret of his success is simple. He's still a character.

Nicknamed for his diving catches, headfirst slides, and all-around daring style of play, Rivera once idolized other pepper-pots like Frankie Frisch and Leo Durocher. Now, he's modeling himself after another hustler. He wants to be a Rick Blaine, that consummate cafe owner/host of *Casablanca* fame, otherwise known as Humphrey Bogart.

Rivera's background is far from romantic. Bounced from one New York orphanage to another, he totally missed high school, and wound up in an army prison, charged with an attempted rape. There he was saved from further problems by two recreational programs: boxing and baseball. Fighting was his first love, but "Baseball was easier on my good looks, especially after I got my ass kicked in the Golden Gloves." It was also cheaper. Rivera only needed former Dodger Billy Cox to buy him a glove, and his fate was sealed.

Now sixty-one, the fast-talking, silver-haired Rivera is Mr. Debonair, wooing hundreds of diners nightly at his lakeside club. He also plays the maracas better than he ever hit major league pitching (in ten years with the White Sox, St. Louis Browns, and Kansas City Athletics he batted .256), and whenever his band strikes up a Glenn Miller tune, his footwork is as fancy as it was in the late 1950s, when he roamed the outfield with other members of the fleet-footed Go-Go Sox.

Turning away from an attractive, long-haired blonde at the bar, he admits, "If I hadn't played ball, I wouldn't have this place. Everything I have is baseball's doing. When I started to sit on the bench I saw the handwriting on the wall, so I bought some bonds and prayed. I only knew the game and how to fight. I certainly didn't know anything about the bar business, not even how to mix a Seven and Seven. But I worked at it. Tonight I'll turn over 250 people in here.

"Usually this wouldn't be possible for a guy who went to jail on attempted rape. Guys like me are finished before we start. I owe everything to men like Al Lopez and Bill Veeck. They had faith in me. Not too many people did. Baseball really saved my hide. It gave me a chance to make something out of myself. If not for the game I'd most likely be in prison today. Or who knows what.

"And the greatest thing of all was that I even got paid to play. That's the kicker. Wow. What a life. I can't believe these guys today who have to be chauffered to the ballpark. What crumbs. I wasn't looking at how my stocks were doing when I was playing. I was playing, I wasn't fooling around with agents, or all those shysters. My only fooling around was having a good time.

"I had a trick with cigarette papers; damn, was it a beauty. I'd be chewing tobacco, and I'd make these balls out of the silver wrapping. I threw them once at someone, and then I'd ask if they could catch it a second time. Instead, I'd take the tobacco and dump it in his palm. The juice would run all over. What a sight that was."

Chuckling, Rivera pauses, and looks out at the marina in front of his restaurant. He finally says, "Boy, baseball was something. It really turned me around.

And in turn I've really done a number on this place. It used to be nothing. No one ever came here, and the place was falling apart. Now I'm really making it, and the people love coming here. They have a good time. I'm not a Bogart yet, but at least I'm a Cesar Romero."

*From stuffed gorillas
to Goldilocks, Bernie Carbo
has always played the
game his own way.*

BERNIE CARBO
Mighty Joe Young Needs a Manicure

Don't call him Mr. Clutch any more. He's now *Monsieur Bernardo*.

Widely-traveled outfielder Bernie Carbo, who'll always be remembered for tying the sixth game of the 1975 World Series with an eighth-inning homer (not for his usual .250 or so batting average, or eight to twelve homers a year), has finally settled down. After playing with Cincinnati, Boston, St. Louis, the Brewers, Pittsburgh, and making an ill-fated return to the minors in 1981 (with the Tigers' Evansville franchise), he's finally hammered his spikes to the wall. He's also exchanged his bats for styling combs, and become the owner of a unisex beauty salon in Detroit.

Women flock there. The cozy, two-chair shop Carbo personally designed has quickly become a mecca for trading beauty secrets, chit-chatting, or leafing through the latest pages of *Cosmo*. The waiting time for a wash or set is usually two to three hours. But, remaining good-humored, the female patrons watch Carbo in awe, frequently commenting, "Oh, Bern, darling, what a beautiful cutting." Or, "Wait till my husband sees me. Oh Bernie, I love you."

A licensed hair dresser after attending beauty school for two years, Carbo can now give any frost or perm a golden touch. Able to caress curls quickly and gently while moving a scissors and comb, he hardly seems like a rookie. But then again, the thirty-six-year-old beautician has always had deft hands; singling, homering, doing whatever was necessary in the pinch.

Take his most spectacular moment, on October 21st, 1975. Before he pulled off his last-minute, heart-stopping heroics, everything looked black for the Red Sox. Already down three games to two, Boston went into the bottom of the eighth inning trailing six to three. With two runners on base, Carbo confronted Redleg reliever Rawley Eastwick. It was no contest. The ball exploded off Carbo's bat, in orbit towards the center-field bleachers. For some Fenway fans, it's still sailing (Carlton Fisk finally won that memorable twelve-inning game by coaxing another home run to stay fair.)

"That home run is my present to the people of Boston," says Carbo, wearing a blue smock, while rinsing off a young girl's hair. "The love affair up there was a mutual thing. The fans appreciated me, and I busted my gut for them. I'd still take a high, hard one on the chin for them, just to start a rally. Too bad management didn't know what they were doing. They never used me right."

Carbo was always outspoken. Regularly platooned with various members of the Cincinnati outfield, or Boston's Dwight Evans, he never felt he was getting enough playing time (he usually did play over a hundred games a year, yet only batted over .300 once, in 1970, when he combined a .310 percentage with twenty-one homers). So he pouted, broke bats against blackboards, or reminded managers with clubhouse grafitti, "Carbo Still Lives." Hard-nosed old-liners like Don Zimmer, the Busch family in St. Louis, or Tom Yawkey were never impressed. Not understanding this new breed of ballplayer, they simply viewed Carbo as a crazy or a troublemaker for his hanging out with flake Bill Lee, dressing in white overalls, or staging the Mighty Joe Young affair.

That latter escapade was another crowd-pleaser—but it also led to more run-ins with management, and a series of short, undistinguished stays with other clubs. Mighty Joe happened to be a stuffed gorilla. Unhappy again about not playing, Carbo dressed his new playmate in a baseball uniform and sat him in the Boston dugout. They later became inseparable—airplanes, restaurants, doughnut shops—wherever Carbo went, Mighty Joe tailed along. They made all the newspapers and the talk shows. Only eventually the other players stopped laughing. They resented the publicity, and Carbo became a marked man whose days in a Boston uniform were numbered.

Now older and supporting a family of two young daughters, Carbo seems quieter, more willing to admit, "I made a few mistakes in baseball." He sometimes thinks of returning to the game, perhaps in Mexico, or some winter Caribbean league. But, in the shop ten to fourteen hours a day, he knows most of these thoughts are just fantasies. His biggest dream these days is establishing a regular clientele, "that will come in, remember when I was a hardball player, and give me enough money to grow old, with a big, always-filled pot belly.

"I've finished 1500 hours of schooling for this. It's going to take two to three years to really get this place to where I want it to be. I know starting a business is tough. I'm scared. Imagine being a rookie again at my age. It's something I always wanted, though. When I was eleven or twelve, aunts on one side of my family wanted to straighten my hair. I wouldn't have any part of that. I'd tell my did that I wanted to do my own hair, and his response was always the same. He'd say I shouldn't be a fag. That hair was a woman's business. It's only lately that he's let me cut his hair. He makes me do it in the house. He still won't come near the shop.

"I guess no matter what I do, I'll be looked at as a freak. Baseball owners in my day were Nixon, and I was Woodstock. They wanted to dictate my life, tell me who my friends should be, what to wear, everything. They wouldn't even let my wife sit next to the other wives. I did a few things wrong, sure. I opened my mouth at the wrong times too often. But I wasn't going to kiss ass the way Rose did, or (Frank) Robinson did. I didn't think everything had to be sacrificed for the organization, or for some owner who acted like a Hitler. Baseball has to be better than that.

"Most likely, people will still think I'm crazy. I'm sure they will when they see what I'm doing. Right away they'll think I'm a fag. I don't care. I'm enjoying what I'm doing, I make people look better. When I was growing up, I wasn't allowed to cry or to express my feelings about men. Now I'm in a field that's very intimate. It's a very personal thing to do someone's hair. I might have to adjust when a guy comes in here and wants me to work on him. But I hope I can grow and do this kind of haircut, or whatever. I want to get close to people. It's something my father, or baseball, has never allowed me to do."

Responding to a patron yelling his name, Carbo moves to the front of the shop and gives the woman a dramatic kiss. After they exchange a little gossip, he comes back smiling. "Just remember, 'Carbo Still Lives.' I'm going to reach all my goals. One day Bill Lee and me are going to own our own club, and stick our tongues out at the other owners. Can you see that?

"In the meantime my roller sets and perms are getting a lot better. I also give great haircuts. I'm really getting this together. No one's hair is turning green or orange. It's a crazy business. But I love it. I've always gotten along better with women than men."

VIC POWER

Bill Cosby Teams up with Martin Luther King

Jackie Robinson, Satchel Paige, Larry Doby; they fought the brave fight. Pioneers against baseball's radical bigotry, they confronted an opponent named Jim Crow, and forced him to give up his "white only" hotels, restaurants, or restrooms. It was a tense, emotionally-pitched struggle. One that evoked a lot of angry words, clenched fists, and tears.

The game's all-time great showman was also on that battlefield. Only this time, Vic Power wasn't dazzling crowds with one-handed grabs, showboating whirls at first base, or his unorthodox, bat-high-in-the-air hitting style. He was deadly serious.

Currently a scout for the California Angels and an advisor to the House of Representatives in Puerto Rico, Power can now recall some of those confrontations without getting angry. But that has only come with time. Thirty years ago, the discrimination was so humiliating Power could only flail out in rage.

"I remember the time I tried to take a leak in Georgia somewhere," says Power, standing on a palm tree-covered beach outside San Juan, near the site of the plane crash where Roberto Clemente was killed. "I was the only colored guy in the Yankee organization then, and the team bus had stopped at a restaurant. Everyone got out to piss, but this guy wouldn't let me go to the

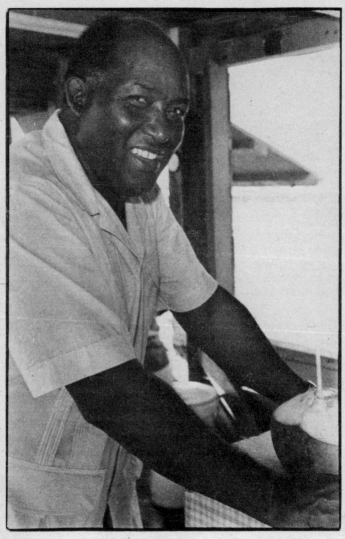

Vic Power, perhaps the
greatest showman the game
has ever known.

bathroom. I asked him, 'Don't colored people piss?' He looked at me and said I couldn't piss there or in the woods. So I bought a Coke bottle, emptied it, and was going to pee in it on the bus. Now the guy said I couldn't keep the bottle. That infuriated me. I threw the bottle at him, and then they called the sheriff. He arrested me, and only after the Yankees begged him did he agree to a $500 bond. I never went back for the trial, and I guess they're still looking for me."

Thrilled by the idea of being a fugitive, Power does a little jig, and then starts to roar with laughter. His big stomach shakes so much, he must soon rest on a log. "I really thought that if I played for the Yankees I could piss, too. But things like that were always happening. I wasn't allowed to go to the white hotel. I stayed in the best house in the colored section, and that was usually a funeral parlor. I slept with dead people at night; or let's say I tried to sleep. I was too scared most of the time. Puerto Ricans are a very superstitious people. Yet the worst thing about all this was that I had to compete with well rested guys. Maybe that's why I didn't make the Yankees."

Instead of brooding about the past, or his dream of becoming the first colored Yankee, Power goes on to talk about his good friend, Roberto Clemente. Once the Pirate slugger's manager, when he took a Puerto Rican all-star team to Nicaragua, Power chokes off a tear and says, "It's true that he was kinda moody, but Roberto did so much for people. He always wanted to give to people. He didn't have to fly that day; it was all cloudy, the food he had for people (in Nicaragua) could've sat one more day. It was such a shock for me. When I saw his briefcase floating in the water, a few yards from here, I knew he was dead. A lot of people still think he's alive, and his warm, giving spirit still is. But I was with him when he bought that case."

Only after Power pays this tribute does he consent to talk about his own career. That's Power; he's always had style.

Or a flair for making baseball more than a game of

balls and strikes. While Willie Mays is synonymous with the basket catch, Vic invented the one-handed grab. This bedeviled managers, cheered fans, and as the seven-time Gold Glove winner recalls, "They called me showboat, but why? I only had a different style of playing. I felt better catching the ball that way. I told sportswriters if the guy who invented the game wanted players to catch with two hands, he'd have put two gloves on them to begin with. Doubleday was no fool. He knew the game was meant to be exciting."

Then there was Power's flashing bat. He'd hold it high above his head, wave it back and forth, then CRASH! BAM! It's amazing that his Louisville Sluggers could handle the action. In his second major league season (after debuting with a .255 mark for the Philadelphia/Kansas City Athletics), he thumped nineteen homers and hit a fat .319 in 1955. Power rarely lost that bang. A .284 lifetime hitter, he became a favorite target for knockdown pitchers the following year, but still batted .309.

No one in the league hit frozen rope line drives the way Power did—and Casey Stengel once told his pitchers, "Forget the beanballs, we don't want to wake this guy up. Let him sleep." But others threw at Power, and war broke out. Either Vic chased them into the outfield with his bat, or fought them on the mound.

"The best fight never came off," says Power, walking towards a nearby beach hut to buy a coconut drink. "It was in Yankee Stadium, and Ryne Duren, that crazy guy with the big glasses was warming up. He didn't see a thing, and he'd always be brought in when there was a shadow. Well, his first pitch was right behind my head. I dropped my bat and went over to the Yankee dugout. I told Casey, 'Listen, old man, if one more pitch comes close to me, I'm not going to fight Duren, I'm going to hit you.' Nothing ever happened, not until we moved on to play the White Sox. Donovan hit me in the back, and we mixed it up pretty good on the ground. You know, though, I still feel that ball's sting."

Disturbed by Power's troublemaker tag and his .259 batting average (1957), Kansas City traded him to Cleveland for Roger Maris. Power immediately liked the Indians, got friendly with Bobby Avila, Rocky Colavito ("if I'm reborn I'd like to come back as an Italian ballplayer"), Larry Doby, and went on the warpath—in ninety-three games he hit .317. The next three seasons with the Tribe were almost as good. Vic averaged .282, played in three All-Star Games, accumulated two Gold Gloves for fielding, and was generally considered the AL's best first baseman, next to NY's Bill "Moose" Skowron.

Equally adept at cracking open a coconut, Vic takes a long sip of the water before he continues to talk. Once his big moments are remembered, he enjoys one of his patented hearty laughs. "What a time I had in baseball. If I came back to this earth a thousand times, I'd always want to come back as a ballplayer. The game was beautiful to me. Forget the money, the relations I made; what nice people, Frank Lane, Gene Autry, Billy Martin, old Casey, Ted Williams—he's my idol—Jackie Robinson, what a group of fellas. I only wish I could've gotten into a World Series and played a little better the last few years."

Power started going downhill with the Twins in 1963. Traded there the previous season for pitcher Pedro Ramos, he initially ignored the cold weather and had one of his customary hot seasons, batting .290 with sixteen homers and eighty runs scored. But in '63 Vic was more than cold ("it got into my bones"); his hitting went into a deep freeze. He only hit .270 that year, with a lowly ten homers and fifty-two RBIs. The worst, though, was yet to come. Playing for four teams in the next two years, Vic's stats plummeted: .239, three homers, seventeen RBIs in 1964, and .259, one homer, and twenty RBIs in 1965. His power was gone, and so was his spirit.

"I was very conscious of what was going on. I saw young kids coming up and knew it was time to quit," says Power, sounding as cheerful as ever. "The Angels wanted me to go to Japan, but I didn't want to do that; I was too scared. Baseball had been good to me, only now it was time to move on, to start a new life. I stayed in Hollywood. I wanted to get into movies. Too bad my English was very bad."

Picturing himself as the new Latin Casanova, Power played the Hollywood studio game—and did get a part. Yet it wasn't the Clark Gable or Marlon Brando variety. Vic was slotted as an extra who had to ride a horse all day, and that quickly convinced him to look elsewhere for heroics.

Returning to Puerto Rico (in 1967), Vic settled for something more familiar—baseball. He managed an amateur team (for six years) and also ran instructional clinics for children. Besides spending his own money for the equipment, Vic brought something else to the ballfield, his undying passion for the game. "I'm going to die on a ballfield. I don't have anything else to give to kids. I don't have a million dollars. I want to keep kids in the ballpark, away from things like drugs, so they'll stay clean and honest. If I know that happens, then I'll be proud."

These activities eventually attracted public attention, and in 1978 a group of legislators offered Power a government position. He now advises the legislature on all sports matters, but is especially interested in amateur athletics. Power's worried that corporations are undermining athletic freedom, and is currently studying measures to keep amateurs distinct from pros. This, combined with scouting for the Angels, keeps Power continually busy. But as he puts it, "I'm having the time of my life."

Hunched over the counter in the coconut stand, he calls for another round while joking with the owner. Smiling, he then says, "The older you get, the smarter you get. I know I'm doing something good. Guys playing major league ball should dedicate themselves to the youth of the world. They should sit down with kids and tell them what Yankee Stadium looks like. The kids in

Puerto Rico especially need help; for them life is hard.

"Let me tell you, baseball works, it inspired me to be a better person. Just being in Yankee Stadium, knowing Ruth and DiMaggio stood there, made me proud, and encouraged me to do my best. I learned so much during my twelve years in the majors. Maybe the Yankees were prejudiced to have a colored player with them, but I was happy to be in America. My English still isn't that good, but I don't say 'son of a pitcher' anymore."

Power then says goodbye to everyone in the hut. He gets a few pats on the back in return, and once outside chuckles, "Coconut water, that was the secret of my success, man. I love it. I always have. It gave me power.

"I even got into trouble because of it in Florida. I saw a fruit stand, and ran across the street to get some. I got arrested for jay walking, and later the judge asked me how I plead. I said innocent. When the judge asked why, I said, 'I go to bars, it says whites only. At bathrooms it says whites only. So when I see people crossing at the green light, I say to myself, the green light is for whites. The red, that's for us colored folks.' "

VINEGAR BEND MIZELL
Mr. Smith Goes to Washington

Star-spangled maps of America predictably include Williamsburg, Monticello, and Gettysburg. They also describe the places where George Washington or Abraham Lincoln slept, or point out famous battle sites, like the Alamo, Bull Run, or Bunker Hill.

Shamefully, one national landmark is always overlooked. None of these maps point the way to the birthplace of the Great Southern Patriot, or detail the stomping grounds of his friends Kit and Charley.

So where can history buffs find these treasures?

Right on the Mississippi-Alabama border, about eighty-five miles northwest of Mobile, in the one-horse/one-mule town of Vinegar Bend.

Vinegar Bend?

That's right! It's here, in the shade of a few weeping willows, that Wilmer David Mizell started pitching, or throwing the right enough stuff to get to Washington D.C.'s power corridors—and eventually to the White House.

Every day, right about noon, Wilmer and his older brother Curtis would get tired of plowing the family corn fields, and they'd sit in the coolest place possible. Since the two teenagers usually had baseball mitts with them, Wilmer would dust off a few fast balls, while Curtis sat behind an imaginary plate, calling balls and strikes. Occasionally Wilmer argued a call. And inevitably this led to some type of fan reaction—for Kit the mule and Charley the plow horse always made their feelings known.

Undoubtedly encouraged by his playmates, Wilmer started working on the Miracle of Vinegar Bend. The town's size prevented the formation of a high school team, but Wilmer was not one to be intimidated. He scouted the area for gloves, bats, and players to go with them, and eventually put together his own version of the Bad News Bears.

Later, when those same boys gave up pop flies for chasing girls, Wilmer showed his singular dedication. He was the ball nut, the one who traveled a few hundred miles to Biloxi, Mississippi, for a tryout with the St. Louis Cardinals (1948).

"It was simply a miracle that I ever got to play major league baseball, and boy, am I ever thankful for it," notes Mizell, still sitting under a tree, only this time it's in the back yard of his North Carolina home. "I waited all that day for a chance to pitch. There had to be a few hundred of us there, and each kid was greener than the next one. Well, finally, I was the last one to go to the mound, and I really did it, I pitched to three batters, and struck all of them out. But that wasn't the most amazing thing. The next day this giant storm came through, and the camp had to be cancelled. If I hadn't squeezed in there at the end, I'd never have made it to the Cardinals."

The following year, a Cardinal scout either (a) remembered those three strikeouts, (b) tracked down Kit's and Charley's smell, (c) recalled the name Vinegar Bend, or (d) all of the above. He found Wilmer in the cornfield, offered him a $175-a-month contract to play minor league ball, and gave him his nickname. With forty acres of plowing staring him in the face, Wilmer didn't even bother to say Jackie Robinson. He hustled up his glove, and was now Vinegar Bend.

Then it was on to places like Albany, Georgia, Houston, Texas, the Army's Fort McPherson in Geogia, and finally, Havana, Cuba. These stops were certainly diamonds in the rough; the hamburgers were greasy, the boarding houses weren't too clean, and some of the ballparks didn't have showers. But Vinegar Bend did perfect his trade. Both in the minors (his three minor league teams won pennants) and, especially, in Cuba.

He went there for winter ball in 1955, after spending two years in the Army. Uncle Sam had interrupted his Cardinal career (Mizell was 23-19 from 1952-53), and all that good Army food had knocked him out of shape. But Cuba, even with its barrage of beans, rice, and pretty señoritas, soon remedied that. Mizell lived there with his wife, and that predictably choked off a lot of rallies in wild, pre-Castro Havana.

Perhaps more partying might've helped. His 1956 comeback was as flat as a three-day-old Cuba libre. Nothing clicked. His fastball and curve didn't dance, and that made him a very mediocre, 14-14 pitcher (3.62 ERA).

The next three years weren't much better. Vinegar Bend typically struggled with his control. "I think things would've come out better if I hadn't torn up my ribs in 1958," says the fifty-three-year-old right-hander, in an unmistakable Southern drawl. "I was really putting it back together that year when I slipped on the mound. I hurt myself good. I got muscle spasms all the next year, and I don't think I ever really got over the whole thing."

The Cardinals weren't too happy either. They saw his record improve to 13-10 (along with a whopping 4.20 ERA) in 1959, but management wasn't convinced that Mizell had gotten back on track. Consequently, once his record fell to 1-3 at the start of the 1960 season, the Cards traded him to Pittsburgh for Julian Javier.

That was Mizell's big year. The Pirates were in a dogfight with the Dodgers for the pennant, and Mizell pitched so well, LA batters weren't the only ones asking "Where the hell is Vinegar Bend, Alabama?" While baseball fans reached for their maps, Wilmer suddenly discovered an off-speed curveball, and rang up thirteen victories with only five losses (his control was also noticeably better, as he only gave up seventy-four walks, compared to his ninety-plus average).

"Maybe I had some great moments later in life, but 1960 was what every player dreams of, a real good scrap for the pennant, and then the World Series. We won all the marbles that year. What else could you ask for? We beat the Dodgers when it really counted, and I won a few of those big games, and then the feared Yankees fell. Nothing could be finer. And I know I made a big contribution. I really pitched. That year made up for all the bad ones."

Mizell did go on to other glories in the political and business worlds. But when he talks about his Pirate teammates, men like Harvey Haddix, Dick Stuart, and Elroy Face, nothing else seems to matter. His eyes get watery, and then they seem to ask, "What happened to those moments, why did they end so fast?"

That story is not so pretty. Mizell soon slipped into mediocrity again, and by the end of the 1962 season he was out of baseball.

His troubles began in early 1961, when he felt something pop in his right arm. Not thinking too much about it, he continued to pitch. That was a mistake. A few days later his elbow got very tender, and he missed about three spring training pitching turns. He did come back for the regular season (7-10), only his fastball deserted him. It lost its velocity, or zip. And without that, Vinegar Bend might as well have been back in Alabama.

The Pirates had even crueler thoughts. They sent him to New York, to the 1962 Mets. That was a joke for most players, but for Mizell it was more agony. His arm still bothered him, and when Stengel put him in the bullpen, the psychological pain also increased.

Finally, the Mets wanted to send him to Buffalo, in the International League. But Mizell, after spending nine years in the majors (90-88, 3.85 ERA), had other ideas. He quickly packed his bags and was ready to go home when Pirate general manager Joe Brown made him an offer—a spot in the Pirate rotation the following year, if he finished the season at Columbus (Ohio).

"I was willing. I went down, and even had some good games," says Mizell, holding his arm out, like he was going to get an injection. "It just wasn't meant to be, though. The spirit was willing, but my arm wasn't. It didn't come around. I don't know why, I just knew I couldn't stand to sit on the bench. There was no other choice. I had to go back home to North Carolina."

Mizell soon went to work for a Pepsi-Cola distributor in Winston-Salem, and enjoyed the "quiet, homebody life"—Sunday barbecues, little league games, church picnics—for four years. Then, admittedly getting a "a little antsy," he took the plunge (1966). As a Republican, he ran for county commissioner and, surprisingly, won by an overwhelming 3,000-vote margin.

Mr. Vinegar Bend then went on to Washington. A Republican hadn't been elected to Congress from his district (Davidson County, or the Fifth C.D.) since Reconstruction, but Vinegar Bend had a secret weapon—his name. Though outspent and outorganized by his Democratic opponent (Smith Bagley, the grandson of tobacco magnate R. J. Reynolds), Mizell took advantage of the 1968 Nixon landslide and rang up the biggest win of his life (a 5,000-vote plurality).

"It was a great victory because it belonged to the people," says Mizell, sounding like Huey Long, Jimmy Carter, or any other true politician. "Thousands of my good friends just went out and knocked on doors for me. They hustled, they worked their tails off for me. We only spent $60,000 or so, as compared to Bagley's $350,000, so that win had to be a nice thrill. It sure was, yes sir, it was a real dandy."

Politicking in Washington was a challenge for a self-described country boy, yet Mizell was good at it. During his three terms he served on two of the most influential committees in the House, Public Works and Agriculture. This gave him clout—and it often brought him to the White House for strategy sessions with President Nixon, or with key Congressional leaders.

But the early 1970s were also a tumultuous time in Washington, and Mizell repeatedly had to defend his conservative policies or trust in Nixon. It saddened him that people were becoming more cynical about government. And while this sapped his enthusiasm somewhat, he still felt "the struggle going on then was real discouraging, yet it was also like a tough ballgame; it had to be played until the last out.

"Sure, there was too much controversy. It took all of the enjoyment out of what I was doing. But I really believed I was achieving something, that I was helping my district. I started a newsletter that each of my constituents got, and I took the issues right to the people. They knew I was on their side. There was just no way to make them forget Watergate. It became the only issue."

That backlash swept Mizell out of office. Up for reelection in 1974, he got crushed by 8,500 votes, and, badly shaken, returned to Winston-Salem. Barely "having time to get back in my overalls," Mizell was then appointed by President Ford as the Assistant Secretary of Commerce for Economic Development. The post was certainly a powerful one: he now channeled funds to small communities so they could rebuild their tax base or attract private industry. But the position was also significant for another reason. It gave Mizell a much-needed boost, especially after Watergate had destroyed many of his hopes.

"Losing my congressional seat really hurt, but even more importantly, I hated to see what was happening in the country," says Mizell, who's now an executive with Southern Tool Manufacturing, a furniture parts company in Winston-Salem. "I saw President Nixon being on the right track in dealing with foreign issues, and he would've dealt with economic problems in his second term. We'd be a lot better off today if he had that chance. The progress we made then, it's been lost, all of it. My losing, that was also a great regret, sure. Today, though, we're taking some pretty tough medicine for not sticking with Nixon.

"My EDA job was somewhat of a consolation. It felt good getting seed money to people, and watching them help themselves. I was from an area that was very similar to the ones I was called on to help. And there were some real success stories. I remember this place in Livingston, Alabama, that didn't have water lines for fire protection. They got an EDA loan, built an industrial park, and in no time, the local high school grew from 300 students to 1,600. That was something. The school even got themselves a baseball team."

Though this reminds him of his own struggle to play back in Vinegar Bend, Mizell cheerfully concludes, "I've really had a great life. It's certainly a miracle that I got to the big leagues from such a small town, and the game opened so many doors for me. The game, it's so beautiful. I would've gotten nowhere without it, or my name."

JAY HOOK
Baseball's Isaac Newton

Forget Ruth's, Aaron's, or Maris's home run records. Joe D.'s fifty-six-game consecutive hitting streak? That was nothing. Don't even give Sandy Koufax, Early Wynn, Bob Feller, or Bob Gibson a second thought. They don't compare to the Great One. The most memorable Met of them all, Jay Hook.

What a ballplayer—just look at these career statistics: twenty-nine wins, sixty-two losses, with a 5.23 ERA. Or even better, catch this breakdown—

with Cincinnati in 1960------11-18, 4.50 ERA
and 1961------1-3, 7.76
Then the Mets, 1962------8-19, 4.84
and 1963------4-14, 5.48

Whew! Truly unforgettable.

When a team needed a loss, Jay was their man.

Except one day he stepped out of character and suddenly became a Clark Kent. And in doing so, made history. Back in 1962, he pitched the Mets to their first victory.

Stengel's miserable, near-handicapped darlings had gotten off to an auspicious start in their maiden season—they had lost their first 9 games (the Mets would lose 120 games that year, a major league record). But on

April 23rd, Jay jumped into a phone booth outside Pittsburgh's old Forbes Field, then held the Pirates to one run (somehow, Choo-Choo Coleman, Marvelous Marv Throneberry, and Co. scored nine runs that day). The champagne flowed. Pennant fever busted out. And Casey quipped, "Hook, what a performance. I'm going to pitch you the next sixty days in a row."

Then reality set in. Choo-Choo couldn't catch on to the signals (this was fatal for a catcher), Marv might've had too many Millers, and Jay, maybe the victim of too much kryptonite, performed more like Jimmy Olsen, inept and stumbling. He lost, repeatedly (as did the Mets, in leading the NL with 210 errors, putting together the lowest batting and fielding averages, .240 and .967 respectively). In 213 innings pitched, Jay gave up 230 hits, only struck out 113 batters, finished thirteen games out of thirty-four, and was generally roughed up—or, in New York terms, mugged.

If the Mets hadn't been an expansion team, the consistently erratic Hook would probably have been a reliever, or a spot starter (that is, if he was in the majors at all). But since the New Yorkers were hungry for anyone who could even grip a baseball, the Northwestern University engineering graduate hung on, and was able to continue his experiments in aerodynamics. The Isaac Newton of pitching, he wrote several articles on the physics of the curve ball for *The New York Times*. And while called "the scientist," Jay was no match for Hammerin' Hank Aaron, who launched nine of these pitches into outer space.

Hook laughingly admits, "I know I wasn't much of a player; ask Aaron, I did a lot for him and his record. But I just wanted to get my five years in so I'd qualify for the pension. As for my curve, what could I do? They just didn't break according to Bernoulli's Laws all the time."

It didn't matter. Even if Hook got shelled it was O.K. The lanky right-hander had something else going for him. No, not a multi-year contract. Jay had his children—and an important godfather in Casey Stengel.

Casey and wife Edna loved Jay's kids. Lacking children of their own, they acted like doting grandparents, and were constantly called upon to babysit. On every visit they'd bring presents or rock the kids to sleep. But the children weren't the only ones who got spoiled.

"It didn't bother me if Casey got mad sometimes. He'd like to scold me, and would always say, 'Hey scientist, if you know so much about why it happens, why can't you do it better?'" recalls Hook, now a group vice-president with a Detroit-based conglomerate (MASCO). Sitting next to a model of a B-1 bomber (he developed marketing strategy for the plane at Rockwell Industries in the early 1970s), Hook explains further, "Casey was more than a manager to me. We got really close. He and Edna were always at the house, they loved the kids so much. When I was waived to the Milwaukee organization (to the Denver Bears during the 1964 season), Casey told me, 'Edna's going to be awfully mad at me. She doesn't want to lose the children.' Well, I guess this had kept me in New York for a little extra time."

The Mets had found better losers by 1964; Tracy Stallard, the pitcher who gave up number sixty-one to Roger Maris, went 10-20, and old, reliable Galen Cisco was 6-19. Hook plainly became expendable. At age twenty-eight he had had it. But before this phase of his life came to an abrupt (but merciful) end, Hook must also be remembered for another stirring bit of history. He added the "Marvelous" to Marv Throneberry's name. WOW!

Delightedly, Hook exclaims, "Marvelous Marv, that's my creation. I was sitting in the Mets clubhouse, and Throneberry came up to me, saying, 'Hey Hook, you went to engineering school, right? You can print good, right? I want you to put up a sign for me.' I really didn't know what to do at first, but I said sure. I finally printed out this 'Marvelous Marv' poster and hung it on top of his locker. The graphics were great. Wouldn't you know, he hit a home run that day, and after the game all the reporters saw the sign. From then on the name stuck."

Fortunately, Hook didn't stick once he got to the minors—and soon had to focus on engineering. That was a wise decision. After landing a job in Chrysler's production planning division (through his baseball contacts), he became a vice-president at Rockwell, moved on to MASCO, and is now a veritable empire builder a la Howard Hughes or Henry Ford.

At MASCO he has the weighty responsibility of buying multi-million dollar companies. His superiors have given expansion a high priority, and so Hook must get into his Lear jet to criss-cross the country (and the world) in search of hot properties. Later on, after deals are consummated, these same companies report to him directly. Hook (at $60,000-plus a year) oversees their financial condition, growth plans, and will often make suggestions to improve efficiency. Quite a resume for someone who never had a winning record and was the constant object of clubhouse jokes. No wonder he's the one laughing now.

"I didn't have too many highs in baseball. I still enjoyed it, but I'm having a much better time now," says the forty-seven-year-old Hook, after returning to his plush office from a high-priority conference. "I enjoy the competition in this world. It's not so obvious, people are more reserved. You don't pat officers on the rear end. But it's pretty much like baseball. It's equally fierce. The difference is that in baseball you have instant response, you've either won or lost. You know the result. In business, the peaks and valleys are more spread out. Things don't break as fast, but that's O.K. Instead of the cheers, I'm excited by the problem solving, the constant challenges.

"I owe a lot of this to Casey. He taught me how to sell, how to work with people. The guy was a genius. What charisma! He did his job in so many ways. Look how he sold the Mets to the fans. That year (1962) we got as much press as the Yanks, and they were headed for the World Series. Writers loved him. And so did the players. No matter how many games we lost, there was never a sense of depression. That was due to Casey's spirit. He made us feel good, and that carried over into bringing people to the ballpark."

At this point a buzzer rings, and Hook rushes out of the office to another business meeting. About a half-hour later he returns, looking tired but satisfied. "There's always a loose end to clear up. That's business. I'm glad, though. We just bought another company, their execs are in the other room. I had to talk with them again and explain some of their financial statements to my bosses. I'm really the one who decides what we're buying, but everyone must feel that they had input. Casey gave me that insight into people. Whenever I got the ball from him, he was helping me develop managerial skills.

"Only there's one big difference. MASCO is growing all over the world. Now we have plants in Brazil, Australia, Canada, and throughout the United States. The Mets were fun. But this time I'm enjoying being with a winner."

What, me worry?

ROD KANEHL
The King of Wilshire Boulevard

Remember Broadway Joe?

He was nothing compared to Hollywood Kanehl. Once the embodiment of "Can't Anybody Here Play This Game?" the former Met utility man has the LA fast lane all to himself. No one's in his league, not when it comes to mingling with the Beautiful People, zeroing in on Margaritaville, or scoring big on a pony. Putting this resume together hasn't been easy. But watching him strut down the street, it's definitely clear, the Hot Rod's all souped up and in high gear.

Life with the Mets was far different. Not able to hit (.241 lifetime), or field (thirty-two errors in 1962), the twenty-eight-year-old rookie quickly showed why he belonged with a team that lost the most games in history, gave up a record number of home runs, and would have been more fittingly called *Les Miserables*. Eight years in the minors did nothing for him. At shortstop, second, third, or in the outfield, the man called Stone-hands proved his versatility; errors were made wherever he went. He did hit the Mets' first grand slam, and Shea Stadium fans still pay tribute every year, with banners pointedly asking, "Why Not Bring Back Kanehl?"

But his relationship to Casey Stengel dwarfs all other claims to fame. The two men were baseball's Odd Couple. While the Old Professor lectured in hieroglyphics,

Kanehl translated to less erudite players like Marvelous Marv or Choo-Choo Coleman (who had his fingers painted to relay signs to pitchers). This won him Casey's undying affection, for several times Rod was saved from banishment to the minors. His string of luck, however, did run out in 1964. Even Stengel couldn't perform any magic with his anemic .232 average, so Kanehl was sentenced to what he calls "Siberia without a paddle," or the Wichita Dreamliners, and to a life of constant insecurity.

Disappointed that the Mets didn't offer him a coaching position, Kanehl first raised turkeys, and when that didn't pan out he sold insurance. He now says that "I was a hell of a salesman, I get the most out of people." But after a couple of years, Rod grew dissatisfied again. He then bought a restaurant on the grounds of LA's Hillcrest Country Club, serving meals to caddies. While cooking exotic sauces excited him, the money was nothing to write to Granny about. He sold the place two years ago, and since then he's spent a lot of idle days, groping for any new angle. Or as Kanehl describes it, "I'm just laughing and giggling. I put a few kids through college. I don't have to worry anymore. I'm surviving. That's what I'm doing. I'm just walkin'-'n'-talkin', walkin'-'n'-talkin'.

"I don't have to do anything now. If you don't want to work today, you go have a drink today. That's LA. It's a fast track. You just have to get a good pair of skates, and you can't lose your skate key. I've worked hard to get where I'm at. Wilshire is my street. From One Wilshire to the ocean, I know everybody. They're my people. I'm like them, a survivor. If you were a ballplayer, what would you put on your resume? What the hell is a ballplayer? That's why I'm walkin'-'n'-talkin'. Oh, yeah, I consider myself a success. I drink and get depressed. I'll even get suicidal sometimes. But I'm still walking down this wonderful street, and I haven't lost my skate key. I'm a fun person, and I owe it all to the Brown Derby (a famous LA restaurant).

"I certainly don't owe a thing to baseball. I thought

*Only "the old professor" could understand
Rod Kanehl's strange signals—or could he?*

the game was all about building allegiances, never-dying friendships, the rah-rah bullshit. I really thought I was going to see all of that when Casey died. I told my wife, 'Let's go to the funeral, and we'll see all the guys.' I was a pallbearer there. But I couldn't believe what happened. It was so unorganized. Billy Martin was there, sitting with Casey's family, and that was it. The people who weren't there, lots of writers, Casey filled their columns for twenty-five years. They didn't come. Mickey, Whitey (Ford), Yogi, they weren't there either. So tell me, how important are allegiances in baseball? I might cry over this. Those people have no excuse. That's sad.

"Casey and me, we understood each other. I could execute. He liked my determination. I'm still hustling. I'm still on Wilshire. Casey would have liked that. For when it came to practicality he was it. He made the Yankees. Everyone says anyone could've won with that team. But he's dealing with a dumb country boy from Oklahoma (Mantle), a dumb dago behind the plate (Berra), a temperamental Italian in center (DiMaggio), and an Indian who barely spoke English (Allie Reynolds). Who else could've merged those personalities? Only Casey made the Yankees work. He's the greatest.

"Maybe if he was still around I'd fantasize about getting back into the game. I only need a year, then I could qualify for my pension. My wife has a good job, and we're comfortable. Maybe I'm not in baseball because I bad-mouthed some alligator before I crossed the creek. Anyway, I'm still on my feet. I'm only forty-seven, and there're lots of things I can do. I haven't lost my skate key yet, either. I can have fun on a rock. Just make me an offer. Any job, anything at all. Just don't give me any 'would-you-takes.' Make me a good offer. I don't want any 'would-you-takes.'"

DICK ALLEN
The Thunder Is Gone

Shakespeare had to be a baseball fan. Only *The Tempest*, his tale of swirling conflicts, captures the spirit of that rebellious giant, the man known as Thunder Dick Allen.

Perhaps the most criticized and unhappiest superstar ever to play the game, Allen had the potential to rank with Aaron, Mays, Mantle, or Clemente. Blessed with cobra-quick wrists, an Arnold Schwarzenegger body, and the strength to swing a forty-one-ounce bat, he inspired his own mythology (could he really split a baseball in half, or lose balls in the upper atmosphere?) while becoming the king of the tape-measure home run. Each six-hundred-foot blast added to the legend, and once Allen won the AL's MVP award in 1972 (thirty-seven homers, 113 RBIs, .308), writers lavished him with praise.

To some he was Hercules, the larger-than-life slugger who could single-handedly lift second-division clubs into pennant contention. While others simply stood in awe of the first man to make over $200,000 and agreed with Tom Seaver's salient quote: "Allen, he's the strongest, most dangerous hitter I've ever seen."

But like other Shakespearean heroes, Allen lived in turmoil, burdened with a tragic flaw. Always quick-tempered, defiant, or suspicious, he had to be the indi-

The controversial Dick Allen always expressed himself—this time with foot graffiti around first base.

vidualist, the proud free spirit in a sport that is known for its conservatism or emphasis on team morale. Far more concerned with his own identity ("Don't-Call-Me-Richie") Allen drank, fought with teammates, bartenders, or race track spectators, and missed games, batting practice, or weeks of spring training. All this made him baseball's bad boy and the target of the most vicious publicity and public harassment in the sport's history.

"Baseball is a form of slavery; once you step out of bounds that's it, they'll do everything possible to destroy your soul," fumes Allen, staring angrily at the grandstands of the Santa Anita (California) race track. Perhaps recalling some of the abuse that fans constantly showered on him, he grimaces, and then continues, "I just wanted to be left alone. I did my thing on the field, but I wanted my privacy. Reporters would never leave me be, and management, they wanted to call every shot, from the way I walked and talked to my clothes or my moustache. Everything had to be Joe College or the corporate image. You ever wonder why baseball loves big, dumb farm boys? Well, big, dumb farm boys don't say very much. I was a grown man, not a kid. I have my own thoughts, and when something happens that I don't think is right, I have to express myself. I guess I have to rebel.

"I'm sorry about some of the things that happened, the fights, managers getting fired. I've made mistakes; I'm not saying I was an angel. But do you know what it's like to have iron bolts thrown at you from the stands? Everyone just wanted to eat me up and leave my carcass for the vultures. That's the American way, especially where blacks are concerned. Management buys you, uses you, then throws you away. They don't shoot black players, but it's awfully close. I'm not a militant, but people wanted to cut my heart out."

Though Allen now owns several promising race horses, and real estate throughout the Southwest, the last few years have not been kind to him. Alone ever since his marriage dissolved in 1972, and unable to get back into baseball (except for a brief stint with the Texas Rangers in 1982), Allen admits, "I've been running away from things for years." That's readily apparent when talking with him. He's decidedly edgy, afraid, hurt, much like a fading, broken-down movie star. The one-time heir apparent to Ruth or Mays will feign a smile, or try to hide his despair in some rough talk about the racing business. But macho gestures are pointless; most of Allen's thunder is gone.

That's unfortunate.

There was once so much promise. Everything about him flared like a raging stallion.

Especially his near-maniacal need to succeed. Feeling compelled as a teenager to prove himself, he'd leave his Wampum, Pennsylvania house around daybreak, pick vegetables all day on a farm for three dollars, and then head for the nearest diamond or basketball court. Allen used this drive to become a sixteen-year-old phenom. He was a high school All-American who led Wampum to eighty-two straight wins (two state championships) by playing baseball with the same reckless abandon as the youthful basket-catching Mays. Scouts came to Wampum the way Arabs traveled to Mecca—in droves—and eventually the Phillies signed Allen for $70,000, which was at that time the largest bonus ever paid to a black athlete.

Sadly, this only meant trouble.

Allen was sent to the Phillies' minor league team in Little Rock, Arkansas (1963), although a black had never played there before. The frightened twenty-one-year-old remembered the city's violent 1956 stance against school desegregation and pleaded with the Phillies for another assignment. This sparked a brief holdout, and once Allen reported some of his worst fears were confirmed. Besides getting prank phone calls, he was greeted with such signs as, "Nigger go home," "Let's not Negro-ize our baseball," and "Chocolate Drop, keep away from white women." Near tears many times, Allen vented his bitterness on opposing pitchers—

besides hitting .289, he led the International League with thirty-three homers.

But despite these successes, and even a personal welcome from Governor Orval Faubus, the die had been cast. Allen felt the Phillies had betrayed him. "When I was first told to go down there, they told me I'd only have to stay thirty days, not the whole season," shrugs Allen glumly. "They lied to me. I didn't want to be there. It was too different. Everyone remembers me for controversy. But what would you do? I was a twenty-one-year-old kid, coming from a town where everyone was close, we all played in the dirt together; then suddenly I'm in a place where once you showered and took off your jockstrap, everyone separated. The whites went their way, to fancy hotel rooms, while the blacks scratched for themselves on the other side of the tracks."

This deep, almost palpable, sense of loneliness never left Dick Allen. In fact, it got worse during his rookie year (1964), when the Phillies moved him to third base. Normally a second baseman, Allen couldn't handle the hot corner. His hitting was spectacular: en route to becoming Rookie of the Year, he slugged twenty-nine home runs, thirteen triples, thirty-eight doubles, drove in ninety-one runs, hit .318, and led the league in total bases, 352; but this wasn't enough for the often bloodthirsty Philly fans (it's said they'd even boo the Pope, or losers in an Easter egg hunt). Mercilessly, they ridiculed his fielding (a league-leading forty-one errors), and blamed him for the Phillies' choking at the end of the season (the club blew their first place lead in the final weekend).

The jeers grew even louder the following season. Allen didn't talk much on the field, and teammate Frank Thomas, the veteran whom Philly fans lovingly called The Big Donkey, often needled him. During batting practice one day, Thomas reportedly said, "You're getting like Cassius Clay (meaning big-mouth)," or "Shine my shoes, boy." Predictably, the racially sensitive Allen reacted. After several warnings went unheeded, he uncorked a strong right which sent Thomas sprawling. Thomas then countered by swinging his bat, cracking Allen in the shoulder. Four hours later the Phillies made their choice; they sided with the twenty-three-year-old Allen over the thirty-six-year-old vet—thus making the popular Thomas a martyr (he wasn't allowed to speak about the incident), while Allen was soon vilified as Public Enemy Number One.

"The minute I stuck my head out of the dugout, people were yelling, 'Nigger' and 'Go back to South Street with the other monkeys,'" recalls Allen, spitting out a wad of chewing tobacco. "I expected to be booed, not stoned. The Phillies could have cleared everything up. They wanted to draw crowds, though. So they let me twist in the wind. It was one more betrayal."

War was immediately declared, as Allen attacked the reserve clause, doing everything possible to get traded. He skipped batting practices. He missed games. He'd come to the ball park glassy-eyed, smelling of liquor, clearly in no condition to play. He was late for team flights, or missed them altogether. He got into fights with bar room patrons and spectators at racetracks. He didn't show up for a double-header in New York, and was suspended indefinitely on June 24, 1969. In retaliation, he held out twenty-six days, missed twenty-nine games, and was fined $10,000.

Meanwhile, the Philly fans counter-attacked. They blamed Allen for the firing of manager Gene Mauch (1968), accused Allen of making too much money (at $82,000 in 1967, he became the highest-paid fourth-year player in baseball history), and proceeded to make his life miserable. A Confederate flag was dumped on his lawn, a BB gun was fired at his house, his car was smeared with paint, a Philadelphia cop clubbed him, and four men in a car chased his wife through city streets.

A self-confessed loner who naturally withdraws or escapes during crises, Allen began to drink more heavily—and played with a vengeance. Even though his right hand had been seriously injured in a 1967 auto accident (his stats before the accident stood at .307, seventy-seven RBIs, twenty-three homers), he clubbed thirty-three and thirty-two homers respectively in '68 and '69. Since his throwing ability was limited, Allen played first base (always in a batting helmet), where he brilliantly countered the fans' taunts with foot-graffiti in the dirt. He scratched "Coke" into the ground to signify his hitting a ball over a Coca-Cola sign, words like "Boo," or "Hit," and when Commissioner Bowie Kuhn objected, Allen fired back with "Why," "NO," and "MOM."

The fun soon ended. Allen missed an exhibition game near the end of the '69 season, was fined $2,500 by manager Bob Skinner, and, when Philly owner Bob Carpenter vetoed the fine, Skinner resigned. Once again, Allen was the scapegoat. Skinner was going to be fired anyway for the Phillies' disappointing fifth-place finish, but the fans didn't care about this. They wanted blood (fans in the bleachers asked him to drop dead), and management obliged. They finally sent Allen to St. Louis for Tim McCarver and Curt Flood (the Cardinal center fielder refused to go, questioning the legitimacy of the reserve clause, and eventually testing its legality in the U.S. Supreme Court).

St. Louis was a lot more enjoyable—at least for a few hours. On opening day Allen hit one of his patented tape-measure jobs, to the delight of an SRO crowd. Then, however, he started to sulk about "the racetracks, they were only open at night, and we played at night," the terms of his contract, and he warned the Cards that they'd only get "one good year." Allen certainly delivered. He belted thirty-four homers in 122 games, with 101 RBIs and a .560 slugging average.

But the misadventures in bars also continued. So the Cards shipped him off to the Dodgers (1971), where Allen was again disappointed and embittered. "I really looked forward to playing there. The Dodgers were always a special team for me. But these guys, they were nothing but a bunch of cry-babies. Maury Wills, he was impossible to play with, and Alston, he threatened to

Content with a life of
seclusion, Allen's now known
as The Shadow.

quit if I played there. How I could've felt comfortable? My hitting wasn't the real story. I just wanted out."

On the verge from retiring from baseball, Allen was talked into playing for the White Sox by long-time family friend Chuck Tanner—and for three years the marriage seemed like it was made in heaven.

The Sox pampered Allen, gave him a separate disciplinary code, and, in return, he made the team a contender. Free at last to "play the game my way," the idiosyncratic muscleman led the AL in slugging (.603), home runs (thirty-seven), RBIs (113), and was only .0005 points short of the league leadership in fielding at first base. Clearly an inspiration to the team, Allen was a near-unanimous choice for MVP, the highest vote-getter in All-Star Game balloting, and a trend-setter—his $250,000 contract made him the Dave Winfield of the early 1970s.

But Allen's inner fires were still smoldering. He was still a man at war with himself. And while observers at the time called him a new man, Allen now dismisses this view and likens himself to "one of those always-singing, cheerful darkies on a plantation. Everyone thought they were happy, but they really had a time bomb in their hands and murder in their hearts."

His own short fuse came from seeing only white managers in baseball, discrimination against minority ballplayers, and the reserve clause; it was only a matter of time before it exploded again.

Allen could never back off from controversy or accept the status quo. Not even in Chicago. Too self-absorbed, he had to be his own man, even if that meant total defiance of team rules and a subsequent breakdown in club morale. While other White Sox players toed the line or suffered through a disappointing season in 1974, Allen again went his own way. He missed planes, batting practices—and then went AWOL for the last three weeks of the season. This even disgusted good friend Tanner. Allen's manager felt stabbed in the back. So the fire this time had to mean another banishment to Philadelphia.

It wasn't a repeat performance on any level. The fans' hostility ebbed, while Allen was strangely silent. And well-behaved. Too many battles had already been fought, and this became a cooling-off period—even for his bat. It died. From the .301 (thirty-two homers) notched with the White Sox in 1974, Allen fell off to .233, with only twelve homers and sixty-two RBIs. In the 1960s these stats might've prompted boos, or the burning of effigies in the stands. But not now. Even Philly fans would admit it's not that much fun to kick a corpse.

"People saw me as some big ballplayer, making a lot of money, living it up with horses, cars, alcohol. They didn't know that once the game was over I had to go back to the other side of the track. It was awful. Everything was burned out of me after a while. I didn't want any trouble. For years I had been made to feel different. I wanted to play ball and live up to my full potential. People wouldn't let me, though. I'm not an outlaw, I'm a person. People didn't know that I was deeply hurt inside, that I was crying to God.

"No one ever knew me, not at all. I don't regret anything I ever did, but the isolation, that's the toughest thing in ball. Having to explain not just my actions, but John Carlos's (the 1968 Olympic runner, who raised a fist in protest over U.S. racial policies), or Duane Thomas's (the controversial Dallas Cowboy running back). Why? The pain was self-explanatory. I wanted to give the game all I had. Everything. Every last bit of me. But reporters, management, especially at the end, in Philadelphia and Chicago, they just looked for controversy. They just wanted to hang me. Imagine what it's like being a man and not being able to open your mouth. I felt like one of those horses in those stalls. That's what baseball did to me."

Allen managed to stay in baseball until 1977. After a few months with the Oakland As (.240 in fifty-four games), he drifted off to places like Wampum, Tijuana, Mexico, or Phoenix, where he could be alone with his horses. A semi-recluse for the past six years, he does turn up at racetracks (usually at dawn, for jockey workouts). And in this world of stable boys, trainers, and assorted hangers-on, Allen has gotten a new nickname. Here, he's simply known as the Shadow.

Wilbur Wood is still serving 'em up.

WILBUR WOOD
Three Hundred Pounds of Clam Chowder

Eyeing every thrust of the long knife as intently as though peering at a catcher for a signal, Wilbur Wood shouts at his teenage assistant, "Make sure you get all the bones out. That bluefish is a real beauty. Be careful. Get the lady out, too, get your little finger in there, and then give it a good rinse. Get all the blood off it. The woman will be by in about an hour to pick it up. And don't forget, she also gets a pound of sea scallops."

Once a supreme sleight-of-hand artist, with his dipping knuckleballs, baffling array of deliveries, and occasional spitter (that's now called a "fishball"), Wood has gone straight—turning away from some of baseball's most noted pranks to own a fish store outside Boston. Here, the forty-two-year-old left-hander, who left the Red Sox and Pirates to notch four consecutive twenty-win seasons with the White Sox, has to be all business. Instead of conjuring up assorted pranks and daydreaming about extended fishing trips, Wood must get to work by seven AM, make numerous deals at the fish market, return to the shop to prepare various chowders, lobsters, or other dishes, and then serve customers with a pleasing smile.

"The store's just a hole in the wall, but to put out all the fish we do, there's a lot of pressure. In this business, too, it's either win or lose. It's gratifying to see customers come back, and to hear them say nice things about your flounders or haddocks. That's winning, and maybe making some money. But if you lose them, or don't give them the right fish, it's like a one-run ballgame when you're on the short side. You wind up with nothing. That's why I'm here usually twelve to sixteen hours a day. You got to carry the best product, and present it to each customer in an attractive way.

"Just look at those counters! Aren't they beautiful? We have the best fish around. We poach salmon, do all kinds of catering for parties, sell crab legs and mussels, and then there's our special chowder. I can't give you the recipe, but we do almost three hundred pounds of it every few weeks."

Enchanted by the sea—and especially the joy of "getting your hooks into a sweet-tasting, whale-sized trout"—since he first went fishing with his father at age six, Wood used to leave the clubhouse surreptitiously after a game to head for the nearest lake. Management was predictably opposed to his risking injury in a boating accident, but no one could complain too vociferously. Besides leading the American League with 24 victories in both 1972 and '73 (he was edged out by Gaylord Perry for the Cy Young award by one vote in 1972), Wood was the workhorse of the White Sox staff, averaging 336 innings pitched a year over five years, with forty-two or more complete games a season. Remarkably, his left arm still feels fine, strong enough to slice away at hundreds of fish daily.

"I can't kick at all. Baseball was real good to me. I had fourteen years, and the knuckleball or those other funny pitches I threw didn't take away anything from my arm. There was nothing easy about pitching, but I was always fortunate. I was with good guys. The only bad thing was that you don't really make friends while you're playing. You only make acquaintances. That's the way it is in uniform. You're like yesterday's newspaper, here today, gone tomorrow.

"I could've kept on playing after '78, but I lost my drive. Seventeen years was more than enough. I completely lost track of who my family was. I had to get to know them again, so when I quit I just stayed around the house for two years. I didn't do a damn thing. It was certainly an adjustment period. After competing for that long and only knowing balls, strikes, or my earned run average, I had to get a good perspective on what I wanted to do, on the real world.

"Right now I'm just starting out and trying to get people's confidence. The hard part of this business is not learning how to buy good fish. I know my dealers. What's difficult is to be a new face in a store that's twenty-seven years old. I have to convince people that they're going to get the same type of service they've always gotten. Eventually I want to be known for my own recipes, not the ones the previous owner left. You just can't drop the bomb right away. It's like setting up a hitter. You have to pick your spots and mix up your pitches. Sometimes you have to go slow in this world."

Wood barks a few more instructions and resumes, "I think my adjustment period is finally over. I'm real happy here. I like getting the best fish for my customers and making this shop go. This business is a challenge every day, that's why I'm involved. I just don't know what's tougher, pitching against Mantle, Carew, Killebrew, or my Fridays."

The Lone Ranger, Roy Rogers, and Hopalong Cassidy had nothing on the Cuban Cowboy—Pedro Ramos.

PEDRO RAMOS
Behind Bars with the Cocaine Cowboy

SLAM!

The prison door clangs shut with a piercing thud.

It's bed-check time. Inmates must lie in their beds and wait for the guards to take a body count.

The routine is always the same. Guards slowly move down the aisles, while prisoners at the Hendry Correctional Institute (on the northern edge of the Everglades, 115 miles northwest of Miami) start making wisecracks, or pull out reading material.

For the Ice Man, or, as he calls himself, the Cuban Cowboy, the regimen is somewhat different. He stretches out on his cot, forgets the eighty or so other men in the barracks, and caresses his Yankee cap. The felt "NY" initials have been stripped off the cap. Prison officials felt they were too divisive. But that doesn't bother Pedro Ramos. The faint outline of the letters still reminds Ramos of better days and gives him the strength to go on.

Serving a three-year sentence for possession of drugs and a weapon, Ramos has been making mistakes ever since the mid-1950s. In those earlier days, the Cuban-born right-hander was tagged for dozens of home run balls. While more recently he has been associated with an even rougher world—the multi-billion-dollar Miami drug scene—where the big hitters play with bullets, underground connections, and kilos of cocaine.

Though Ramos has been arrested for various drug-related offenses, he stands by a prison gate making excuses, like a disappointed pitcher after a tough one-run game. "I know I shouldn't be here, I know I shouldn't have lost my freedom, no matter what the police say. I know I've made a few mistakes in the last couple of years, but what about the rest of my life? It was a different Pedro Ramos. They arrested me for cocaine, but I don't even know what that stuff looks like. I still don't know if the stuff they (the police) found in my car was real. I know I'm in here now, and that makes me a convict. But I shouldn't be here, no one should."

Despite Ramos's protests, he still has quite a record. And that doesn't mean won-lost totals for the old Washington Senators, Cleveland Indians, or Yankees—the self-billed flame thrower only had two winning seasons in fifteen years, led the AL in losses four times, and career-wise was 117-160, with a 4.08 ERA. Those figures are somewhat excusable; Ramos often played with second-division clubs. But it's his other record, or run-ins with the law, that can't be so easily whitewashed. Or sweet-talked away.

Aside from his colorful antics, like challenging Mickey Mantle to footraces in the outfield, or his long Cuban cigars, or ten-gallon cowboy hats, Ramos has walked on the wild side, straight into a subterranean world, known as the Istanbul of the West—or Miami's Cocaine Connection.

His official involvement began on September 3, 1978. That night Ramos was arrested in a bar for carrying a gun (which he also did as a ballplayer) and a small amount of marijuana. Ramos then owned a small cigar manufacturing company in Miami's Little Havana (its large community of Cuban exiles), so prosecution was deferred on the condition that he attend a drug counseling program. And subsequently the case was dismissed.

Then came the Big Bust. On July 31, 1979, an informant tipped the police that Ramos was making a large cocaine delivery. A tail, or police surveillance team, was assigned to Ramos's house, and they watched him get into a car carrying a thin cigar box which held a kilo of coke. In that same car sat the brother of a man who's described by Federal narcotics agents as a drug-trade millionaire.

Once the police stopped the two men, they found the cocaine plus two loaded guns. But that was only the tip of the iceberg. Afterwards, two more kilos of coke were discovered in Ramos's house, in a briefcase inscribed with the initials, "P. R."

Ramos was released on $16,000 bond, and his case moved through the courts for two years. Finally, after a judge ruled that the search of his house was illegal and suppressed certain evidence, Ramos was freed.

"I don't want to talk much about this, but I don't even know what real cocaine looks or tastes like," says Ramos, who's been called the Cocaine Cowboy by the local newspapers. "I simply asked my friend for a ride. I don't know why the police would want to be after me. The whole thing was a trap. Why set me up, why did they want to screw me up? I've been around, sure, with a lot of women. Maybe someone was jealous. I don't know. They said I was a dealer. If I was involved in cocaine, I'd like to know where my money is. I have nothing.

"I can't say any more. On these things you either go to jail or go six feet under. If you open your mouth you're dead. You can get out of here, but you can't get away from that. I just can't talk."

It's now unclear if Ramos can safely return to Miami and lead a normal life. But until August of 1980 he'd been lucky. He hadn't been convicted of anything—and he strutted around Little Havana like a member of the Chamber of Commerce, gladhanding residents at street corners and passing out cigars from his tobacco company.

He had gotten into this business soon after leaving baseball in 1970. Along with a $1,000-a-month pension, the small company had kept him going. And besides, it was the only thing he knew. Baseball had been his entire life; he even tried to make a comeback with the Mets in 1972. But zeal or desperation doesn't equal smoking fastballs. He had been used too many times as a starter and reliever (fifty to sixty games some years), and his right elbow was a painful mass of swollen scar tissue.

So perhaps Ramos dreamed of making other big scores. Always a happy-go-lucky type, he hit the night-spots with various unsavory characters, and on August 18th, 1980, was arrested for threatening a bar owner with a two-inch Colt revolver. This resulted in an aggra-vated assault charge, a felony, and Ramos was eventu-ally placed on eighteen months probation.

The count had reached two strikes.

Then came the sucker pitch—a high, hard one, that caught Ramos completely off guard. It whizzed by him. But it wasn't just a strikeout. He was going down for the ten-count.

Ramos violated his probation. The police arrested him on August 24th, 1981, for speeding, drunken driv-ing—and the biggie, carrying a concealed weapon. This was a probation violation and it meant time, the type convicts call hard time. In Ramos's case, because there had been other probation violations or arrests, it re-sulted in a three-year sentence. Ramos was lucky. He could've gotten thirty big ones.

"It's all a big mistake. The gun was my wife's, she left it in the glove compartment," argues Ramos, moving across the grassy Hendry prison yard towards the mini-mum-medium joint's recreational area. After avoiding a few armadillos, he continues, "They said I broke proba-tion, but the gun was found after they arrested me. Something wrong was going on. I shouldn't have pled guilty, that was a mistake. The whole thing was en-trapment. I don't know why they're after me."

Paranoiac musings?

Real conspiracies?

Excuses or hidden subplots?

None of this matters anymore. Ramos's dream of coaching in the big leagues or of working with young ballplayers must be deferred.

Instead, he must adjust to the Routine—the six AM wake-up siren, the frequent body counts, the rotten food, the military-like discipline, the idiosyncrasies of certain officers, the violence among inmates, and, most importantly, the loss of freedom.

No wonder his once-powerful voice has turned into a mere whisper. Or that he's overly thankful for any little privilege, like having a cigar, or a weekly visit from his new wife. Ramos is simply trying to survive, to retain his sanity.

He's playing it day by day. He just goes about his business, saying yes sir or no sir to every guard around him. Hendry's no place for dreams; a man could go crazy thinking about the future. So Ramos must content himself with another type of coaching—he's the prison's recreational supervisor, who doubles as the joint's official softball pitcher. The vet who's on the mound one minute and with his memories the next.

"For a kid from Cuba, I didn't do too bad. I even got friendly with Nixon," recalls Ramos, speaking of his days in Washington. "He was my friend. I used to invite him over for black beans. That's not too bad, considering that I worked as a water boy in a cigar field as a kid. I still don't even read English. But I've been with the highest and lowest. I met Castro at the Cuban embassy, a long time ago (1960), and Nixon, he'd telephone me to congratulate me, or wish me luck for some game."

These phone calls, though, didn't come too regularly. Ramos rarely won. After playing with a Senators farm team for $150 a month, he launched his big league career with a 5-11 mark in 1955. His stats were noticeably better the following year, 12-10, but from 1958 to 1961, he averaged eighteen losses a year, with only eleven to fourteen wins. The Cuban Cowboy simply didn't have a blazing six-shooter.

Mickey Mantle found that out. Ramos would try to intimidate the Yankee slugger with menacing looks, and

But sometimes, even the best shots go astray.

once challenged him to a $1,000 footrace. That confrontation never came off and the give and take was always in good fun. Ramos idolized the blond "Jankees" centerfielder. One day, though, Mantle got one of Pedro's fastballs and pulled it—or more accurately, detonated it—against the upper deck facade in Yankee Stadium, about a foot short of the top and eternity (no one has ever hit a fair ball out of the House that Ruth Built). And, as Pedro says, "I thought that ball was going to New Jersey."

Ramos shrugged off the blow and kept throwing his spitter, or Cuban Palmball. The Yankees even picked him up for pennant insurance in 1964 (for a steep $75,000)—and Ramos really delivered. He saved seven games that September, without giving up a walk in twenty-two innings of relief.

But that was Ramos's last and only flirtation with glory. From 1965 until his retirement in 1970, he was nothing more than a workhorse. Managers would throw him into games long after they had been decided. With the Phillies, Reds, Pirates, and new Senators during his last few years, Ramos was the mop-up or garbage man—who left fans with a distinct sense of deja vu. Pounded as a rookie and as a vet, Senor Pedro exited on the same discouraging note.

Still, Ramos remembers the game fondly, and holds on to that Yankee cap. "There's nothing like baseball. The game is what life's all about. The people I met, the traveling, the fun, playing ball was my rainbow, my dream come true. Then I never thought of tomorrow. Only now do I think of tomorrow. It's always a struggle to get there.

"I'm only forty-seven, I still have enough life in me to come back. But jail is so terrible, I can't describe how bad it is. It's especially terrible for a guy like me, who led the life I led. It's nothing here, you're just breathing, you're just a number, 390330. I used to be 14 with the Yankees, but my number now is such a bad, awful number. I guess I'll never be able to take it off my back."

Ramos's voice trails off now, to an indistinct murmur.

His eyes close, and except for a few quarreling inmates in the distance, there's silence. Finally, the croak of an alligator in a nearby creek makes Ramos snicker. Shaking his head, he then glances at a barbed-wire fence and sighs. "I can't believe I'm here. The Cuban Cowboy in a place like this. Shit. Not being free, that's the worst. I see men crying in here, I see so many men desperate. I'm so lonely, too. Maybe I'll contact some big league clubs when I get out. But in the meantime, it's so bad here. Most nights, I'm also crying myself to sleep."

DICK RADATZ
Frankenstein Revisited

GRRRR! AAAGGHH! GRRRR!

Beware! The Monster is stirring. Not in any fenced-in bullpen; that's long behind the 300-pound King Kong, otherwise known as one-time star reliever Dick Radatz. The first fireman to be selected to an American League All-Star team (1963), he dominated that game so completely, National League stars looked helpless. Now he wants to unleash those frightening moves and noises from a different lair: the dugout.

Out of baseball for more than fourteen years, Radatz has finally overcome the pain of being traded from Boston to Cleveland in 1966 (and then to three other clubs in quick succession). Unable to even think about the game for years, he's hoping to land a coach's position at Michigan State or on some other college campus. The decision to go job hunting wasn't easy. After floundering in the business world for ten years—changing jobs as frequently as he used to change pitches—Radatz has been making good money as a manufacturer's rep for a Lansing, Michigan chemical company. But he admits to feeling lonely, fidgety, unmotivated without baseball. If his initial overtures to colleges are as successful as his 1962-64 stats (9-6, twenty-four saves, 15-6, twenty-five saves, 16-9, twenty-nine saves), he'll be

Early in 1964, All-Star Game pitcher Dick Radatz is at the top of his form.

hired in a hurry, and opposing schools will be howling in panic.

A Frankenstein on the mound, Radatz knew (and can still teach) pitching. Armed with a blurring fastball and a diversified collection of junk, he struck out five of the six National League stars faced in the 1963 All-Star Game, including Mays, Snider, and Willie McCovey. He didn't have this same kind of stuff the next year. Mays rattled him for a rally-starting walk, and Johnny Callison hit a game-winning homer. Seemingly never able to recover from the shock, Radatz suffered a general decline, struggling the next four years with twelve wins, twelve losses, and a combined 5.0 ERA. Yet his resume boasts something more important than won-lost totals. Having overcome several work and family-related problems in the last fourteen years, he can help a team or individual make its own type of comeback.

Sitting in his plainly furnished Lansing duplex, he recalls his days on a Boston radio sports talk show (on WBZ in the early '60s), and then sighs, "That city meant everything to me. For years I couldn't understand why I was traded, or get over the pain of it. Damn, all the fun went out of the game for me. Was I depressed. There was no living with me. I just went through the motions with all the other clubs (besides Cleveland, he also played with the Cubs, Tigers, and Expos).

"I was making decent money by the mid-'60s, about $45,000, but I started to run into control problems. I really didn't care, but my friends persuaded me to go to a shrink, and even a hypnotist. Once I got sent to the minors the next year I really had had it. Everything was going downhill. That winter (1969) my son asked me one day to go fishing with him in the summer, so I decided to stop the bouncing around. Right then and there I quit.

"Maybe I should have done it earlier. Baseball means too much traveling. It puts a lot of doubts in a wife's mind. The strains are terrific. While you're away she's thinking, or making up stories in her mind as to what you're doing in a hotel room or a bar. In my case, she disliked the game and what it was doing to our social lives. She also thought I was with every woman in town. That was a lot of nonsense, but baseball is a single man's game. It kills family life. But a man's got to do what he's got to do. I had to persevere. I had to be a success. The divorce rate for cops is high, but I think it's even higher for pro athletes. I have a lot of friends in the game who couldn't stay married. Maybe if the marriage wasn't so strained I would've pitched better at the end.

"Now that all of that is past, at least I know what I want. I'd been in the insurance business, but that's a sham. So are some of the sales jobs I've had. I did it all for a while. I like what I'm doing now, only I really want to get back into the game. It's me. I know how political it is to find a coaching slot with a major league team. I've tried, man, I've tried. Letters, phone calls, everything. I'm just hoping I can get this Michigan State thing, or some other place. I only want a chance.

"Maybe then I won't have to get involved with any pranks. Because of my size, people are always approaching me with some kind of hustle. Denny McLain and a few other businessmen once asked me to be the Incredible Hulk. They wanted to paint me green, put me in a box at a shopping center, chain me up, and then I was supposed to bust out with a roar. All this, on Saturday afternoons, for $250.

"I won't really calm down or feel good about myself until I'm doing something with that little white ball. My life's not anti-climatic now, but these years have been as tough as hell. I didn't experience a gradual letdown. It was like I fell off a cliff. Only now am I getting back into the swing of things. I have new purpose. I want to be part of the game again. It was good to me. I can open the scrapbooks once in a while, and like magic, I'm twenty-five again."

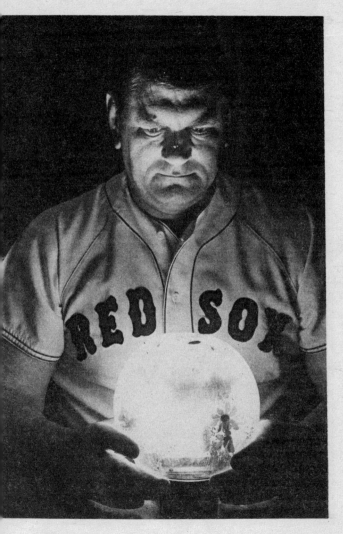

The Monster working in the lab, late at night.

Charmin' Harmon flexes those famous muscles.

HARMON KILLEBREW
Vietnam and Other Memories

The Killer terrorized opposing pitchers. Fifth on the all-time home run list with 573, he had league-leading totals of 42, 48, 45, 49, 44, and 49, and hit 25 or more in thirteen of fourteen seasons. The third baseman-turned-outfielder and first baseman also drove in a hundred runs or more nine times, won the MVP award in 1969, and now has a great shot at being elected to the Hall of Fame. In short, he had an illustrious career (twenty-two years, mainly with the Washington Senators and Minnesota Twins), one that was filled with heroics.

Goliath-like stats, however, are not the entire Killebrew story. He's certainly proud of jumping straight out of high school ball to the majors, and socking more home runs than any other right-handed hitter in American League history. But he also has a soft, kittenish side. Not a rah-rah, give-em-hell type of guy, he has a patient, subdued teaching style as a part-time batting instructor for the Oakland As. And despite his sledgehammer arms or Nautilus-welded physique, he often becomes sentimental, reminiscing about famous acquaintances like Eisenhower, Nixon, and Kennedy.

Predictably more gruff-sounding when broadcasting for both the As and Twins or in recalling his achievements, he says, "I have to be proud of what I did in the game. Those homers and RBIs are what it's all about. I could've done a little better; my .256 average wasn't so hot. But I more or less accomplished what I set out to do. It was a dream come true for me to just be in the major leagues. What a thrill it was to get a $6,000 bonus, or be competing against guys I once idolized, like Chico Carrasquel, Nellie Fox, or Mickey Mantle. It was also great to come back in 1969, after I had ripped up my foot in the 1968 All-Star Game, and to win the MVP, home runs, and RBIs. Those days are special, especially because a lot of people said I'd never make it back. I showed them, huh?

"That's not all I think about, though. These days I like remembering the people I met in baseball, the presidents and senators I was friendly with, and the trip I took to Vietnam with Aaron, Musial, Mel Allen, and Brooks Robinson in 1966. That was an experience. We went through jungles and saw what our boys were going through. Sheer hell, that's all it was. What a place. It made us all feel so good to bring them a little happiness. I'll never forget that baseball players were so important to them."

Modestly denying that he's a Minnesota folk hero, or that this reputation could be turned into a new kind of clout in the political arena, Killebrew says, "I've been approached, I've gotten a lot of offers to run for political office. But politics is one thing that doesn't interest me. Who needs the headache? It's nice to get mail from people urging me to get involved. I won't, though; it's not something that excites me. Plus, I don't need ferocious competition anymore. I'm happy just being on TV and staying close to the game, even if it means a lot of motel rooms, airplanes, and living out of suitcases."

Reminding himself that it's often difficult for him to carry those bags because of knee injuries sustained as a player, Killebrew snickers and says bitterly, "Do you know that the average salary today is more than my all-time high? ($125,000) That's tough for me to swallow. I don't understand what's happening today. Either these salaries are a joke, or I was born ages too early. I guess

I'm just going to have to live with it. Maybe there are other compensations that might be just as important. I don't know, I hope so.

"Whenever I start getting angry or too annoyed, I try to think of other things that aren't affected by money. I can't feel too sorry for myself, not with the things I saw in Vietnam. That experience colored a lot for me. I was also around in the '50s. That era has to be one of baseball's greatest, and while a million dollars would be fun, playing back then was very important to me. I'll never forget, Eisenhower was president, and he called me over to his seat to ask me for an autograph for his grandson David. A few years ago I saw David, and I asked him if he still had that ball. He said he did."

What can you say? It's Gus Zernial's lucky day.
(He's second from the left.)

GUS ZERNIAL
Money Is the Best Revenge

Ozark Ike's dream is always the same. It begins with him grabbing a bat, striding to the plate, and a sell-out crowd roaring in the background, "We want a hit. Come on, Gus, we want a hit." Zernial knows he must deliver. It's the bottom of the ninth, two men are out, and the bases are loaded.

After taking a few warm-up swings, Zernial positions himself in the batter's box. The pitcher eyes him coldly, but Ozark feels confident, thrilled by the confrontation. Then the ball is thrown, Zernial hitches his bat—and suddenly it all goes blank. Without having gotten a chance to swing, he wakes up in a cold sweat.

Connecting never used to be a problem. Instead of feeling frustrated or impotent, Zernial made pitchers toss in their sleep, winning both the home run (thirty-three) and RBI (129) titles in 1951, along with hitting a respectable .268. Primarily a left fielder for the Philadelphia Athletics and three other teams (from 1949-1959), the six-foot-three slugger played most of his career in the shadow of another giant, Ted Williams. Ozark is still disappointed that "Casey (Stengel) never picked me for an All-Star team." But that oversight, and even nagging shoulder problems, didn't prevent him from flirting with stardom. Besides clouting a home run in every seventeen at bats (a ratio that puts him twenty-second on the all-time list), he was one of the American League's most consistent clutch hitters, averaging twenty-eight homers and ninety-six RBIs for six years (1951-55).

Only recently has Zernial been troubled by not delivering. Desperately hoping to become a broadcaster for a major league club, he gave up his car leasing business five years ago and started announcing college sports in California's San Joaquin Valley. This led to two TV tryouts, one with the White Sox, the other with the Texas Rangers. Insisting that "politics sabotaged me," Zernial didn't get either job. Usually mild-mannered, he angrily lashes out at "the two b_____ who wanted me to fall on my face," and calls the setback "the biggest disappointment of my life."

"I really thought I was going to be hired by the White Sox. A few of the execs liked me a lot. But one night, there I was, sitting in the booth, and this other announcer says, 'Here's big Gus to do the play-by-play.' No one had said anything about me announcing that night. It was a totally cold mike. Did I bomb. Geez! I was so upset. I still can't stop thinking about how this screwy guy undermined me. It was so cruel."

Now sixty, Zernial has tried to find solace in religion—or by managing real estate investments for a born-again Christian company called Maranatha. Based in Fresno, he shows people how to invest, manage properties, and set up tax shelters. Saying, "I get a lot of joy from leading people out of economic confusion," he cradles a few portfolios in his Kluszewski arms and continues, "It's Christian to see people making money, lots of it."

His heart, however, remains on some playing field. At his own expense, he drives two or three hundred miles most weekends to announce a high school football, or baseball game. It's the one way for him to keep his dreams alive, of becoming "a nationally known announcer like (Tony) Kubek or (Joe) Garagiola." And interviews with young athletes also "bring out the kid in me. I never want to change."

Zernial first started broadcasting at age six, in the living room of his Beaumont, Texas house. The son of a deputy sheriff, he'd imitate a radio announcer, and bang a chandelier with a wooden spoon everytime a home run was hit. After being chased out of the house, he'd clout his own shots in various cow pastures. Ozark eventually made it to what he still calls the biggies, the Hollywood Stars of the old Pacific Coast League. Wearing a five-dollar pair of shoes and a borrowed uniform as a rookie (looking like a character out of "Lil' Abner," from where he got his nickname), Zernial forced the parent White Sox to look at him, hitting .344 with fifty homers and 159 RBIs.

He's perhaps better known for introducing Marilyn Monroe to Joe DiMaggio (he first showed the Yankee clipper a photo of Marilyn, and then later arranged a meeting) than for his major league stats. But the right-handed pull hitter did sock ten pinch-hit home runs, two homers in a game thirty-two times, and is the only player to win both the home run and RBI crowns after being traded (from the White Sox to Philadelphia). Yet, plagued by ninety to a hundred strikeouts a year, he now jokingly remarks, "It hurt then, but I've been looking at my not living up to expectations in a new light. Why shouldn't I be in the Hall of Fame? I helped put about seventeen pitchers there, Lemon, Wynn, Feller, Ford . . ."

Then, the glint in his blue eyes fading, and his choir-boy voice suddenly sounding weary, he adds, "I only wish the DH (designated hitter) rule was in effect back then. I could've played at least five more years. 1950 is as vivid to me as yesterday. Baseball was the ultimate. I was lost when I left it. It took me more than five years to get it out of my system. I can't really describe the feeling of suddenly being away from a sport you love. It was like I had a giant emptiness inside my gut, I felt so

Today Gus's twinkle comes from a different light.

incomplete. Let's say it's a deep, deep loss, like how you feel if your mother or father dies.

"That's why broadcasting or being close to sports is important. It keeps me active, in the game. There's nothing like it. I've been in the auto glass business, stocks and bonds, car leasing, but none of that sweeps you away into a different world. Sports is close to religion for me. It has its own spiritual beauty.

"Not being allowed back into that world, I've done the next best thing; I've learned how to make money. It's quite a feeling to see others investing and doubling their money in three or four years. We haven't had a loser yet, and I'm talking about $30,000 to $50,000 a shot. I'm just a salesman, one who knows about tax shelters, or what property is worth. But when I see my clients scoring big, it tickles me to death.

"Now I can really say I'm on an up trend. Baseball put me up and put me down. Broadcasting did the same. But in this field I'm really moving upward. We're buying more and more buildings, and, who knows, maybe I'll even become a partner in a few years. It's a miserable world out there, and I only want to help people better themselves. Economic security can help them keep the faith."

His eyes again twinkling, Zernial then says, "Even though this sounds crazy, I'd go back to baseball in a minute. I get a lot of happiness from helping people manage their money, but if the right baseball offer came along, I'd go back immediately. I guess the game will never leave my system."

Once a flashy fielder, Leo Cardenas now wields a speedy squeegee.

LEO CARDENAS
"Fill It Up, Mac!"

The Sohio gasoline station at the corner of Kenwood and Montgomery in Cincinnati is much like any other pit stop in Mid-America. Its chrome pumps glisten in the noonday sun, smiling teenagers clean your windshield, and the price of gas is too high. Only one aspect of the place is a bit peculiar—one of the service attendants is Leo "Chico" Cardenas, the often acrobatic sixteen-year shortstop for the Reds, Twins, and three other clubs, who's been pumping gas for the last three years.

Released by the Rangers in 1976 after hitting .257 lifetime, Cardenas suffered through "an empty, body-dragging six months, a time when I couldn't even get out of the house or be with my friends." For a peppery firebrand who had played in one World Series and two league championship playoffs, work was a letdown. He just couldn't adjust to standing on an assembly line in a local machine shop, and soon moved on.

Now Cardenas is supposed to report to the gas station five days a week at six AM. As unpredictable as when he refused to go after a Frank Thomas pop-up in the last feverish days of the 1964 season (thus costing the Reds the pennant), Chico *might* be batting .400, showing up two days out of five. He's too busy to take work seriously, playing about three hundred fifty games of softball a season for a local bar, the Caddy Cap Lounge. At age forty-five, he must "practice, practice, practice," and get ready for the next big game.

"Still being part of the game is beautiful. It's what life is all about. There's not much else. Playing hard, going out every day, getting a hit with men on, all that keeps me going. I still got the reflexes, I haven't lost anything. I'm not getting old, that's for other people. I can still get loose quickly. It comes from staying in good shape and keeping my mind pure. It's got to be this way. The guys respect me, they know I come to play. It's always been this way, and things won't change. I'll always get pumped up for key games.

"How could I be playing this way if I had some other kind of job? I enjoy the gas station. That's where my kind of people are. It's just like a ballpark, people appreciate what you do for them. They come in there and tell me how glad they are to see me. I love it when they talk about seeing me in Crosley Field, or about the plays I made. If I was a coach in the minors I'd have to play politics, or play the hustle game. That's not for Chico. I wouldn't be able to keep my soul, and I certainly wouldn't be able to meet all the nice people I do today. I'm myself at the gas station. It's okay to be here. It's nothing bad. I'd rather make a couple of hundred a week and be me.

"Things will be even better at work after the Caddy Cap wins the league championship. I'll be pumping gas and whistling all winter long. We're in tough races every year. The competition around here demands the most from me. It's just like the big leagues, and getting to the World Series against the Yankees. Boy, were those '61 Yanks tough. I still remember the double I got in that Series. But my teammates now really play too, they're always hustling. You got to, to play as much as we do. I really love them. I don't smoke or drink. I don't. So I don't see any reason why I can't go on playing with them forever."

WOODIE HELD

"Make Mine Anchovy with Onions and Mushrooms"

High-flying pizzas, topped off with rich sauces from secret recipes.

Snowmobiling races across the most deserted, hair-raising slopes around Lake Tahoe.

Acrobatic stuntflying, in a motorized hang glider, high above Yellowstone National Park and the surrounding Rockies.

Or all-night marshmallow sessions with buddy Billy Martin.

Versatility, that's the key word here. Name a pleasure, a Walter Mitty-like fantasy, or a daredevil thrill, and Woodie Held has done it with GUSTO. Baseball's quintessential jack-of-all-trades, Held has made "here today, somewhere else tomorrow" his own special trademark, both on and off the field.

During his fourteen-year career with seven different clubs, Held was the Heinz 57 Varieties man. Third base, left field, short, first, center, or batting practice pitcher —it didn't matter where. He hopscotched from one position to another—and would've undoubtedly invented a new place to play, if not for the constraints set down by the Lord himself, Abner Doubleday.

Apparently convinced that life needs a lot of spice, Held hasn't been content with the plain old salt and pepper of most workaday lives. Once out of baseball, he has even outdone the great Lon Chaney, that immortal man of a thousand faces, by writing his own version of "1001 Jobs Made Easy."

Pizza parlor proprietor.

Electrician.

Lumber yard owner.

Bartender.

Construction worker.

Professional snowmobile racer.

Waterskier.

Iron welder.

Yellowstone tourist guide.

You name it, George Woodson Held has done it. For him, mastery of any single ballfield position was never important, and similarly he's becoming a true utility man in the business world. Everything goes, as long as he's having fun-fun-fun.

"You only go around once, so why get stuck or not live it up to the hilt?" asks Held, clutching a bottle of his buddy's favorite beer, Miller Lite, in the living room of his Dubois, Wyoming home. Naturally cooled by the cold winds blowing off the nearby Rockies (Yellowstone's only about eighty miles away), the beer goes down easily, and seems to loosen Held's tongue. "Money, what the hell does that mean? I never played baseball for the bucks, and I'm not going to sell my soul now. I want to live, do everything I can to enjoy myself. Me and Billy had a ball, and that's what I'm into now. I don't care if the snowmobiling or the plane means some terrifying moments. Life has got to be an adventure."

So was baseball.

Impressed by his father's semi-pro career in Idaho, Held used "all of my thirteen-year-old smarts" to become the bat boy for the Sacramento Solons, in the old Pacific Coast League. Here, he took infield practice with the team, and got playing tips from a few ex-major leaguers. Apparently, their encouragement paid off. After three years of handing out bats and washing out jockstraps, he got some clout of his own—a $6,000 bonus from the Yankees to play Class C ball in Twin Falls, Idaho (1951).

Going north to this "wild bear and delicious trout country" first seemed like he was following his father's footsteps. But all similarities end right there. Held had power, and even more importantly, managers saw him as a "tenth force. They felt I had as many purposes as a good box of tools."

Held then took his chisels, hammers, and drills to Boise, Quincy, Illinois, Kansas City, and, finally, to every carpenter's dream, Yankee Stadium. Unfortunately, at the end of the 1954 season management was still content with old saws like Gil McDougald, Phil Rizzuto, Andy Carey, Gene Woodling, and Hank Bauer, so Held only got to play in four games before being sent down to the Denver Bears for the 1955-56 seasons.

"Those are the breaks in baseball; you got to be ready for knocks, even while you're having fun," concedes Held, nodding his head knowingly. "I was awed being up there, but, truthfully, I really wasn't ready for the big stuff. I don't know why, I just didn't feel comfortable. Besides, it was such a tough lineup to crack. I understood why I was cooling my butt on the bench so much."

Things got a lot hotter in Denver; Held started to scorch the ball. His totals were so impressive in 1956, .280, 125 RBIs, thirty-five homers, the Yankees called him up for another look-see, only this time Held refused to go back to the minors, and was finally traded to the Kansas City Athletics (along with Billy Martin) for Ryne Duren and Suitcase Harry Simpson.

Thrilled to be in the majors after six years of "run-down hotels and two-bit hamburger joints," Held had one of his better big production seasons. While only batting .239, he hit twenty homers, knocked in fifty runs, and characteristically struck out eighty-one times in ninety-three games (he's baseball's all-time Big Whiff, or strikeout per at bats leader, fanning 944 times in 4019 appearances, for a .235 average).

Looking for a more consistent slugger, the As sent Held and Vic Power to the Indians in exchange for Roger Maris (1958). That year was a bust; Woodie only hit .204 with seven homers. But his next six seasons with Cleveland weren't too bad. Though never a Colavito or a Kaline, he had some big home run years (twenty-nine in 1959, twenty-three in 1961), and consistently drove in sixty to eighty runs, while playing mostly at short or second.

"I don't know what it was, but I was able to bear down more when men were on base," recalls Held proudly. "If I had concentrated all the time I would've hit for thirty or more points every year (his lifetime average was .240). I just didn't. I always wanted to hit well, but I liked clutch situations. Boy, could I get a hot streak. My first five hits in 1959 were home runs. I could've been a real terror if I'd tried harder."

A "terror?"

Held had time for all sorts of fantasies the last few years. Sitting on the bench most of the time, with a .140 to .200 average, he knew the handwriting was on the wall—so why not play mind games, or dream the Impossible Dream?

Sixty homers a year.

An MVP award.

Ruth, Cobb, Williams, Held.

The Hall of Fame.

Crash! These reveries finally ended in Chicago, when the White Sox had had enough of his .143 batting average. It was now time to go on to a whole new set of delicious daydreams.

Pizza.

Held saw himself as the Pavarotti of pie twirling; perhaps in sunny Italy, near the blue Mediterranean, mixing sauces and making people smile. He had to settle for Dubois, Wyoming, but the scenery was still beautiful, and those pepperonis, mmmm, they were a grand slam.

Unfortunately, Woodie started to smell like a pizza. The odor became so unbearable, he installed his wife in the store and went to work as an electrician. Comfortable with this for four years, he then got another dose of wanderlust and headed for the slopes in his snowmobile. Nothing came before his Suzuki Artic Cat. Neither his wife nor the several jobs that got him through the '70s—welder, bartender/owner, millwright, tourist guide. Woodie was truly happy. Racing professionally was one more thrill in his never-ending quest for excitement.

"You gotta live dangerously sometimes; that's where the fun is," says Held, pointing to a dozen or so snowmobiling trophies on a mantel. "I can't eat those things, but I like to try everything, have a blast. I don't care about breaking my bones, or ribs, or going through walls (he had a bad accident in 1971). Life is there to be enjoyed, to be lived.

"That's what baseball was all about. I had a damn good time. It was a ball. Today I've got to be doing something different all the time, and that's what I liked about the big leagues, it was something new every day. You had to be alert. It was pressure, conflict, a test of strength. And the final result was always a mystery. I really miss it, but now I'm getting my highs in other ways."

Indeed.

George Woodson Held has become the Lindbergh of the Rockies. Whenever construction and other odd jobs around Dubois prove too confusing, Woodie runs out of the house and hops into his motorized hang glider. Then, with a "downdrafts-be-damned" attitude, it's full-throttle time, or peace of mind at 12,000 feet.

"There's nothing like flying for a real feeling of independence. Playing the outfield was somewhat similar, but when you're high above the Rockies you have the whole world at your fingertips. Sure, it's kind of scary—but when I'm up there, cruising about forty-five MPH, I'm not a middle-aged man any more (now fifty-one). I feel like a twenty-five-year-old kid."

*Joe Christopher, unraveling the
mysteries of the cosmos.*

JOE CHRISTOPHER
Looking into a Crystal Ball

Is it a science, or a lot of hocus-pocus?

Darken the room, sit in front of the mysterious-looking charts, and let the Calypso-accented spiritualist unravel the secrets of the universe. This is no ouija board, tarot card, or palm-reading session. Heavens, no! Joe Christopher's particular brand of soothsaying revolves around theosophy, or the "cosmic philosophy based on mathematical principles"—and if you give the Met/Pirate outfielder half a chance, he'll assess everything from Dave Kingman's latest batting slump to your girlfriend's favorite ice cream flavor.

Just give him a birthdate. Then the ghosts of Isaac Newton, Johannes Kepler, and Copernicus take over.

"February 11th, 13 times 11 equals 143. That means this person is looking for truth," chants Christopher, surrounded by his three, squealing children in a small, Queens, New York apartment. "Yup, he's an honest person, who was conceived in Taurus, born in Aquarius, that makes him honest, very sensitive."

A thousand moons better at numerology than at hitting curveballs, Christopher continues, "April 20th, 13 times 20 equals 260. This person is very earthy. You know, down to earth, real, nothing false. He or she's very changeable, but also very sweet. There's a heart of gold there."

Really wound up now and looking skyward for more inspiration, Christopher forgets that a client is due any moment for a reading, and says, "Through my mathematical system, I can give you the spiritual characterization of any man, or coordinate him to nature. Remember, the ancient word for mathematics is sperm. Numerology is sacred. You just have to gain entrance into the hidden order, learn the equations, and the potential for any person becomes visible. The inner man must be understood. No philosophy in this country tries to do that. Instead they teach a bunch of lies. My system is different, it takes people to a different realm."

Flourishing such terms as "coordinated action," "the earth's four corners," and "spiritual alignment," Christopher describes how he uses these same theosophic principles to run a baseball school. Everything about the forty-eight-year-old Virgin Islander echoes a dark, unexplained world—from his intense, brooding eyes to his Belafonte-like accent—so why should the school be any different? Unlike most players who take youngsters to sandlots, to teach them the science of fielding a ground ball, Christopher conducts seminars in his living room, where he examines "their place in nature," probes their spiritual and mental attributes, and shows them "how they can align their bodies to the planets, to become fuller, more complete ballplayers."

This approach wasn't pulled out of a hat, even though it sounds a little strange. Christopher has been gazing at the heavens for years. As a teenager in St. Croix, the "higher laws" intrigued him so much he started studying for the priesthood. This pursuit is now called "my true calling and destiny," but at the time, the Lord lost out to Joltin' Joe's family. Life on the Christopher farm was a struggle. So Joe turned to baseball.

Modeling himself after his brothers, he became a catcher, and was eventually signed by the Pirates at the National Baseball Congress tournament in Wichita (in 1954, at age nineteen). Christopher then took off on his own baseball journey through the galaxies—Salt Lake

City, San Juan, Mexico City, Columbus, Ohio, Lincoln, Nebraska, Phoenix; wherever there was a minor league franchise, Joe mystically appeared. Finally, in early 1959, Joe's wanderings came to an end; he met his patron saint.

"Branch Rickey (the inventor of the farm system, who brought Jackie Robinson into baseball) enhanced my spirit; what a courageous man," says Christopher, suddenly lowering his voice in reverence. "He knew all about the hidden order, and the way to higher realms. That's how he found Robinson; he understood Jackie's spiritual characterization. I learned an incredible amount from him, especially how perceptual laws worked. He understood the relation between why and how. And yet he was never overbearing, unlike some of today's owners. The men you don't hear from too much are usually the strongest."

Rickey might've been a god, but he still couldn't move mountains. Roberto Clemente was securely fixed in right field, and Christopher had to content himself with backup duty. Whenever the Great One, Bill Virdon, or Bob Skinner needed a rest, Joe would have to forget his "astral geometry" and try to apply some elementary physics, i.e. glove catches ball, bat meets ball. Moderately successful with his mitt, he was a near-disaster at bat. Over the three-year span, his collective batting average was .244 (sixty-two hits in 254 at-bats) with one homer and seventeen RBIs.

The Pirates had no choice. Even the devout Rickey couldn't show any mercy. Christopher was sent to purgatory—or put on the 1962 expansion draft list, and taken by the Mets.

Other castoffs, guys like Rickie Asburn, Frank Thomas, and Choo-Choo Coleman, shrugged their shoulders and accepted their destiny calmly, with even a laugh or two.

Not Joe. He grabbed his astrological charts and cursed the stars.

"Why me?" he wondered. "What did I do to deserve this damnation?"

Screaming and hollering like a kid who doesn't want to go to the dentist, he reluctantly reported to spring training, and clashed with manager Stengel concerning his playing status. Demanding to be a regular starter, Joe finally got his wish. He played every day alright, but for a Mets farm team in Florida.

We all know, however, that cream rises to the top. Joe paid some more dues, and then came back to the Mets by mid-season. He should've stayed put. The club certainly didn't need another .240 hitter who could barely fight off the sun to catch a routine fly ball.

Miracles do happen, however. After another infamous season in 1963 (he hit .221 with one home run and eight RBIs), Christopher played as if he had sold his bat to the devil. The Amazin' Met incarnate, he swatted a hefty .300, sixteen homers, and knocked in seventy-six RBIs. No one could believe it. Not the Old Professor, the fans, or even Joe himself. Was it divine intervention? Were Joe's stars in the right conjunction? Or did Joe find some new Italian restaurant?

"It was simply a question of the higher laws, understanding myself, and feeling comfortable with my surroundings," explains Christopher, while yelling at one of the children for spilling milk on the kitchen floor. "Damn! I can't think straight. Oh, yeah. My batting. Rickey was a great man, but the Pirates changed my hitting style. I felt strange, my body didn't feel coordinated to nature, since they wanted me to hold the bat still. I did this for years. Then in 1964 I went back to the hitch. I had to generate some movement; I didn't keep the bat still any more. And look what happened, I wound up in heaven. I always told them I could play with the biggest stars in the league."

Once Joe came back to earth, he was more like a meteor—he had fizzled. In 1965, he was again the Christopher we all came to know and boo—he hit .249. Then, in twelve games with the Red Sox in '66, his batting average sank, and sank, and sank . . . to an unmentionable .077—and Joe didn't need any tea leaves or palm readings to figure out his future. It was time to retire. In fact, that time had been long overdue.

No longer a star, Joe struggled for months to get a job. His heart was never in it, but, because three children had to be fed, he took a salesman's position with an insurance company. Admittedly, "It was doomed from the start." Joe didn't like "the concept of selling people pie in the sky," or the feeling of being tied down. So, looking towards the heavens once more, he started to study physics, geometry, astronomy, and now feels that baseball should benefit from his special talents.

"Most people think I'm into some kind of black magic, but baseball spends millions of dollars on a player's physical attributes, while they should be spending it on his spiritual attributes. The game has to come out of the Dark Ages. I can show them the way to insight. I don't want any money right now. First I just want a chance to prove myself. I can get players out of slumps and make a club a pennant contender. This isn't voodoo, this is truth.

"I'm studying all the time now, and my brain is always working. A major league club should take advantage of this. I will do what hasn't been done before. I will get to the true soul of a player, and through my mathematical system he'll stop wrenching with the pain of uncoordinated motion. George Foster, Dave Kingman, Winfield, they wouldn't have to suffer any more. They wouldn't go through slumps once I get finished with them."

Christopher must pause now. World War III has broken out in the bedroom, and the kids' screams are louder than ever. Upon returning, he musters a smile and boasts, "I could even show teams who their number one draft picks should be, what trades to make. Everything's in my numbers. When they hear what my capacity is, and how I function, all these teams will be knocking my door down."

Leo "The Lip" Durocher counseling Ernie Broglio on how to pitch to Lou Brock.

ERNIE BROGLIO
Immortality

"I'll give you one Lou Brock for one Ernie Broglio."

"Broglio for Brock?"

"That's right, straight-up, take it or leave it. Brock for Broglio."

"Really?"

"Yup. Broglio for Brock."

"It's a deal." (Pats on the back, smiles, and handshakes all around.)

And so the two names are linked forever. One lives on in glory, the other lives on, trying to forget. In fact, the mere mention of either name (especially in Chicago or St. Louis) prompts immediate sneers, or hysterical laughter.

For this wasn't a big swap on a street corner between two bubble gum-chewing youngsters. This was the real McCoy. This was perhaps the worst trade in baseball history.

Sure, there've been some other beauts: the Mets exchanged Nolan Ryan for Jim Fregosi; George Foster was traded by the Giants for Frank Duffy; and the Reds swapped Frank Robinson, a future triple crown winner for right-hander Milt "Gimpy" Pappas.

But Brock for Broglio? F. K. Wrigley is still swallowing his gum over that one.

Brock, the all-time base-stealing king (118 thefts in 1974) who was always near .300, will soon be in the

Hall of Fame (an eighteen-year man, with 3,023 career hits, and an incredible .391 World Series average).

As for Ernie, well, what can you say about a 77-74 lifetime right-hander? He's a great guy, very friendly, talkative, real salt of the earth—and you should see his hairdo, a silver-gray duck's ass, a la Ed "Kookie" Byrnes of 77 *Sunset Strip* fame.

Oh, there's also a bit of Billy Martin or Leo "the Lip" Durocher in him. He has quite a temper. His verbal pot shots were like his curves or fastballs, they always got him into trouble. He could get away with mouthing off in 1960—his record with the Cards that year was a mean 21-9 (with a 2.74 ERA). But a 9-12 (1961) or 1-6 (1965) pitcher can't make demands about starting assignments or hotel arrangements. He has to be low profile, quit his yapping, and be thankful he still has a job.

Poor Ernie. He couldn't do this. And so, he was always in the doghouse. Or in baseball terms, on the shelf.

"I've always had a hot Dago temper, or a big mouth," admits Mr. Silver Streak (or, as his boss calls him, the Silver Fox), in the back yard of his San Jose, California house. His hair is blinding in the noonday sun, and it's understandable why he was constantly in trouble. The guy is all energy. "I just couldn't sit still on my butt and sulk. I got scratched a couple of times when I thought I should be pitching, and I had to come back with choice words for my manager. My mouth usually got the best of my mind.

"Baseball to me was just like punching the clock. I had to take orders from all kinds of dumb guys, and that didn't go over too well with me. I wanted a lifestyle of independence. I couldn't understand why clubs or managers didn't give me the respect to make my own decisions. Yeah, I was struggling at times, and pitchers like that are a dime a dozen. But if I performed on the field, why should management have the right to tell me where I should live? In St. Louis, I lived in Gaslight Square. It was quite a lovely place. It got my Mediterranean juices going."

It also made August Busch's beer boil. The Cards wanted Broglio to be an upstanding member of the community, not an all-night reveler in the shady section of town. They also had other thoughts about his performing on the field, so the coup was engineered.

Broglio for Brock.

Ernie's mouth had roared once too often. In heated talks with the Redbirds' top brass, he insisted on staying in Gaslight Square. It was that or nothing. The Cards quickly obliged him. They sent him northward. And by the end of the 1964 season, Broglio was 7-12 (compared to Brock's .348)—as Cubs fans got ready to lynch every Wrigley Field official.

" 'Where's Brock, where's Brock,' that's all I heard for years," says Broglio, nervously lighting a cigarette. "It bothered me, it had to bother me. That chant and the talk hung over me for years. It really hurt. I was trying to impress not only myself, but the Chicago organization as well. I wanted them to think that they made a really good trade. So I really had to prove myself two times over. I guess that broke me down."

Desperately trying "to make management happy this time around," Broglio also strained his arm. Only appearing in eighteen games, for the Cubs in '64 (4-7), he hoped the off-season would be a cure-all. But that was a pipe dream. The end was already in sight.

While Brock's story became baseball's *Chariots of Fire* (from '64 to '66, he stole 180 bases), Broglio labored. Still bothered by arm trouble (bone chips), he went 1-6 in 1965 and 2-6 the following year. His ERA (near 7.0) wasn't the only thing that soared. So did his frustrations.

"I was giving it everything I had, I was busting my butt, and nothing worked," says Broglio, with a trace of regret in his voice." I even thought I was doing a decent job at times. I guess Durocher (the Cubs manager in 1966) had different ideas. I was supposed to start

Ed "Kookie" Byrnes meets The Silver Fox.

against the Mets, and he took me out of the rotation. That had to bother me. It was an embarrassment. Afterwards, I had some choice words for him on the bench. I told him to get f_____."

Two days later Ernie was playing in Tacoma.

Two years later, after flopping around the minors and a tryout with the Reds, Broglio was out of baseball.

Characteristically, though, Ernie retired with flair. He piled his jockstrap, uniform, socks, shoes, hat, and glove on the front lawn and set them on fire.

After that, he got a job as a liquor salesman. Broglio admittedly likes to belt down a few. But the job didn't work out, because "all my clients expected me to spend the day with them, constantly drinking, at every bar in town."

Now Broglio's much more content. A self-described physical person, he's a warehouseman (or packer) for a liquor distributor. Every night, from eight PM to seven AM, he lifts cases of Jack Daniels, Cutty Sark, or other such items off the warehouse floor and loads them into trucks. It's grueling work, but Ernie enjoys it. He makes more than he ever did in baseball (his top salary was $25,000). While the night shift is often relaxing, the Silver Fox can pull out a crate and talk baseball with the guys.

"It took me three or four years to get over the game and the treatment I got, but now I'm doing okay. It doesn't bother me any more that I'll always be remembered as the other guy in the Lou Brock deal. I did things on the field that I'll always be proud of. If sports writers want to remember me that way, what can I do? I didn't make the trade. What can I say? One of us had a super career, the other turned out to be very mediocre.

"Look, if I wanted to make the whole thing a downer, I could. But what's the point of that? You grow. I tried my best. The only thing I'd do differently is I would've learned to keep my mouth shut. I would've studied the game more. I'd like to be a coach. This job's okay, but it's not something I really get too much joy from. Only my wife and kids make me feel good."

Broglio pauses and looks at a ceramic Madonna, sitting in his backyard. "My life isn't anti-climatic now. Baseball never meant everything in the world to me. The sport, the pressure, you never have any time for yourself. I was always getting ripped. Now, though, I'm a long way from that. I just want to get some time off, go sailfishing in the Baja, and maybe do what I've always dreamed of, take a trip to Italy."

VINCE DIMAGGIO

And here's to you!

The name is a national treasure. It instantly evokes all the innocence, joy, and promise of the game—especially the way it was played in a less confusing time. Then men seemed more heroic. So it's understandable that this name is wrapped in fantasies: of Joltin' Joe, that poker-faced kid who did all his talking with a bat; or later, of a dizzying, glamorous world, filled with wild Hollywood parties, Marilyn Monroe, and the million-dollar drip-drip-drip of Mr. Coffee commercials.

But the name also belongs to older brother Vince, a quiet man content to live in the shadows of a legend, who at age seventy-one is a Fuller Brush salesman in Los Angeles. Though a competent, .249 lifetime-hitting outfielder with teams like the old Boston Braves, Phillies, or Pirates (from 1937 to 1946), he never enjoyed any fame, or the riches that usually go with it. Unlike Joe (or younger brother Dom, who controls a number of businesses in the Boston area), Vince has had to scramble to survive. His retirement from baseball meant one job change after another, from bartender to carpenter, from milkman to liquor salesman.

Now a ten-year veteran of traveling door to door with cosmetics, oils, and brushes, he often leaves work early to go fishing, tend to his garden, or to study the Bible in pursuit of "that higher league." Insisting that he's found

A fielding magician, our white knight Vince steels himself for battle.

*Quite content, Vince no longer lives
in the shadow of Mr. Coffee.*

inner peace, only one thing disturbs him. Except for a phone call every six months, or a fleeting glimpse of his brother on TV, Vince, like the rest of us, has been forced to wonder, "Where have you gone, Joe D.?"

"Joe's always been a loner, and he always will be. When the folks were alive we were a lot closer. But I guess in the last four years I've seen him two or three times. What can I do, I'm Vince, and he's Joe. He's always had a living style higher than mine, or higher than I cared to live. It's only a shame that we have gone such different ways. That's real sad. Family should stick together.

"I remember taking Joe over to meet the owner of the San Francisco Seals. I had been playing for them, and I told them about my kid brother. They needed a short-stop, so I got Joe the tryout the last day of the season. Once they saw him they liked him, and my older brother Tom negotiated the contract. It's funny how all this began. Maybe if I had kept my mouth shut, I'd be remembered as the greatest DiMaggio.

"It hasn't been that tough living with my name. The only pressure of being a DiMaggio was trying to convince people that I wasn't Joe. I've tried not to use it to get my foot into the front door. I want to do things on my own. But I guess no matter what I do, I'll always be under Joe's shadow. He was one hell of a star, and I was just an ordinary star. I could play the outfield better than him, but when it came to batting, forget it. I would've liked to have given him a better battle. I'm a proud man. I just didn't have his eye."

STEVE BLASS
Watch Out for Tight Underwear

It's a mystery worthy of Sherlock Holmes, Hercule Poirot, and Sam Spade combined. What ever happened to Steve Blass?

A consistent 15-to-19 game winner for four years (103-76 lifetime), the Pirate right-hander suddenly lost everything in 1973, and was soon out of baseball. It's the most puzzling turnabout in diamond history, and no one has ever explained what went wrong.

Blass had been one of the National League's most feared money pitchers. He just didn't win ballgames. Blass was the man the Pirates depended upon in the closing weeks of the 1971 pennant drive. His 15-8 record, with a 2.85 ERA, shows how he performed under this pressure, and why Pittsburgh picked him to be the stopper in that year's World Series.

When Baltimore jumped to a two games to zero lead, Blass had the unenviable task of starting against perennial twenty-game winner Mike Cuellar. Undaunted, he pitched a three-hitter and kept Pirate hopes alive. But the heroics didn't end there. Matched against Cuellar again in the seventh game, he handcuffed the Orioles once more, giving up only one run on a brilliant four-hitter.

Blass was equally stunning the following year, matching a 19-8 record with a 2.49 ERA. He still remembers

Pirate Steve Blass, alone with his treasure.

feeling stronger than ever at the end of the season, and adds, "By depending more on my sinker or slider, instead of a fastball, my arm felt as fresh as it ever did in spring training. At that point I really thought I could go on pitching forever." (Though the Pirates eventually lost the final game of the league championship series to Cincinnati that year, Blass again pitched a four-hitter for seven innings.)

But then came 1973. While still in great physical shape, Blass struggled throughout the spring. Only 3-3 by early June, he pitched twice against Atlanta one weekend, and his combined stats for five innings show how far he had fallen: twelve hits, eight walks, three wild pitches, one home run, and twelve runs scored. And by the end of the season, even worse than his 3-9 record (9.85 ERA), he sometimes couldn't get the ball to home plate without bouncing it on the ground or heaving it into the stands. What went haywire? Why did Blass suddenly lose all of his control?

Forced to leave the game at age thirty-one, after spending most of the 1974 season in the minors (2-9, with a 9.74 ERA), Blass never came up with any answers. Back then he visited hypnotists, psychiatrists, faith healers, anyone at all who had a theory about his inability to throw a ball (he was often afraid of hitting batters with fastballs, and had to be coaxed to pitch). Though no one helped him, he remained high-spirited. Even during his most intense moments of self-doubt, he was still the inveterate prankster, giving reporters hotfoots, or tying teammates to chairs (he once angered manager Danny Murtaugh by persuading a bus driver to drive the Pirates to the airport, telling him a game had been cancelled).

Sitting in the den of his suburban Pittsburgh home, near a collection of 1971 World Series photos, Blass continues to joke about his "pre-pre-pre-premature retirement," quipping "That was the earliest final shower on record. I had to get out of the game. I wouldn't have been able to live with myself if I was making today's salaries."

Now selling high school class rings for a jewelry company in Pittsburgh and operating summer baseball camps, the forty-one-year-old Blass has recently been thinking of returning to the game as a coach, "to make sure the sheriff doesn't knock on my door for the mortgage payment." He seems content talking about baseball dreams fulfilled, and of discovering "a special inner strength from all those sleepless nights."

Smiling and always sounding as upbeat as a Dale Carnegie sales lecture, he goes on to say, "I had a hell of a career. I can't feel bad about what happened. It was terribly painful to lose what I had in the clubhouse with the other guys, the camaraderie, the closeness shared with men like Clemente, or the fighting through baseball's wars. Even when I was struggling it was fun to go out to the ballpark. I accomplished so much. When I was a kid I used to fantasize about pitching in the seventh game of the World Series and winning it. Well, I did it. I won that game. That's beautiful. I had lots of fun for seven seasons. What's there to complain about? I had so many successful seasons. Why should I think about two lousy ones?

"Really, the only thing I remember about the whole thing was how supportive people were. I was getting about two hundred letters a week from people telling me to keep my spirits up or giving advice on what I was doing wrong. One guy from Virginia even called me up and told me that whenever he missed a shot hunting it was due to his underwear, and that I should make sure mine wasn't too tight.

"Even my work has turned out really well. I'm on the road a lot in the Pittsburgh area, making contacts with principals and student committees, but I enjoy it. I'm my own boss, and this business is exciting because it's so competitive. We have a fine line of rings. That's important for me. Less and less kids know what I did, so (laughing) I have to rely more and more on my selling skills. I'm learning something everyday, and that's keeping me young."

After passing around a few of his rings to show off

heir quality, he becomes more serious. Looking at a
plaque that commemorates Roberto Clemente's baseball achievements and charity work, he continues, "We
flew home together after a World Series game and
talked a lot about pride. He wouldn't allow himself to
be mediocre, and though we were never that close, that's
one lesson I learned from him. You can't lose your
dignity. I wanted to come back and be great again, sure.
But if it wasn't to be, I had to keep things on an even
keel, in perspective. I wasn't going to destroy everything
I had accomplished.

"People just shouldn't pity me. The past is the past.
Even the greatest pitchers don't go on forever. I laugh at
the whole thing now. I got closer to my wife and family
after all the disappointments. And as I tell my buddies, I
had far too much integrity to make the bucks guys today
are making. Besides, I would've made a lousy millionaire."

A real prize in 1964, baby-faced Dean Chance
won the *Cy Young Award*.

DEAN CHANCE
From Cy Young to Stuffed Giraffes

"Come on, step right up, folks, don't be afraid. Three balls for a dollar. Knock down two clowns and be a winner. That's all it takes.

"Just a dollar. Look at those teddy bears. Or how 'bout that giraffe? Everyone's a winner. It's easy. Just look."

As part of his spiel, the carnival man flips a few soft tosses at a row of wooden clowns. Except for one little boy, no one on the midway is impressed. Some spectators even snicker. Before anyone walks away, the vendor keeps hustling. He knocks down a few more clowns, while his verbal pitch suddenly changes.

"Tonight only, a special price, 50 cents. Come on now, 50 cents. Only two clowns down, you're a winner. Come on, step right on up."

Always at home in a nether world, Dean Chance is still reeling off slippery curves. From living in the Hollywood fast lane with Angel teammate Bo Belinsky to owning a piece of heavyweight fighter Earnie Shavers to pitching penny-ante games, the 1964 Cy Young Award winner has never stopped hustling. For him, life is a roller coaster that has taken him from wild Beverly Hills parties to hopscotching from one state fair to another in a forty-five-foot tractor trailer. And while his friends once numbered Hugh Hefner, Ann Margret, and Mamie

Van Doren, he's now traveling in far different circles. Today, Chance teams with midgets, fat ladies, assorted gypsies, and hundreds of stuffed animals.

Once one of the game's premier pitchers, the six-foot three-inch right-hander (with a 128-115 lifetime record) says he became a barker on the midway because "nothing else was available. I just wasn't prepared to do anything else." That may be true. But there's also another reason for Chance's bizarre circumstances. As a player, he simply squandered his talent.

Chance not only won ballgames. At times he was virtually unhittable. Though his first three seasons with the Los Angeles Angels weren't too impressive (he had a 27-30 record with the weak-hitting second division club from 1961 to 1963), Chance added a slider to his repertoire—and that "brought me the fame I had always dreamed about and desperately hoped for." In 1964, he was 20-9, with an amazingly low league-leading 1.65 ERA (in 278 innings pitched), eleven shutouts, and 207 Ks. With those credentials it didn't matter if the nation's sports writers objected to his palling around with Hollywood jet-setters or Bo "Bad Boy" Belinsky. They still had to honor him with pitching's most coveted prize, the Cy Young Award.

The two-time All-Star Game starter didn't do as well the following two seasons. He was 15-10 in 1965, and then fell to 12-17 after suffering from a slight case of tendinitis in his shoulder. The Angels gave up on him in 1967, trading the $50,000-a-year hurler to the Twins, and, as Chance now recalls, "This really hurt. All my friends were in LA, and it was like the Angels were telling me, 'you're all washed up.' I had to prove them wrong."

He did just that. Voted the 1967 Comeback Player of the Year by baseball's Bible, *The Sporting News,* Chance became the Twins' most dependable arm, recording a 20-14 mark, a 2.73 ERA, 220 strikeouts, and a league-leading eighteen complete games. Equally noteworthy, in August he pitched a perfect game against

Boston for six innings, and then came back to hurl a no-hitter against the Indians.

But mowing down batters was never enough for him. Chance wanted to be a name, a celebrity, someone who made the gossip columns or got preferential treatment at the swingingest clubs. In other words, he needed a spotlight that was bigger and brighter than any sports page.

"My friends in California encouraged me to be an actor," says Chance, climbing into the cab of his tractor trailer, to show off a recently purchased CB. "Driving this thing around the country ten months a year isn't the greatest. But after a while I learned that I wasn't the type to sit around in casting offices waiting on someone else's decision. I don't think I was short on ability. I just didn't have the desire to be in movies. It was glamorous alright. I liked that part of it. Being in Walter Winchell's column, along with Bo, that was okay. It was exciting."

Laughing, he then continues, "Maybe I'm too quiet for that sort of life. I'm more of a homebody. Anyway, acting is like what I'm doing today. It's too chancy."

Boxing, namely Earnie Shavers, was supposed to be more of a sure thing. It interested Chance for two reasons: the glamour was there, and so were the fast bucks. Plus, getting a fighter was easy. Chance had connections. He knew all the right people in the Ohio fight game (his home state), including boxing czar Don King. By 1969, he had secured a fifty-percent interest in Shavers, and accordingly, fantasies of pitching in the World Series or an All-Star Game were replaced by another dream. To get Shavers a title shot against Muhammad Ali.

"Boxing was really a fun thing for a long time. I first got involved with a friend of mine, Ed Mears, who put on fights in Canton, Ohio. (Chance now owns a farm in the central part of the state.) He said we couldn't miss, that there was a lot of money to be made. Well, we did a (Jerry) Quarry bout, and then later got Shavers. We damn near won the title. I had a lot of money tied into him, but I lost it all. Every last penny. That's the way it is in boxing. You get close to fighters, almost become part of them, and then it's all gone. Fighters get to believe their own press clippings, and it's goodbye. What can you do? I'll never forget, I was there when Earnie knocked out (Ken) Norton in the first round. Damn, was that sweet."

But boxing and baseball don't mix. Not when late-night meetings, a bad diet, and keyed-up emotions hurt a player's conditioning. Chance inevitably developed arm trouble and lost his fastball. During the 1968 and 1969 seasons he slid into mediocrity (21-20, even though his ERA stayed below 3.0), and was traded by the Twins to Cleveland. The fans adopted him immediately, but at $70,000 a year, he was a bit too expensive for a 9-8 record. So the Indians dumped him with the Mets (0-1 in three 1970 games), and the following season he struggled to finish 4-6 in Detroit. The fun had gone out of baseball.

"I just didn't have it. Not only was the strain too much on my muscles, but I couldn't get the juices going. I couldn't get all that excited. I'm not sad about those last years. When I look back I have no bad feelings at all. I gave everything I could. I know most players feel hurt when it's all over, or can't think about the game. But believe me, I have real good thoughts about what I accomplished. The only mistake I made was not thinking about what I'd do after it was all over. I was too busy having a good time. Baseball gives you a slight edge in the outside world. But let's put it this way, being a name won't help you if you can't do the job."

Never having worked in the off season, Chance was totally unprepared to start a second career. So he did what came naturally. He hustled. Or looked for an easy racket.

And while he can sweet-talk a crowd with his "games of skill, not chance," the forty-two-year-old self-described "wheeler and dealer" hardly has a rollicking time under the big top. Besides being on the road constantly or living in motels, he must set up his games, hire dependable people to run them, and purchase stuffed

His new friends agree, Dino's still tops in their league.

animals from an assorted cast of gypsies and con men, whom he describes as "a band of cut-throats. They'll trick you for a piece of popcorn." Admittedly, it's a lonely, confusing life. One that mocks his often-repeated midway shout, "Just step right up, everyone's a winner."

For, as he confesses with a brooding look on his tanned face, "This racket is a tough buck. Hanging out at these places is not all that bad; at least I'm eating. But looking back, I never should have gotten involved. You have to deal with two many characters, with too many people who want to rob you blind. Plus it's feast or famine. You're always depending on the weather. Maybe in a year I'll be in a different business. I don't know. I'd give it up now, but I can't find anything better to do.

"It's not too easy getting up for this work. It was a lot different when I had to face Mantle or Maris. Then I was really psyched. Now what I'm really doing is selling toys. You have to set the game so you lose the item. But back when I was playing, everything was out front, it was me straight up against the batter. One on one. Pure excitement. The survival of the fittest. There's no better confrontation in sports. And guess what, I often came out on top.

"Baseball was great to me. It was not just thrills. It was also beautiful feelings. A sense that I had really achieved something. That I was getting close to people because of what I was doing. After that no-hitter I got a call from Vice-President Humphrey. When the game was over, I felt so good I can't even describe what was going on in my mind. Words can't do it justice. But no matter what people say about me, I wasn't out for personal glory. We (the Twins) were fighting for the pennant, and I wanted to contribute. A win would've been as good as the no-hitter. I just wanted to do something for the other guys."

Ignoring the carnival noise around him, Chance picks up a large giraffe, props it next to his chest, and says, "Geez, I never thought I'd be giving these things out for a living. I guess I made a few mistakes along the way. Maybe I should've led a life more conducive to preserving my skills. Why knows? Anyway, no matter how I'm remembered, I at least know one thing. Once you play in the big leagues, no one can take it away from you. Why, it seems like only yesterday that I was up there, playing hard and hanging out with Bo. I'll always have those experiences, no matter what. That Cy Young Award, that's mine, forever."

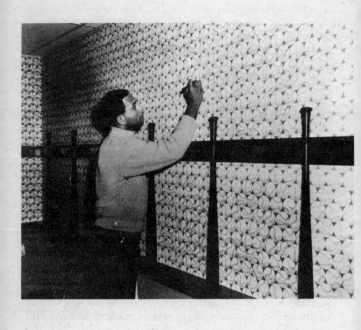

ORLANDO CEPEDA
Marijuana Claims a Victim

Being Babe Ruth's son hasn't been easy. It's meant living in the shadow of a legend—living with constant self-examination, insecurity, anger, and heartbreak. Very few men can cope with such pressure. Even fewer can come back from a scandal to plunge ahead, to excel again.

The "Baby Bull," Orlando Cepeda, is one such man. He's had to struggle constantly. Dogged by the fame of his father, Peruchio, the home run king of Puerto Rico, Cepeda had to measure up, or set his own slugging standards. That was quite a task, playing for the Giants in the 1960s alongside Mays and McCovey. But the Bull came through. He was Rookie of the Year in 1958, the first man unanimously elected Most Valuable Player in the National League (1967 with the Cardinals), and overall he batted .297 with 367 home runs.

Individual honors, however, never satisfied him. He always had something else to prove. The Reggie Jackson of his day, he had frequent run-ins with Alvin Dark in 1962, after the Giant manager allegedly had called Latins "dumb and temperamental." This feuding eventually wreaked havoc in the Giant clubhouse, took the team out of the pennant races, and sent Cepeda packing (to five more teams before he retired in 1974).

Life wasn't any simpler back in Puerto Rico. The mind games continued. Along with the painful self-doubts. Cepeda searched for answers, or an axis for his post-baseball life. And he found one. Only it turned out to be illusory—a near-devastating, nightmarish mistake.

In 1975, Federal agents arrested him for drug smuggling at the San Juan airport, after they discovered 160 pounds of marijuana in his car trunk. The shock waves were immediate. Cepeda's entire world was now in ruins. Besides expensive legal fees and an eventual five-year prison sentence (he served ten months at Elgin Air Force Base in Florida), Cepeda had to face the wrath of his neighbors. The whole island turned on him, and, as he now sadly remembers, "The isolation, the disgrace, the feelings of numbness, they were horrible. I knew I had done something wrong, that I had to pay for my stupidity. Yet I wasn't a criminal; people didn't have to kick me while I was down. I remember this guy who was supposed to be my friend saying, 'If I'm with my kids and I see Cepeda coming, I'll walk the other way.'"

Cepeda would battle back later on, by opening a baseball school for children in San Juan. But at the time everything in his life was blurry, torn apart, or destroyed. Hell is always a shattering ordeal, only in his case it was worse. For years he had heard only cheers and talk about his eventual enshrinement in baseball's heaven, the Hall of Fame.

Deservedly so. Cepeda broke in with a bang, and soon became one of the greatest hitters in the game. As a rookie first baseman, he hit .312, had twenty-five homers, and ninety-six RBIs. No great believer in superstitions, so he then tamed the sophomore jinx, and racked up more Ruthian figures—.317, twenty-seven homers, and one hundred five RBIs. After slumping somewhat the following year (.297, with twenty-four homers and ninety-six RBIs), the Bull roared again in 1961, and the din continued for most of his career:

1961—.311, a league-leading forty-six
home runs, and 142 RBIs (his

.609 slugging average placed him
second to Frank Robinson).

1962—.306, thirty-five home runs, 114
RBIs.

1963—.316, thirty-four home runs, 97
RBIs.

1964—.304, thirty-one home runs, 97
RBIs.

Cepeda hurt his knee in 1965 and missed most of the
season. In his absence, the Giants used Willie McCovey
at first base without losing anything offensively. So
Cepeda became expendable. The Giants had gotten tired
of his yearly salary disputes, and the Alvin Dark controversy had always been a sore point with management.
They were into a general housecleaning anyway (Felipe
and Matty Alou, Jose Pagan, and Harvey Kuenn had all
been traded before the 1966 season), so Cepeda was
sent to the Cardinals for pitcher Ray Sadecki.

Feeling more at home in St. Louis ("guys like Curt
Flood and Bob Gibson put me at ease right away"),
Cepeda gave the Cards the extra punch they needed to
be a contender. With him batting third or fourth, other
teams couldn't pitch around Flood or Lou Brock. And
consequently each batter was strengthened (once
Cepeda and Maris played full-time in 1967, Flood's
average jumped from .267 to .335, and Brock's from
.285 to .299).

As for Orlando, he first hit .303 for the Cards, then
.325 (one hundred eleven RBIs), during the team's drive
towards the 1967 pennant. His World Series totals are
far less impressive—three hits in twenty-nine at-bats for
a .103 average—but that doesn't prevent him from saying, "The Cards were special. I was supposed to have
been washed up because of my knee, and yet I came
back to produce. Don't get me wrong, the pressure was
on to prove myself all the time. It just never bothered
me. I kept playing and I got it out of my mind on the
field. Plus St. Louis, it was good there. People were nice,
and I was the first Latin to break into a white section."

Making about $90,000 in those days, Cepeda was expected to produce. When he didn't (due to sore knees, he hit .248 with sixteen homers in 1968), the Cards quickly traded him to Atlanta for Joe Torre.

Again Cepeda was supposed to be finished. And again the experts were wrong. Even with his bad knees, he was an adequate first baseman—and pitchers still had to fear him. He could always deliver the timely hit or crash the long ball.

His batting average slipped to .257, reminiscent of his debut season with the Braves, yet he still clubbed twenty-two homers, twenty-eight doubles, and had eighty-eight RBIs. Most ballplayers would have been satisfied with these totals. Not Cepeda. Calling 1969 an off season, he then played ball all winter and came back to hit .305, with thirty-four homers and one hundred eleven RBIs.

Cepeda was living on borrowed time, however. His knees couldn't withstand the grind of a 162-game season. He had to be a part-time player. That was obvious with the Braves in 1971 (he only played 71 games), and it led to his being traded to the Red Sox. In the American League, Cepeda could be a designated hitter—and an awesome one at that—as he batted .289 in 1973, with twenty homers and eighty-six RBIs.

That was Cepeda's last complete season. With Kansas City at the beginning of the 1974 season, he had to retire after only thirty-three games. Numerous knee operations simply made it impossible for him to go on. But Cepeda had accomplished what he set out to do—he was no longer living under his father's shadow. By registering 379 homers, 2,351 hits, and a .297 batting average, he was now legendary in his own right; and his induction into the Hall of Fame was only a matter of time.

Now, however, that call may never come.

Cepeda got busted.

One cold statistic—160 pounds of marijuana—has changed his entire life.

Instead of plaudits or awards, there's only censure or disgrace.

That ball is going-going-gone.

And lingering questions. What was the true extent of Cepeda's drug involvement? How was the shipment arranged; why were federal agents tailing him; and was he tied into the underworld?

The case remains shadowy, since Cepeda refuses to talk about these issues or the past. He'll only say, "Fooling around with drugs was a stupid mistake; it never should have happened."

It's only known that he served ten months of a reduced sentence (KC/Philadelphia second baseman Cookie Rojas led a petition drive to get Cepeda out of jail), and then participated in drug rehabilitation programs at various halfway houses. In 1979 he worked briefly for the Phillies, and was later a batting instructor for the White Sox.

Today he's still trying to lead a normal life. But putting the drug issue behind him has been a constant struggle ("people still call me an addict"). Bitterly, he complains that police agents are watching him, tapping phone conversations with friends, and trying to sabotage his school. His face coloring with anger, he insists, "People want me to burn. It doesn't matter that I did so much in baseball. Or that I only made one mistake. People don't think I'm a normal person. They want me off this island."

Sitting in a San Juan stadium dugout, Cepeda watches one of his students bungle a play and hurriedly jumps onto the field. Upon returning, he quickly says, "You got to teach these kids the fundamentals. Otherwise coaches will label them lazy and dumb. There's still a lot of discrimination in the game. I could see it when I was with the White Sox. But I didn't care about that when I was a kid. Then, just to be in the majors was roses.

"The one guy, though, who should speak out about what goes on is Mays. He's the best player ever, he gave so much. It's a shame he can't be in the game. (Mays has been barred from baseball because he's working for a casino in Atlantic City). He should be an ambassador for baseball. He is baseball. Humpty Dumpty officials shouldn't be able to keep him out. No one should.

"Baseball is so damn political sometimes. You have to walk a tightrope, and the Hall of Fame, that's like running for president. You need people behind you, promoting you, and lobbying for you. Because I was busted, I won't make it, most likely. Every time there's a Hall of Fame vote, they use the bust to keep me out. But it won't drive me crazy, or make me lose sleep if I don't make it. Baseball tries to keep its straight image; that's a lot of bullshit."

Cepeda grabs a bat, handles it, and soon shakes his head disgustedly. "I paid for my mistake. I just want to be left alone now, I just want to be with my family. I cried for two weeks when I was sent to jail. I paid for what I did. I lost everything I had. I bought land for a health spa, put a mortgage on it, and then, when I had to hire lawyers, I lost about $300,000. But most of all, I lost my freedom. Do you know what prison's like? What more do people want from me?

"I don't care if they want me off this island. I'm going to help kids here. People to this day are lumping me with criminals. The police weren't too happy that I was coming back from jail, that I'd be in society again. They started to talk about my needing protection, as if drug bosses were going to hurt me. There were even newspaper articles that talked about my dealing with the Mafia. My mother couldn't take this stuff. It finally killed her.

"But I'm not bitter. I think my name's stronger than ever. I visited some inmates in a local jail recently, and they gave me a great reception. That gave me new faith in myself. I'm going to come back, even if that's a lot harder than hitting a home run."

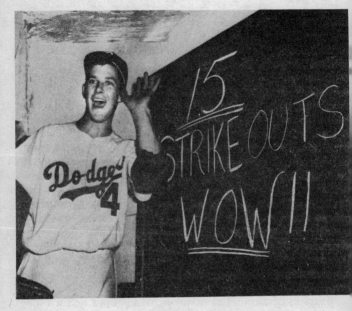

King Karl got the call in 1954, and the Flatbush faithful were soon shouting "sooner with Spooner."

KARL SPOONER
Striking Out in the Grapefruit League

The record book only tells part of the story: 1954, two wins, no losses, 0.00 ERA; 1955, eight wins, six losses, 3.65 ERA; or overall, 116 innings pitched, 105 strikeouts, and three shutouts.

It doesn't describe the disappointments, the broken dreams, or the pain of being washed up at age twenty-four.

What can capture the feeling of losing everything? Maybe a Frank Sinatra ballad, or an Ingrid Bergman tear-jerker, works for the love-torn. Maybe. But what about a ballplayer when that fastball or curve disappears as quickly as an ex-lover, where does he turn for support? Certainly not to the past. Memories of sun-drenched, boyhood days on the mound are only more mocking. He goes on, tries to forget or hopes for the best.

Only it's not too easy being billed as the next Carl Hubbell, or another Bob Feller, and then winding up on a garbage heap. Some flashes in the pan never get going. Others, like Dodger lefty Karl Spooner, literally shovel shit, work three jobs, and pray.

Things have gotten better. Spooner is now a manager of a grapefruit-packing company in Vero Beach, Florida, only a few miles away from the Dodgers' spring training home. It's a fairly easy job; he simply has to make sure the conveyor belts run properly and that the women packers do their job. The money's also good, and, while Mrs. Spooner still works on an assembly line at a nearby airplane factory, the family lives like any other American household. That is, except for Karl. He's still haunted by a dream turned nightmare.

How could he forget? His major league debut was utterly sensational. Called up by the Brooklyn Dodgers at the end of the 1954 season, the $500 bonus baby quickly fired off a hail of bullets—all blanks.

A four-hit shutout against the Giants to clinch second place for the Bums.

Then a three-hit zipping of the Pirates, with the same result, lots of strikeouts.

Twenty-seven Ks, in fact, for the two games.

Newspapers immediately dubbed him King Karl, and lamented. "Why wasn't Spooner brought up sooner?"

An instant celebrity, Spoon was invited to the Ed Sullivan show, toured the banquet circuit, and, to celebrate the coming of 1955, threw expensive parties at restaurants like Al Schacht's (the clown prince of baseball). Brooklyn, too, toasted their new hero. He had "la difference," he was the man who would team up with Erskine, Loes, and Newcombe, to bring Brooklyn its long-awaited championship. So, with great anticipation, fans waited for the season to begin.

Nineteen fifty-five would be a banner year. Flatbush got its World Series win—Sandy Amoros's catch, and Johnny Podres's pitching made sure of that. Yet the joy only went so far. Once the faithful's hero, Spooner was now Brooklyn's Invisible Man.

For him, 1955 was a disaster. Or, more bluntly, the end.

His downfall began early that spring, in an exhibition game against the Cardinals. Podres was pitching, and manager Alston hoped he could go three or four innings. That would give pitchers like Billy Loes and Carl Erskine some needed rest, since they had been complaining about sore arms. But Podres got shelled, and asked to be taken out in the second inning. No one, however, was ready in the bullpen, least of all the Spoon.

"What a mistake. I really thought I was set to go," recalls Spooner, looking balefully out his small office window. Nearly trembling when lighting a cigarette, he remains speechless for a few minutes, and only then continues, "I just wasn't ready. What else can I say? I felt something pop almost as soon as I got out there. Afterwards it really started to hurt. In those days they called it tendinitis. It was really a rotator cuff. And you know what that means, you're finished."

Spooner did pitch again that year, but every toss was a struggle. Out of action until June, he lost his free and easy delivery, and was below .500 for most of the season. Not able to get it cranked up, it's understandable why he says, "I can't remember too many of those games; everything is in a cloud." Everything was. His pitches were hit so far they could've been used for rain pellets. Or, in his case (two complete games out of fourteen starts), for lots of showers.

Flashes of the 1954 Spooner were evident in the second game of the '55 Series, with his striking out six Yankees. But his worst shellacking occurred in the sixth game. The Bronx Bombers are known for their explosiveness, this attack looked like a repeat of Hiroshima. Before Spooner even looked up, five runs had scored in the first inning, three on a towering drive by Moose Skowron. When Alston walked to the mound, there was no booing. The stadium crowd knew the Spoon would never be back.

Still optimistic, however, Spooner played winter ball in the Dominican Republic that year. He thought the adhesions, or scar tissues, in his left shoulder would heal, and that "even without a good, overpowering fastball, I could learn to be a different type of pitcher." It was not to be. Whether it was exams at various hospitals, brief stints with minor league teams, or yearly spring workouts at Dodgertown, the results were always the same—pain, and nothing on the ball.

"I just couldn't get going. I'd feel good for a moment, and then the pain would start all over again," confides Spooner, his voice cracking. "I wanted to throw hard so badly, the image of it was so clear to me. But it was so physically unbearable, what a frustration that is. You get down on yourself. As long as there was a chance I had to try. You hate to say die. Baseball was glory, it's something you love to do. But when it's not there, what can you do? You try to forget, no matter how much it hurts."

Spooner finally did give it up in 1959, after the Cardinals released him during spring training. Yet that immediately posed another problem: what would he do to earn a living? Only trained to throw a baseball, he didn't have too many choices. It was either odd jobs or Skid Row.

"I've tried to forget the misery I went through after the World Series. That was certainly a high point, winning the championship. But let's be honest. After pitching didn't work out, I was heartbroken. I couldn't get my mind straightened out. It might not be right for a grown man to cry, but baseball had meant everything to me. I couldn't believe it was over. My arm went dead on me, and I couldn't understand it. I was nowhere.

"What was I supposed to do, be a brain surgeon? Luckily, I got a bartender's job at night, and was also able to do some construction work during the day. I remember shoveling shit just to make ends meet. It was especially tough seeing my wife go to work. Oh, did that hurt. She pulled me out of my depression, and I guess she's still doing that. But she had to get a job. Otherwise we would've gone bankrupt."

The Spooners struggled for six years. During this time, Karl never ventured near Dodgertown, afraid that "the place would touch off too many memories." In fact, he didn't even throw baseballs to his son or go to Little League games. It was okay for the kids to play it, but in the house baseball had become a taboo.

Karl's outlook brightened once he got a regular job with the Haffield Citrus Corporation in 1965. At first a

Quality guaranteed: that's a Spooner trademark.

receiving clerk, he studied various aspects of the company's expanding business, and now supervises sixty employees. In short, Karl's the owner's right-hand man, a strange—but also welcome—turn of events for the newly smiling southpaw.

"Yeah, overall, I feel a lot better these days," grins Spooner, leaving his office to inspect a new shipment of grapefruit on a conveyor belt. "It still hurts to think of baseball, of what might have been. I'll most likely never get over that. But the kids (five of them) are growing up, and doing real well. That's satisfying. Plus the job's working out okay now. I'm real glad I don't have to tend bar any more at the Blue Goose, Lenney's, or any of the other places I worked. Boy, that was nowhere. The people here have treated me so much better. Like a person. It's helped, a lot."

Pleased with the quality of the grapefruit, Spooner grins and shouts a few instructions to a group of workers. He then recalls how his former employers treated him. "The Dodgers were great; they gave me every chance to come back. I had always been a Dodger fan, especially of Preacher Roe, what an old hillbilly he was. What a fine individual. I was just a wild-assed kid when I got to Brooklyn, and he took me under his wing. He really taught me a lot.

"I certainly had a lot in those days. I guess my biggest frustration nowadays is reading the sports pages and seeing those six-figure contracts some guys get. They're not half as good as I was."

JOHNNY BLANCHARD
To Hell and Back

It's finger-biting time.

The game is on the line in the bottom of the ninth, and either Hoyt Wilhelm, Hank Aguirre, or Stu Miller is pitching. Of course, runners are on the bases, itching to scramble home. Yankee manager Ralph Houk is also nervous. He looks down the dugout for a pinch hitter, only the choice isn't an easy one. He has a host of power at his disposal—Elston Howard, Bob Cerv, Dale Long, or even Yogi Berra at times. Each of them is given one more look, then Houk plays his ace. "Go ahead, Johnny. Grab a bat. Let's get this thing over with."

Big Bad John was always ready. It didn't matter that he'd been sitting on the bench for three hours, twiddling his thumbs, desperately hoping to play. Blanchard was clutch. He strode to the plate, flexed those coal miner's muscles, and took a few cuts. Meanwhile, fans in right field scattered. They knew what was coming. A cannon shot. None of them wanted to die in the South Bronx, or be another victim of the man the Bombers dubbed the Killer.

In his eight years with the Yankees, Blanchard murdered so many relief pitchers he could've opened his own funeral parlor. No one was safe from his screaming liners. Blanchard could face the cream of American League pitching—Frank Lary, Camilo Pascual, Billy

*You'd smile too if you won as many
games single-handedly as pinch-hitter
deluxe, Johnny Blanchard.*

Pierce—and the results were usually the same. Another Yankee victory. Besides stroking dozens of game-winning hits, he socked seven pinch-hit homers (tied for ninth on the all-time list), is one of the few players to hit pinch-hit home runs in two consecutive at-bats (July, 1961), and then went on to tie the record for home runs (four) in most consecutive at-bats.

Blanchard only had one problem. With Howard and Berra around, it was a little difficult to crack the lineup. The Yankees tried him in right field, but Maris was then in his prime, so Johnny had to be content with seventy to ninety games a year. This didn't do much for his batting average or self-esteem. Usually called into a game cold to face fresh relievers, he was a lifetime .240 hitter. But from 1961 to 1963 Blanchard still produced more RBIs than any of the other Yankee subs—and was often called the best tenth man in baseball.

Especially in 1961. Given a chance to play more regularly (ninety-three games), Blanchard clubbed twenty-one homers, had fifty-four RBIs (out of seventy-four hits), and raised his batting average 63 points, from .242 in 1960 to .305. Nagged by self-doubts throughout his career ("I always felt I had to prove myself, that I was only as good as my last at-bat."), he now felt like a full member of the Yankees' new Murderers' Row, a vital part of the wrecking crew that destroyed the Reds in the World Series. In that lopsided four-games-to-one affair, Blanchard went four for ten (a slight drop from his 1960 Series clip of .455, or five for eleven), with two home runs and three important RBIs. Once again, as his overall Series batting average of .345 indicates, he had been Killer John.

"Yankees have pride; I had to produce when the chips were down," says Blanchard joylessly, sitting in a restaurant that overlooks Lake Minnetonka in Minnesota. Staring into a cup of coffee, he sits silently for several minutes, his deeply lined face frozen in despair. "I felt alive in those days. I felt special every time I went out on the field. How things have changed. Boy! It was unbelievable how many games we won in the last few innings. As time goes by I've really gotten to appreciate just how good we were. Anything sets me off, a parade, someone mentioning New York. My daydreaming maybe starts off in 1960, but it always winds up in 1961.

"I would've won the car (for most valuable World Series player) that year if Ford hadn't pitched twenty-nine and two-thirds innings of shutout ball. I was the happiest guy on the team that year. I knew I was on the best team ever assembled. Mantle. Berra. Richardson. Ford. Terry. Maris. The Yankees had been my whole life, ever since I was a kid. The night they traded me was the worst, what a blow. I went from first to tenth. Damn, I really started to drink. It was the end of the world. The whole thing just stunned me."

Blanchard would eventually admit to being an alcoholic, and go through years of treatment. He now says that the trade (1965) which sent him to Kansas City along with Rollie Sheldon for Doc Edwards, depressed him for years. Describing himself as "a competitive animal" who believed "winning was everything in life," he felt betrayed by being dumped with a loser. Ever since leaving college to sign a pro basketball contract with the Minnesota Lakers, he had been with front-runners. The Yankees even made him feel more important when they lured him away from the hoops with a $30,000 bonus. But the trade changed everything. Convinced that he was washed up, Blanchard could only reach for a bottle.

"It was a tough time coming home to Minnesota. I always had a reputation for being a boozer," admits the fifty-year-old ex-catcher, who tried to hook up with several teams as a coach after being cut by Milwaukee at the end of the 1965 season. "I think that's one big reason I couldn't get back into the game. I don't think anyone wanted to take a chance. So I hit the booze even more. I was an alcoholic, no way around it. No way I'm going to bullshit myself. My friends even called me Bud, for the beer. Did it strike me that I had a problem?

Nope. It was dumb. If I hadn't gone to ruin, I'd be a manager in the big leagues today."

Instead, he wound up in the real estate business. And alcohol haunted him again. Recovering from hangovers, he'd miss appointments or forget where he was supposed to be. Some of this drinking was done at the liquor store he had opened a few years earlier with World Series money. He always thought "I'd need something to fall back on," and once his real estate bosses fired him, the store was just that, "a place where I could run and hide."

Around 1972, Blanchard tried to sell cars. But by this time his drinking had gotten even worse. He'd get into fights at bars, wouldn't come home at night, and, inevitably, his marriage started to fall apart. Threatened with a divorce, and beginning to feel "something had to change, or I'd have committed suicide," Blanchard sought professional help.

"I was dying. I was lost without baseball," he says, gulping another cup of coffee. "My friends were leaving me, and my home life, that was falling apart. Everything was going down the tubes. I was in a self-pity bag. I had no job to speak of, my children were getting uptight, I couldn't even remember where I had spent the night sometimes. One day I had blood on me, and I said to myself, 'This is bad news. This is the end.' A half-hour later I was in a treatment center."

Blanchard stayed there for thirty-four days. A few months later he sold his liquor shop and got a job with the T. C. Johnson Company, a firm that manufactures heavy-duty cranes for laying railroad track. With them now for nine years, Johnny says, "I've become a great salesman for a great company, and there's no way I'm going to touch anything but a tonic water. I haven't had the hard stuff for eight years."

Looking out over the lake, he leans back with his head sunk on his chest. He seems to be contemplating his struggle for self-respect. Then, with a slight smile, he starts talking again.

*It's been a cold journey, but Johnny's
on the comeback trail.*

"So many guys leave the game and flounder. I'm sure they're into the sauce pretty good. Just like that (snapping his fingers), they turn the lights out, and you're gone. Ninety-nine percent of the guys can't live with that. The game's fun for years, it's a kid's game, and you love it. But then all of a sudden you're thirty-five and the bubble bursts. What do you do then? Hey, pal, being told you're over the hump at thirty-five, that's a lot to take.

"You turn to booze. You have to. When you're in the game and things are going good, you can't celebrate with milk shakes. So you tip a few. Then, when you're on the way out, the drinking has to get worse and worse. You can't talk to anyone about it, it's too macho a world. You have to maintain your manhood, and a conspiracy of silence develops. Don't get me wrong; I loved being with the Yankees. With my limited ability it has to be the biggest accomplishment of my life. But I'd bet that twenty-five percent of that '61 team was alcoholic."

Thoughts of that year now evoke a wider smile. Chuckling, he recalls the slider Bob Purkey threw him in the World Series, when his homer tied the score in the third game. Then, watching a sailboat float by, he talks about the future.

"Every time I see that lake I love it more. The sunfish out there are great. When I was in the Boy Scouts, thirty-seven years ago, my father and I would go out there and build an ice house. We'd stay out there for two weeks. I can't wait for this summer. I want to take my sons fishing. Maybe we'll get lost out there together."

Connie Mack's words of wisdom must have paid off; Bobby Shantz became one of the best fielding pitchers in baseball history.

BOBBY SHANTZ
No More Hershey Chocolate Bars

Gutsy. That's the only way to describe five-foot six-inch left-hander Bobby Shantz. Back in 1952, though pitted against giants like Mantle, Doby, and Minoso, he combined a 24-7 record with a 2.48 ERA to win the American League's MVP award.

But those batters were only dangerous to a degree. Still working in the bullpen, Shantz faces an even tougher lineup today. One that's almost impossible to resist.

For behind the counter of his Bullpen Dairy Bar in Chalfont, Pennsylvania, the scorecard reads, "double-decker ice cream cones, butterscotch sundaes, 'baseball-bat-sized banana splits', malteds, shakes, hoagies, hamburgers, and Italian sausage sandwiches."

Whew!

Shantz has had to prepare these treats (without weakening) for the last five years, ever since he sold his twelve-lane bowling alley next door. Not easy work, the pressure has finally taken a toll. Shantz doesn't get much satisfaction from the Bullpen anymore.

Throwing Big Mitt hamburger patties on a grill has gotten to be as routine as an intentional walk, and food prices are escalating like ballplayers' salaries. Even more disheartening, scooping ice cream for a bunch of squealing children has far less glamour than a 1957 World

Series start, a 119-99 lifetime record, or eight Gold Glove awards, which rank him as the best fielding pitcher of all time (four awards in each league, as Shantz played sixteen years for eight teams, including the Philadelphia Athletics, Yankees, Pirates, and Cardinals).

As the fifty-eight-year-old Shantz sadly explains, "The people who come in here are only interested in good ice cream. What do they care what I did in 1952, 1957, or whenever? That MVP year was the best year of my life. But no one remembers anything, or even wants to. They just want a big piece of cheese on their hoagie, or an extra helping of hot fudge. Not memories from some old ex-ballplayer."

Before elaborating, Shantz displays some of his old form, slinging a dozen steaks onto a grill to get ready for the noonday crowd. He's then interrupted by a counter lady, who calls him over to a balky Coke machine.

"This damn thing gets clogged up all the time," hisses Shantz, straining to get a close look at a spout. "That's why I gave up soft ice cream; the machine broke down every day. A lot of things fall apart in this place. I'm not too mechanically inclined. I even have trouble putting in a light bulb." Pausing for a moment to consider what must be done with the machine, he eventually stammers, "This equipment is a pain. Most of the time I have to call repairmen. I really don't know what I'm doing here."

Once Shantz finishes struggling and gets the carbonation working again, he resumes, "It used to be great here. I used to love the hot fudge sundaes. I was just like a kid, I couldn't get enough of them. And oh, those Hershey chocolate bars. After a while though, I lost interest. Maybe I have more will power these days. I don't touch much of the stuff here. It's all good, but I see it all the time. This is a real grueling racket. There's no limelight here."

There was glory, lots of it, during Shantz's playing career. Before his remarkable 1952 season, he won eighteen games for the As in 1951, and was consequently awarded a special privilege. While only earning $12,000

Strawberry sundaes are only one Shantz specialty.

the following season, he was allowed to sit next to manager Connie Mack on the bench. This "favorite son" treatment helped him learn the subtleties of the game—and it later paid off. Shantz was the experienced veteran chosen by Casey Stengel to start against Lew Burdette in the second game of the 1957 World Series. And in 1962, during the twilight of his playing days, the Houston Astros honored Shantz by letting him launch their first season in the league.

"I go to bubble-gum card conventions now, to stay close to the game. People give me a couple hundred bucks to stand somewhere and sign autographs. I've been to five or six of them. They're real fun. I just have to sign the cards. I don't even have to talk that much. Going to them, or to Old-Timers' games, that's a way to keep in the public eye. I don't get bored that way.

"I really have to look for some business I like. I'm the worst person in the world to have this kind of place. I threw a baseball for twenty years. What do I know about running any kind of business? I'm only here because I can't screw up a hamburger. I cook, chop onions, mop the floors, clean the toilets, anything the others (four employees) don't want to do. I'm never going to get rich. The only way I'm ever going to make money is to open one of these places on a college campus, or across from a ballpark. In the meantime, I make more money golfing."

Shantz now moves away from an ice cream freezer and points to a trophy case in an adjoining dining room.

"I was so small I didn't think I was going to make it to the majors. My father was a glazier, and I thought I'd wind up in a sawmill at seventy-three cents an hour. But I actually stayed sixteen years in the big leagues. Not too many guys can say that. But most likely I should've quit a lot earlier. My arm was killing me the last few years. I didn't know what to do at the time. I had the bowling alley, but I really didn't want any part of that. I just love baseball, that's me, and I've never wanted anything else.

"Those years with the Yankees were the best. Wow, I can't even begin to tell you how much fun they were.

Things will never be as good. I liked playing for Connie Mack, what an old guy he was. He was like a father to me. But being in pinstripes was different. Bauer, Mantle, Kubek. I knew I'd get runs. I just couldn't believe it. Here I was, winning ballgames in Yankee Stadium. Richardson, Berra. What a bunch of fellas. They treated me like one of the guys."

In Spanish, or any language, Yo-Yo Arroyo spells R-E-L-I-E-F.

LUIS ARROYO
Big Cigars Are Like Security in the Bank

Joe Page. Johnny Sain. Ryne Duren. Sparky Lyle. Goose Gossage.

Along with providing instant R-E-L-I-E-F, all of these pitchers add up to a long line of P-E-N-N-A-N-T-S. They were the Yankees' own SWAT team, the troubleshooters who left the bullpen to face dangerous situations, douse last-minute fires—and to make the Bronx the home of champions.

On equal footing with any of these aces, Luis "Yo-Yo" Arroyo was another Mission Impossible specialist. While his own stay in New York was a short one (1960-63), the pudgy little left-hander from Puerto Rico carried the Yankees to two pennants, in 1960 and '61. Throwing nothing but screwballs or curves, he went 20-6 over those two seasons, with thirty-six saves and a razor-sharp 2.53 ERA. Arroyo was such a soothing sight jumping over the bullpen fence, Whitey Ford called him "my personal bodyguard, the guy who kept me in the big leagues." (Over half of Arroyo's twenty-nine saves in 1961 came after Ford pitched.) The fans, equally enthusiastic, signaled their respect by making LUIS-LUIS security blankets the hottest item at Yankee Stadium concession stands.

Arroyo first joined the Yankees halfway through the 1960 season, after four rather disappointing seasons in the majors (with the Cards, Pirates, and Reds in quick succession). The Yankees were then six games out (on July 22nd), and, to complicate matters, one-time star reliever Ryne Duren was becoming progressively less effective. In desperation, the Yankees brought Arroyo up from the minors. Now manager Stengel had no choice. He had to rely on this relatively untested junk-throwing pitcher.

"Man, I couldn't believe it, none of it," exclaims the fifty-six-year-old Arroyo, shaking his head until his Yankee cap falls off. Now a scout for New York in Puerto Rico, he dusts off his pride and joy and continues, "Only a few months earlier I'd been pitching for a Reds' farm team in Jersey City; now I was with the champs. Man, I'll never forget. I was told to go to Yankee Stadium. I looked in the paper to see who was in town, and saw the White Sox were there. I never thought of the Yankees. I couldn't believe it. Nope. I could only think, 'Here we go again. Damn, why couldn't it be the Yankees?'

"Imagine my surprise. Especially when I was told I had to get to the Yankee locker room that night. I didn't know how to get there, so I took a taxi. It cost me sixty dollars, but it was worth it. I took out a cigar, walked up to the players' entrance, and the guard said, 'Who the hell are you?' The next thing I knew, I was walking into the clubhouse, puffing away, and there was Mantle and Maris, looking at me kinda funny."

Poor Baltimore.

Pity the White Sox.

And goodbye to the rest of the league.

Casey's experiment immediately worked. Arroyo was hot. He won five games and saved seven, as the Yankees went on a tear. They won sixteen of their last eighteen games, and Arroyo had the honor of nailing down the pennant-clincher, by getting the Red Sox' Pete Runnels to pop up to Clete Boyer. No one laughed now at Arroyo's name (Stengel couldn't pronounce it, hence the Yo-Yo). For little Luis, it was big cigar time.

Arroyo had fantasized about becoming a Yankee

since childhood, when he worked on his father's farm outside Ponce. He once saw Johnny Mize, Joe D., and Cliff Mapes at a local stadium, and the image of the flannel pinstripe never left him. It didn't matter where, or what he was doing—milking the cows, cutting sugar cane, or feeding the chickens—Arroyo carried his glove around with him, dreaming of playing on the same field with his heroes.

Only attending school until the eighth grade, the squat, five-foot-eight lefty signed his first pro contract with a Ponce team, and then it was "a lot of banging around, hamburgers, and bad buses." As he pointedly says, "I really got a chance to learn English. I saw every small town in America . . . the smallest places you could image, that didn't even have sidewalks." Making about $250 a month (in the early 1950s), he spent six years in the minors, moving from one team to another as rapidly as kids trade baseball cards. The struggle to make it often seemed futile. But despite feeling depressed at times, he was more worried about adjusting to America. "The first few years in the minors were the toughest. I didn't want to make a fool of myself in restaurants. I had to learn how to eat hamburgers, french fries, shakes, to really be one of the guys."

Forced to overcome various arm or shoulder injuries, Yo-Yo didn't make it to the biggies until 1955. He then broke in with St. Louis as a starter, and dazzled the league by winning his first nine games. Leo Durocher selected him for the All-Star Game, and Arroyo seemed headed for a brillant career. But, inexplicably, he soon flip-flopped, going 2-8 the rest of the year.

"I still don't know what happened," says Arroyo, who only won three games the following year, and then had a disastrous 3-11 mark in 1957. "Nothing was bothering me; I felt fine. I was a fastball pitcher then, and I guess the batters caught up with me. Nothing worked. I couldn't even fool a rookie. I soon knew I had to come up with another pitch, or it would be back to the sugar cane fields."

Consequently, it was screwball-screwball-screwball.

Except for an occasional curve or slider, batters saw nothing else. And today Arroyo's two middle fingers are permanently bent, seemingly wedged together in a question-mark-like shape. They're also painfully arthritic. But the tricky pitch did keep Arroyo in the majors. In fact, the difference between the two phases of his career can only be described by one of Phil Rizzuto's Holy Cows. From that 3-11 record, Arroyo screwballed his way to 5-1 in 1960, and then a sensational 15-5 mark with a 2.19 ERA in '61. Those latter totals made him *The Sporting News'* Fireman of the Year—and for a little icing on the proverbial cake, he won the third game of the World Series that year by retiring six straight Cincinnati batters. Oh, what sweet revenge.

Twisting his left arm, as if throwing a screwball could magically recreate 1961, Arroyo says, "The Yankees did a super job of taking care of me that year. Houk never pitched me more than three innings. I was once in nine straight games, but other than that, everything was super. What an organization. We had speed, defense, power. Going to the ballpark was better than being at home. At least six or seven times Mantle or Maris hit a homer in the ninth to win the game for me. I couldn't do anything wrong. Even my batting average was good (.280)."

In two years' time, however, Arroyo was out of baseball. A candidate for the Cy Young Award in 1961, he would've had trouble getting his grandmother out the following season. His screwball no longer danced or fluttered; and as for his curve, some of those are still in orbit. Statistically, he was 1-3 in 1962, with a 4.81 ERA, while the next season his 13.5 ERA (in six games) put him on a train to the minors with a one-way ticket.

Why the nosedive? Why did he become totally ineffective?

Blaming himself for "getting fat and lazy," Arroyo says his conditioning habits completely changed after "I got that Series money in my pocket." He had always played winter ball, but the Yankees convinced him not to that year, and that led to a lot of eating and drinking on the banquet circuit. Even though the Yankees strongly influenced his decision by giving him a check for what he would've earned in Puerto Rico ($6,000), Arroyo shows no signs of being bitter. Instead, he talks glowingly about manager Ralph Houk, the old, pre-Steinbrenner Yankee management, and the team's giving him a full 1963 World Series share.

"The Yanks are class. They did everything they could to get me through a tough time," says Arroyo, sitting in a cafe near a stadium in Ponce.

"It bothers me a little that I didn't get more years in (he played eight) for my pension. I should have continued to play winter ball. It never hurt me to do that. But all that's in the past. When I quit, the Yankees made me a scout. I used to have the whole Caribbean. Just last week I signed a kid. It's getting tough, though. While kids used to sign for four to five thousand, now they're looking for twenty to twenty-five thousand. It's unbelievable."

Taking out a long black cigar, Arroyo flashes an equally big smile and concludes, "Not only am I proud of what I did in baseball, but it's also the best sport around. It treats people good. When I hear guys complaining about baseball I get really pissed off. It did so much for me. Right now my son's going to dental school at the University of Michigan. He's getting a great education, thanks to the Yankees and my screwball."

Prized Angus cattle, and even guys like Aaron and Mays, have had to eat out of Harvey Haddix's hand.

HARVEY HADDIX

The Only Kitten in the Hall of Fame

It takes talent to pitch the greatest game in baseball history and still lose. Not too many men can pull off such a trick. They have to be a breed apart—kittens with a special meow.

Finesse, stealth, quickness—these traits produced (1) Harvey Haddix's nickname, the Kitten, (2) a 136-113 lifetime record, and (3) his unforgettable taming of the Milwaukee Braves.

On May 26, 1959, while pitching for the Pittsburgh Pirates, Haddix hurled twelve perfect innings against such sluggers as Hank Aaron, Joe Adcock, and Eddie Mathews. The crafty little left-hander was always pretty reliable. He had gone 20-9 with St. Louis in 1953, and his ERA was usually near 3.5. But on this day, against the defending NL champs, he was simply awesome. Despite having a touch of the flu, Haddix had retired thirty-six straight batters, and was already headed for baseball immortality when the roof fell in.

In the thirteenth inning, the Braves' Felix Mantilla hit a routine grounder to third (Don Hoak), which was thrown away. Mathews then sacrificed, and Aaron was intentionally walked. Haddix had to forget his no-hitter, his other thoughts of glory. The game was now on the line as the always-dangerous Joe Adcock stepped to the plate.

This was no time for purring; prayers were in order.
Haddix hung a slider, and that was it. Adcock hit one
into the right-field stands—and while he was only
credited with a double (for passing Aaron on the
bases)—the final result didn't change. The Kitten had
scratched and clawed, only to wind up a loser.

"The whole thing was goofy," laughs Haddix, on his
465-acre Twin Lakes farm in Ohio. Surrounded by "the
boss of the place" (his dog, Tony), and dozens of
mooing cows, the fifty-eight-year-old Haddix quickly
adds, "My opponent, Lew Burdette, was right. He said
an experienced pitcher like me should've known better
than to bunch my hits. What can you do? I wasn't upset
at the time."

Not about to cry over spilt milk, Haddix soon went
on to other heroics. While only 11-10 (3.97 ERA) the
following year, he stifled the Yankees in two key World
Series games. With the Series tied at two games apiece,
Haddix only gave up five hits and two runs in six and a
third innings (Elroy Face got the save in the Pirates' 5-2
victory). Then, called in as a reliever in the seventh
game, Haddix squelched a Yankee rally and walked off
with the victory.

"Those two Series wins, they can't be topped by
nothin', not even if one of my bulls won a blue ribbon at
the state fair," says Haddix, who's also a pitching coach
for the Pirates. "For us to come back after the way the
Yankees stomped us, whew, not too many guys beat
them in those days. We were just a bunch of old rats,
(Dick) Stuart, old Strangeglove, he was quite a character, Elroy, Bill (Virdon), Maz (Mazeroski), what a
bunch. We were partying so much you could drop a
bomb on our hotel at four in the morning and we'd still
field a team the next day."

Getting to that Series hadn't been easy. Debuting with
the Cards in 1952 (2-2), Haddix overcame the sophomore jinx to go 20-9, but the following year he slipped
to 18-13. A foreshadowing of things to come, Joe Adcock played the villain. Haddix was well on his way to
another twenty-game season (thirteen wins by July

13th), when the Braves' first baseman lined a ball off his kneecap. Haddix came back a few weeks later, but he'd never be the same again. "I lost my spring after that; all the tendons on the left side of my knee were ruined."

Incredibly, Haddix could still bounce off the mound to make great fielding plays, and would win three Gold Glove awards later in his career. Curiously, however, this cat-like touch did little for his curveball. It got belted. Once Haddix posted a 12-16 record in 1955, the Cards traded him to Philadelphia (13-8 in '56). Then he had two very mediocre seasons (10-13 in '57, followed by an 8-7 mark with a 3.52 ERA for the Reds in 1958).

Cincinnati then sent him and Smokey Burgess to the Pirates for Frank Thomas and Jim Pendleton. Aside from his perfect game, Haddix had a so-so season, combining a 12-12 record with 149 strikeouts. The next few years, Haddix started to use more off-speed pitches and was suddenly more effective. He was only a spot starter, but his totals from 1961 to '62 were respectable, 19-12 with 200 Ks.

Haddix had nagging arm and knee problems, and he finished his fourteen-year career in Baltimore. Used exclusively as a reliever, he still loved "the challenge that only baseball provides." But his body couldn't withstand the constant traveling, and (at age forty) he longed to be back on the farm, where "there's real fresh air, and wild deer in the back yard."

Farm life was pleasant for awhile. Haddix enjoyed his hogs, and the price of grain remained high. By November 1966, however, he got itchy, and the grass looked greener elsewhere, especially on a ballfield, in a baseball uniform. He contacted the Mets, and was soon working with their young pitching staff (Tom Seaver, Jerry Koosman, Nolan Ryan, etc.). Haddix stayed there for two seasons, then moved on to the Pittsburgh and Cincinnati chains. This latter assignment lasted a year, and by 1972, the Kitten was back on the farm.

Haddix played around in the hay for three years. He soon realized that he could have the best of both worlds—working as a pitching coach in the summer and as a farmer in the off season. He put this strategy to work in 1975 with the Cleveland Indians. The commute wasn't a long one, and he remained with the Tribe for three years. Then he worked out the same arrangement with his true love, the Pirates, and he's currently trying to bring Kent Tekulve and John Candelaria back to their 1979 championship form.

Helping younger players excites Haddix, but while tending to his cattle he says, "Coaches just don't get the respect they used to. In the old days a coach was the boss, even if he didn't do much. Today players get to the big leagues a lot much quicker, and you have to teach. These young guys don't know the game, and coaches have a much bigger job. I might not do this for that much longer, the money's just not there.

"But I wouldn't trade what I've had for anything. I've had the best of lives. I travel and see the sights in big cities, then I can get back here and have the quiet. I grew up twenty miles from here, and I'm never going to leave this place. Farming is tough; the prices for wheat are going so low. It also takes two years to raise a steer. But even though I never have time to loaf, I'll be durned, working hard is okay. You got to if you're going to amount to anything.

"How do you think you become a pitcher? It's work, lots of it. I wasn't all that great; the perfect game is my only claim to fame. But if I hadn't sweated I'd have nothing. And that game is really something. What the heck, they got a nine-foot picture of me in the Hall of Fame, alongside DiMaggio and (Ted) Williams."

Haddix then strolls past a bunch of cows to get to the barn. Ignoring a loud chorus of moos, he grabs a bucket and starts feeding his hogs.

"You know they don't call hogs right on TV. Whooow! Whooow! That's how you call them. The guys thought I was nuts because I used to practice my calls in the clubhouse. I still do. There are contests around here for people who can call the best, or the loudest. I only have a few hogs left here. I'm more interested in these steers. Cows are money. But the contests are fun. Besides, I really want to win. The Haddix family has had great hog callers long before there was ever a game called baseball."

George Altman quickly adjusted to baseball in Japan—many a ball went *sayonara!*

GEORGE ALTMAN
Bulls, Bears, and the Hogs

Chaos reigns.

Groups of wildly shouting men seem locked in combat. They stand chin to chin, pointing frantically with their fingers or thrusting papers in each other's faces. Periodically, eyes dart upwards toward an electronic board flashing sets of numbers—and as the figures race across the Chicago Board of Trade tote board, the yelling turns into a stream of gibberish.

"Am Pax, Am Pax (soybeans), 10,000 at $8."

"Yeah, yeah, 20,000 at $8.50, and 5,000 Xylo, 2,500, at $3.50."

"Seed Mor at $4.25. No. 10, 3,000 at $5.35."

"I'll go 10,000, No. 1 at $9. Then sugar No. 12, 6,500 at $18.25."

"Look at the board, look at the board, No. 12, 7,500 at $18.50."

One of the booming voices belongs to George Altman. Once an outfielder for the Cubs, Mets, and Cards, the tall, lanky Altman has entered another fiercely competitive arena: the world of the bulls and the bears—the commodities market. A speculator who deals almost exclusively with futures contracts (like soybeans, wheat, or oats), he can make thousands in a few minutes, or get clobbered.

Prices of commodities change instantaneously, and,

like a batter at the plate, Altman has to be ready for every different move. He must know the other bidders, their strengths and weaknesses. And in this ballpark courage is essential. Risks must be taken nearly every minute. There are no guarantees, ever; but as Altman has painfully learned, the fearless usually survive, while the fearful get buried in a sea of ticker tape.

Amid this turmoil Altman remains composed, even mellow. For all the wheeling and dealing, he's now the consummate switch-hitter: aggressive when the market is bullish, patient when losses must be absorbed. Knowing how to ride a market to its logical end usually demands years of seasoning. Altman, a relative newcomer to the commodity business (six years on the Chicago Exchange), has developed this skill the hard way. *Seven* seasons with the lowly Cubs was an initial endurance test; and then Altman confronted the ultimate pressure—he had to battle cancer.

"To go down in the trading pits, you just can't have an MBA, you have to come prepared," jokes Altman, standing in a recessed part of the trading floor with one eye fixed on the flashing electronic boards. "I guess you could say I've been through a few things. They've built character (laughing), and given me the right concentration. Because of that I haven't come close to losing my shirt. I still make a lot of bad moves. It's a slump, just like a baseball. But the game showed me that life was one battle after another. That's a good lesson; it keeps you from getting too greedy when you're playing around with the big boys, the bears or the bulls who throw around hundreds of thousands."

Altman's baseball days started off on a much more modest scale. Unable to pursue a pro basketball career because of aching knees, he signed a $200-a-month contract with the Kansas City Monarchs (of the old Negro League) and toured the country. He then played Army ball (1957-58) in the same outfield with future major leaguers Willie Kirkland and "the craziest guy I've ever met," Leon Wagner. The threesome had lots of zany times, but Daddy Long Legs (as Altman was called), wasn't too optimistic about making it to the majors.

"I was twenty-six at the time, and just about ready to go back to my father's auto shop in North Carolina," recalls the fifty-year-old Altman. "One day the Cubs were practicing near my base, and when they went to get their picture taken, I jumped into the batting cage. I hit a few balls out, so they invited me back. Believe it or not, a few days later I found myself in the lineup. Then the next thing I knew I had a contract. I guess I was just in the right place at the right time."

Maybe Wrigley Field didn't always bring out the best in ballplayers. Let's face it, getting it up for a last-place ballclub wasn't easy.

It might have been the right time, but Wrigley Field the right place? Let's face it, getting it up for a last-place ballclub isn't easy. Altman struggled. He hit only .245 in his rookie year, with eighty strikeouts in 420 at-bats (that's about twenty percent of the time), and only had twelve home runs. Nineteen sixty wasn't much better. He only raised his average twenty-one points, and still didn't deliver the power the Cubs expected (thirteen homers with fifty-one RBIs).

The next two seasons, however, were a different story. Suddenly, Daddy Long Legs started to crash the vines. He hit forty-nine home runs the next two years (ninety-six RBIs in 1961), and his combined batting average was .310. This turnaround delighted fans, helped the Cubs win a few more games, and surprised the hell out of George.

"I was always serious about the game, but playing for the Cubs, that was never too easy. I could never relax. When you're with a losing ballclub there's a greater chance of getting injured (Altman's knees constantly bothered him, and he also suffered other injuries). When you can't relax, you pull muscles. Plus that sun in Wrigley Field is a detriment. It takes a lot out of you. I feel bad. I never played up to my potential."

Summing up his career as "busted great expectations," Altman played a lot worse after the Cubs sent him to St. Louis in 1962. He hit .274 that year, and then went into a complete tailspin. Barely hitting his weight, he dipped to .230 in 1964 with the Mets, then returned to the Cubs, only to hit .235, .222, and .111. By 1967, George was disgusted. His knees were hurting as much as his ego, so he left the Cubs and headed for the Land of Second Chances—Japan.

Noting "I was big over there," George didn't need his Berlitz training to discover one important fact: ballparks are smaller in Toyota country. Playing for the Lotte Orions in Tokyo, he was suddenly the samurai slugger who drove pitchers to hara-kiri.

Typically a .300-plus hitter, with thirty homers and one hundred RBIs, Altman describes his eight years in Japan as "the most tranquil time in my life. I felt good over there because the whole scene went along with my personality. It was peaceful. When you study the Oriental psyche you can see how it is not to be so aggressive. People might not be so happy, but they never express it; you never see temper tantrums. American players don't usually fit in because they're so outspoken. They'll complain if they have to do an hour's worth of exercises before a game. I didn't have to let off steam.

"Besides, I understood that my lifestyle would be different, that I wouldn't be pampered like I was in the major leagues. If you can't adjust to that, you'll run into problems. That never bothered me. The only conflict I did have was with the manager. I started to get sick in 1974, and he couldn't understand why I was still around. He leaked the news to the media that I was ill, and that made me more adamant to play. I was having my best year when he couldn't take it anymore, so he had to release me."

"Getting sick" is Altman's way of saying he had cancer. A malignant leg tumor was discovered, that forced him out of baseball into a chemotherapy/radiation program. He lost thirty pounds in 1974, but that didn't sap his enthusiasm for the game (or Japan's big bucks). He rushed his rehabilitation, and played one

Now that his soybeans are a valuable commodity, George is lighting up a different kind of scoreboard.

more year for the Hanshen Tigers before returning to the States in 1976.

Money wasn't a problem, not just yet. But Altman had to make another quick decision. What was he going to do with the rest of his life?

A stock broker during his Chicago playing days, he was now afraid of managing other people's money. So he looked for an investment business of his own. Friends pointed him to the Chicago Board of Trade, and, after talking to a group of traders, Altman plunked down $135,000 for a seat. He's never regretted it.

Wearing his new uniform, a snugly fitting gray jacket, with a "Chicago Grain" badge on the lapel, he cheerfully says, "This is a super business. It's just like baseball, you have to go for the jugular. There's so much tension, it's nervewracking. But that's okay. It's almost as exciting as playing before a big crowd, and getting an important hit.

"The main risk here is buying thousands of bushels of something, and then the price goes down immediately. The idea is not to be stubborn. You have to take your loss and get out. The tendency is to say, 'I can't take this loss.' But you have to get out sometimes. I didn't once, and it cost me close to $10,000. I've learned my lesson. I just want to live comfortably. The bulls and bears make money, the hogs get slaughtered."

Altman steps away for a moment to check the prices of various soybean issues. He also talks with a clerk, and upon returning laughingly remarks, "Talking to you, it's already cost me $500.

"You have to move and think fast here. That's why it's so much like baseball. In a split second you can lose thousands, or get your grand slam. Just like in the game, you can't let the noise affect you. Your reflexes and discipline must be above that. Baseball is a great training ground for all of this. It taught me timing, and how to get used to winning and losing.

"I'm grateful for that. A few years ago I could've gotten in on this fantastic silver market. I wanted in at $4.90, and it came down to $4.95. I said to myself, 'Be patient.' Then it went to $5.40. I wanted to kick myself, I just couldn't chase it any more. Here you're talking about a million dollars. Or a guy hitting a long, long flyball with the bases loaded. It's quite a shot, but you missed it. Because of baseball, I can lose one trade and still say to myself, I'm going to win the next one, and a lot more after that."

Hobie Landrith never worried
about facing Ford; now he's going up
against Toyota and Datsun.

HOBIE LANDRITH
Old Shoes and Positive Thinking

It's Pearl Harbor all over again. The Japanese have landed, and casualties are mounting. Especially in Detroit. There, some say it's *sayonara* time for Ford, GM, and Chrysler.

Volkswagen is also on the skids, but they've been luckier. They've found their own John Wayne to halt the Toyota-Datsun advance. The unlikeliest of heroes, he's a .233 lifetime hitter who was the Mets' first selection in baseball's 1962 expansion draft—Horatio Alger himself, Hobie Landrith.

As an assistant regional sales manager, Landrith has utilized dugout folklore to outmanuever the Japanese and to rally his own VW troops. Trained in salesmanship by some of the greatest psychologists ever—Rogers Hornsby, Casey Stengel, Freddy Hutchinson, and Birdie Tebbets—the "Punch and Judy" catcher has not only sold a lot of Rabbits and Sciroccos. He's also scoring in Germany, with his new, improved statistics. Only connecting for thirty-four home runs and two hundred three RBIs in his fourteen-year baseball career (that he was able to hang on for so long is incredible in itself), Landrith can now compare his region's one-percent rise in VW sales to Toyota's seven-percent drop, or to the mother company's four-percent national decline.

"Baseball taught me how to deal with crises, how to

be a winner," says Landrith, looking like the quintessential high roller, with his legs propped up on a desk. "Non-Japanese cars are in a horrible slump right now. I wish I could put my finger on the cause of it. But we're going to get our momentum back. No question about it, all the difficult moments I experienced as an athlete helped me deal with the circus that's the business world. The pace is so hectic here, it's like the ninth inning of a game when you have men on base and you're trailing by one run. My sales people are going to get that hit."

Landrith has always shown such self-confidence, or determination. He's been forced to. He's had little else going for him. As a sixteen-year old in Detroit, he didn't even have the money for a pair of spikes, and had to sweet-talk his way into the ballpark. One day (in 1945), hoping to see a game and maybe get himself a job, he volunteered to shag fly balls for Hank Greenberg, who was taking extra batting practice after returning from the war. The Tigers were so impressed with Landrith's attitude they kept calling him back—and eventually Hall of Fame catcher Mickey Cochrane gave him a pair of his old shoes.

The die was cast. Landrith decided to be a catcher. He didn't know anything about handling pitchers, and certainly couldn't hit. But he was determined to be a backstop. Though his strict German father wanted him in the family refrigerator shop, and scolded him constantly for devoting too much time to "a ridiculous game," Hobe kept practicing. When a diamond wasn't available, he'd throw a ball against Briggs Stadium, play imaginary games, and dream.

"When I was working for the Tigers it was always 'kid, kid, kid, get me this, wash the floor, or pick up my dirty laundry,'" recalls Landrith, smiling boyishly, his blue eyes twinkling. "But none of that stuff ever mattered. I was rubbing shoulders with guys I had only read about. Besides, I was able to learn so much. If any of them told me to push a peanut down Main Street at midnight I'd do it, in a minute."

The Tigers were more merciful. They used Landrith to

catch batting practice for a year, and at age eighteen he was signed by the Cincinnati Reds for their minor league farm system. Hobie found paradise at Tulsa, in the Texas League. The "dream of every clear-thinking kid" was within sight until a grinch intervened. Landrith's resiliency was tested as he broke his leg in the first game of his second minor league season. Near tears, Hobie went home and didn't play until August. Then he got an unexpected boost from Lady Luck. The Reds were set for an exhibition game, but their regular catchers, Walker Cooper and Dixie Howell, were both sidelined with injuries. Landrith played despite the pain in his leg, and was soon called up to the majors (1950).

For yo-yo duty.

Neither Cooper nor Howell could be displaced permanently; Landrith just didn't have the power or defensive ability. So when he wasn't on the bench, Landrith was constantly on the move, up and down between the Reds and one of their farm teams. This went on for six years. Ed Bailey and Smokey Burgess had become the Reds' catchers by 1955, but nothing really changed for Hobie. He only got to play forty-odd games a year. And while other players would've become disgruntled or disgusted, Hobie only took advantage of the situation.

"I knew crashing that lineup was impossible, so I learned how to get motivated in different ways," explains Landrith, now fifty-three. "The first thing I had to do was to listen to Birdie (Tebbetts), he was such a gifted manager. He really understood the psychological aspects of the game. He told me, 'You'll have a pitcher out there struggling, you'll be the one who'll have to steady him down.' What he really was teaching me was how to get negative thoughts out of someone's mind. That's an invaluable skill; I'm using it today. I can't tell you how many times some of my sales people go into slumps and I have to be there for them. Ballplayers, car dealers, it doesn't matter who, you got to keep forging ahead, you gotta dig in there. Dig, dig, dig."

Unfortunately, Landrith could never get out of his own slump. The Reds sent him to the Cubs in 1956, and

Hobie did get to catch a lot more. But he didn't hit, there or with any of the other six teams he'd eventually play for—St. Louis, San Francisco ("the place I loved the best"), New York, Baltimore, Washington. At every stop in his wanderings, Hobie was the hitless wonder who somehow became the manager's right-hand man—so he stayed in the majors for fourteen years, even though a great season for him was a .240 batting average with thirty RBIs.

Once Landrith retired in 1963, he again used his charm and personality to get ahead. Through friends in San Francisco he was referred to key officials at Volkswagen, and apparently his aggressive style was an instant hit. VW coaxed him into working for their public relations department (with a sizable contract), even though Landrith had gotten several baseball coaching offers. Four years later Hobie moved on to sales, and today he directs the sales activities of forty-five VW dealers in Northern California. Ultimately responsible for the movement of 25,000 cars annually, he's often called to meetings in Germany, where he's treated like royalty. Is he happy? Part of him certainly is. Yet he often sits in his office, waiting for the phone to ring—hoping it will be an offer to manage a major league team.

"Getting my mind off baseball is sometimes impossible," admits Landrith, a reddish glow coming over his face. Presumably thinking of some distant ballfield, he grows silent for a moment, then continues, "That competitiveness stays with you. No one in the game ever thought I'd turn down those coaching offers. I had to then; my wife and kids needed someone at home. Plus the business world has a lot of excitement. In baseball, if you counsel a person you can enjoy his performance, and it's the same here. You taste success. If the national company does five percent and you do seven percent, you should be pleased. You're a winner.

"I felt the same way as a player, even though I was on some rotten teams. I always tried to get the most from my pitchers. I don't think I was a throwaway, not even in the '62 draft. It did something for my ego that I was selected first. I can still see Casey, standing with just a shirt and socks on, greeting us with that gravel voice of his. He was saying 'Don't think for a moment you're here because you're not too good,' but some of us had different thoughts. What a team! We really had some wacky times.

"Leaving all that, the game, it was a real downer. But you have to forget, and move on. You can't cripple yourself. That's why this business is so rewarding for me. The rapport I had with people in the game, I can also have that here. You have to be able to chew your salesmen out and then be a human being. We're all in a slump now, Toyota's really doing a job. But we'll be back soon."

Landrith then glances at the telephone and smiles knowingly. "It doesn't matter how things are going here, all my fantasies are still in baseball. I'd like to get back in it. There's an environment, an atmosphere, that you can't give up. As an athlete you make a mistake and everyone knows. Here, I can wipe out mistakes with an eraser. So it's funny, I still want to be back there, no matter what the realities or pressures. There's nothing like a first love."

BOOG POWELL
Barracudas, Whales, and Sassafras

Ten miles off Key West in the Gulf of Mexico, amid swarms of barracudas, eels, and sharks, a 290-pound creature sticks his head out of the water and shouts, "I'll poke them in the rear with my spear. You get them when they come out the other side of the coral head. And move it. There's a lot of good eating down there."

Boog Powell is still intimidating. He's now chasing lobsters instead of ground balls, but once his friends on the boat get their instructions, they exchange beer cans for nets and put on their snorkels. Even though they've been hunting for six hours in the scorching Florida sun, no one complains. They just plunge into the water. No one's going to argue with a whale-sized figure who crashes around the ocean floor with the same authority it took to hit a Sandy Koufax fastball.

Batting averages are a foreign dialect in these parts. Casting rods have replaced Louisville Sluggers, and instead of World Series photos or Gold Glove awards, T-shirts line the walls reading "Divers Do it Deeper." In fact, the nautical trading post known as Angler's Marine—the 175-boat marina on Stock Island—barely has space for all its fishing gear, Evinrude motors, and shiny new outboards.

Most of the time the owner can't be found. He's

usually off somewhere, deep-sea fishing, snorkeling, diving for buried treasure, gourmet cooking, or promoting beer (Miller's, of course). For John Wesley Powell is still Boog, that fun-loving hell-raiser who's always been a curious blend of Harpo Marx and Errol Flynn.

Or, as the forty-year-old former Baltimore Orioles outfielder-turned-first baseman puts it, "Huckleberry Finn has nothing on me. What mischief did he do that I'm not capable of? Nothing. Everything's got to be for laughs, that's the only way I live. I could've played ball in Japan for big money, baseball was the only thing I ever wanted from life. But at the end I just wasn't happy. I was all the way on the downside.

"Now look at me. You call lobster-hunting work?" continues Powell, once he returns to shore with thirty lobsters in a cooler that was recently filled with beer. "I can go fishing whenever I want, drink Miller's all day long, and I'm living in the craziest party town in the world.

"Some of my stunts with 'Cuckoo' (Curt Blefary), Gus (Triandos), and Eddie Fisher were something. And do I miss those guys. But hell, those times were nothing compared to what goes on down here. That's the best part of the marina business. People want to have fun, and you're there to help them."

In Key West since his mid-teens, Powell bought the marina in 1975 while still playing for the Cleveland Indians. After two seasons with the Tribe he was picked up by the Dodgers, who used him as insurance for Steve Garvey. Always known for the long ball (in 1969, he coupled 37 home runs with one hundred twenty-one RBIs and a .304 batting average), Powell was suddenly cast as a spot pinchhitter, the third man behind Manny Mota and Vic Davalillo. That transition was far too frustrating for someone who had hit 339 lifetime homers, and who had combined with Brooks and Frank Robinson for four Baltimore pennants. So, after briefly considering a $150,000 offer from a Japanese club, Powell wrote a letter to the Miller Brewing Company asking for a spot in a commercial, and made the break. He bought a van and drove to Florida with his wife, three children, and the family dog, Sassafras.

"It wasn't my style to just sit around, waiting for the call that never came," says Powell, while nervously watching a forklift operator move boats from storage racks to berths in the water. "It hurt, it has to, no matter what some guys say. But at least I had the marina. Most guys have nothing. When they're playing, they're sheltered and not ready to do anything else. Then all of a sudden it hits them in the face. They have to face the cold, real world. And if they haven't prepared for that, they're gone."

The marina business isn't just tropical cruises, marlin fishing, and sleek powerboats. Powell does have problems. Reliable forklift operators are hard to find. Mechanics can be too demanding, and in a time of spiraling inflation luxury items like boats are not on many shopping lists. Then, there's one added worry in Key West: hurricanes.

Apparently, Powell has weathered these crises, for he's come a long way from his "rookie" season when he only had a few employees and boats in tow. Now, he's a virtual rear admiral, commanding fifteen assorted salesmen and maintenance people, and a boatyard frequently jammed to capacity.

"I used to beat the hell out of the Yankees; now I do that to my help," says Powell jokingly. The 1970 American League Most Valuable Player award winner (thirty-five homers, one hundred fourteen RBIs and a .297 average for the Orioles) smiles puckishly, smoothes down his curly blond hair with the end of an ever-present beer can, and adds, "It's very tough to be a success at this business. The hardest thing is being nice to the guy who hotrods his boat into shore at ninety miles per hour. Then there are the guys who get hot when the forklift isn't operating right. They come here on their day off expecting a good time, and then, watch out, that damn thing doesn't work. That's when I really have to do some fast talking. Baseball, I guess, taught me how to react.

"At first I didn't know what I was doing here. But I decided to give it a shot, since I saw too many ball-players getting burned with restaurants, or letting their names be misused. I'm still not too good with floor planning, or inventories. You can't have boats sitting around here like a used-car lot, you have to know what's selling. The tricky part is that people need cars. They don't need boats.

"But my biggest headache is keeping forklift operators. I've been through about forty of them in the last three years. It's a very delicate thing when you're handling someone else's boat fifty feet in the air. I have a heart attack everytime I see $40,000 sitting up there, rocking up and down on those forks. I die a little every time. It's even harder to handle than going up against Koufax's fastball, or the guy who always gave me fits, Jim Kaat. And they were tough. You were really earning your salary then."

Competing for customers in a market that's as fierce as any baseball rivalry, Powell has little time for memories. Most of his trophies or other mementos are crammed into boxes, and while he still follows the game, mounds of magazines in his recently built ocean-side split-level point to a new obsession—gourmet cooking.

"Leg of lamb, there's nothing like it in the world," muses Powell, donning an apron before deftly slicing a smoked Italian ham. "Most people overseason it. It just put a little garlic on it, some rosemary, and crushed black pepper. Conch is also special, and I do a swell vichyssoise. My dad was a super cook; I'm just good. I don't do anything that fancy, but I enjoy the hell out of it.

"I guess I really got into it when we were living in Baltimore. This guy always came by in the morning, yelling outside our house, 'Soft crabs, get your soft crabs.' Brooks, Dave McNally, and Triandos, were all living pretty close by, so we'd fire up a barbecue at one in the morning after a night game and really have a party with those crabs. We even had this cart, filled with booze, that had a toilet seat on it that we used as a cooler. Those were some days."

Grinning like a mischievous child, Powell is about to relate other escapades when his wife, Jan, shouts, "What are you going to do with the garlic bread? Are you going to heat it?"

That interruption is followed by wild noises, as Sassafras has jumped into the channel to bark at a passing outboard.

Once the dog is quieted, Powell relaxes on the patio with a vodka and orange juice, then resumes, "I know why I love that dog; it's a lot like me. It only wants to get into trouble.

"I remember the time Eddie Fisher and me traded this hobo a broom so we could get his hat. It was crazy, the ugliest thing you ever saw. We talked and talked, and finally, by about three AM, the guy agreed. When we got back to our hotel room we almost died. The hat was lined with fifty-dollar bills. Eddie got so excited he had to tell Cuckoo. So we went to his room, but the f_____ wouldn't let us in. That didn't stop us. We broke the door down."

Laughing hysterically now, Powell takes a bite out of an overstuffed hero sandwich and throws a piece of salami to Sassafras. His baby blues are also starting to dance by this time, and, in a voice choked with emotion, he goes on to say, "Moments like that I miss. They were such a big part of my life. I'm very content now; I have very few problems. But the guys you play with, they're irreplaceable. You blow a ground ball in the last inning, lose a game, and someone in the dugout says, 'Forget it, you'll drive in the winning run tomorrow.' That's what the game is all about. It's a brotherhood you'll never forget."

After all these years, the face of
this outstanding relief pitcher has barely
changed. Who is this Dorian Gray of
baseball? (For the answer, turn
the book upside down.)
Don Mossi.

ABOUT THE AUTHOR

EDWARD KIERSH is a journalist who has covered many subjects, including sports, for *Newsday, Inside Sports,* and *Sport Magazine*. He has also written for the *Village Voice*, two Ford Foundation criminal justice publications, and *Travel and Leisure Magazine*. Currently living in New York City, he grew up on a Brooklyn ballfield, where like Vince D. he was "good field, no hit."

HARVEY WANG is a New York photo journalist who has worked for the *Village Voice, Working Woman,* and *American Lawyer*. He has had several exhibitions, but is still looking for a pitch he can hit.